Linda Bickel • Alan Mansfield • Sarah-Jane Clark
Catherine Richards • Conrad Tetley • Lynda Fitzmaurice

edexcel
advancing learning, changing lives

Level 2 Higher Diploma

Business, Administration and Finance

A PEARSON COMPANY

Published by Pearson Education Limited, a company incorporated in England and Wales, having its registered office at Edinburgh Gate, Harlow, Essex, CM20 2JE. Registered company number: 872828

www.heinemann.co.uk

Edexcel is a registered trademark of Edexcel Limited

Text © Pearson Education Limited 2009

First published 2009

12 11 10 09
10 9 8 7 6 5 4 3 2 1

British Library Cataloguing in Publication Data
A catalogue record for this book is available from the British Library

ISBN 978 1 846904 14 1

Edited by Susan Ross and Bruce Nicholson
Designed by HL Studios, Long Hanborough
Original illustrations © Pearson Education Limited 2009
Illustrated by HL Studios, Long Hanborough
Picture research by Kath Kolberg
Cover photo © iStockphoto/Lise Gagne
Printed in the UK by Scotprint

Acknowledgements
The author and publisher would like to thank the following individuals and organisations for permission to reproduce photographs:

Advertising Archives p73; AFP/Getty Images p154; BANANA PANCAKE/Alamy cover; BBC/Marriott, Rolf p5; Bob Johns/expresspictures.co.uk/Alamy p35; Corbis p150; Craig Holmes Premium/Alamy p128; Dan Lamont/Corbis p181; Friedrich Stark/Alamy p175; Gary Cook/Alamy cover; Getty Images pp2, 142, 158, 171, 178; Getty Images/Caroline von Tuempling p23; Getty Images/Chabruken p164; Getty Images/Digital Vision p147; Getty Images/Hola Images p90; Getty Images/Image Source p32; Getty Images/Joel Kiesel p187; Image Source cover; Image Source Pink/Alamy p61; istockphoto p144; iStockphoto/Alex Brosa p7; iStockphoto/Cecilie Johanse p93; iStockphoto/Daniel Rodriguez p77; iStockphoto/Digital Property Ltd p51; iStockphoto/ideeone p62; iStockphoto/Lise Gagne cover; iStockphoto/Martin Purmensky p169; iStockphoto/MBPhoto p196; iStockphoto/Michael DeLeon p225; iStockphoto/Steve Cole p24; iStockphoto/Vasiliki Varvaki cover; iStockphoto/Yuri Arcurs p16; iStockphoto/Zsolt Nyulaszi p220; JUPITERIMAGES/BananaStock/Alamy pp131, 167; JUPITERIMAGES/Creatas/Alamy p20; Motoring Picture Library/Alamy p174; Paul Doyle/Alamy p82; Paul Rapson/Alamy p67; Pearson Education Ltd/Jill Birschbach cover; Photodisc/Alamy cover; Randy Faris/Corbis p54; Rex Features pp10, 207, 229; Shutterstock/magicinfoto p123; Stan Gamester/Alamy p30; Steven May/Alamy p182; UpperCut Images/Alamy p231; Vico Collective/Alamy cover.

Every effort has been made to contact copyright holders of material reproduced in this book. Any omissions will be rectified in subsequent printings if notice is given to the publishers.

Disclaimer
This material has been published on behalf of Edexcel and offers high-quality support for the delivery of Edexcel qualifications.

This does not mean that the material is essential to achieve any Edexcel qualification, nor does it mean that it is the only suitable material available to support any Edexcel qualification. Edexcel material will not be used verbatim in setting any Edexcel examination or assessment. Any resource lists produced by Edexcel shall include this and other appropriate resources.

Copies of official specifications for all Edexcel qualifications may be found on the Edexcel website: www.edexcel.com

Contents

Welcome to the Business, Administration and Finance Diploma!

The Business, Administration and Finance Diploma is a ground-breaking qualification created by employers, the Government and the leading education bodies. The Diploma will give you skills and experience that employers value and will provide you with opportunities to progress on to further studies.

The Diploma will introduce you to a broad range of topics relevant to the real world of business including marketing and sales, customer service, communication, personal finance and financial services, business administration and accounting.

You will learn how to develop new business ideas, and will be given the opportunity to develop and run your own business. You will learn about the issues affecting businesses today such as new technologies and environmental issues, and what businesses should do to remain competitive. This Diploma will equip you with knowledge of how businesses work and the skills you need to work in the business sector.

You will cover three main themes:

* Business enterprise: Looks at how to develop ideas, how to carry out research and promote products or services.

* Business administration: Introduces business administration and its importance to organisations.

* Finance: Looks at the knowledge and skills needed to manage personal and business finances.

Get stuck in!

The Higher Diploma is about the same size as 7 GCSEs at level 2 (e.g. 7 GCSEs at grades A*–C) and includes the following elements:

Principal learning The knowledge, understanding and skills essential to working in the Business sector, covered by this book.

Generic learning Functional skills in IT, English and Maths, and personal learning and thinking skills have been embedded in this book to give you opportunities to develop and practise your skills.

The Project You will complete a Project – for which you will set the brief – to demonstrate the skills and knowledge that you have learnt.

Additional/specialist learning You can choose from a wide range of different qualifications to support your Business principal learning. You might choose something that will further support you in a career in business, or something that relates to your other interests in order to broaden your skills.

Work experience Your Diploma will give you the opportunity to do at least 10 days' work experience. You should consider which local companies may be willing to offer you work experience as early as possible.

Going further

This Diploma is available at Foundation (Level 1, equivalent to 5 GCSEs at grades D–G), Higher (Level 2,equivalent to 7 GCSEs at grades A*–C) and Advanced (Level 3, equivalent to 3.5 A Levels at grades A*–E). The Advanced Diploma is recognised by universities and you could achieve up to 420 UCAS points.

From the Higher Diploma, you can progress to:

* Advanced Diploma

* BTEC National or other Level 3 vocational courses

* Apprenticeships

* GCE A-levels

* Work

We hope you enjoy your studies on this cutting-edge course and that you feel inspired by the real-life scenarios in this book. Good luck!

About this book

This book has been divided into nine units to match the structure of the Principal Learning for the Higher Diploma in Business, Administration and Finance.

Features of the book

There is a chapter devoted to every unit, and each chapter opens with the following:

* Overview – a description of what is covered in the unit
* Learning Outcomes– a checklist of the Learning Outcomes covered in the unit

Each unit follows the Edexcel learning outcomes and each topic covers an individual theme.

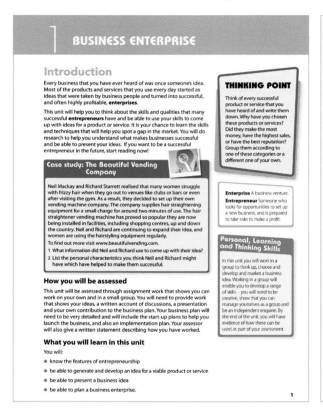

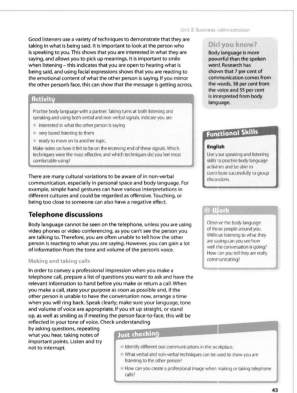

Features

Starter stimulus: A discussion point or short activity that will introduce the key concepts of the double page spread.

Key words: Key concepts and new words are explained clearly and simply to make sure you don't miss anything important.

Did you know?: Extra pieces of interesting information.

Functional skills: These features highlight opportunities to develop and practise your functional skills in English, IT or Maths. Remember, you will need a Pass in all three functional skills to achieve the full Diploma.

Personal, learning and thinking skills: These features highlight opportunities to develop and demonstrate your personal learning and thinking skills.

Case study: Case studies show how the concepts covered in this book apply to the real world. Questions and activities will encourage you to push your understanding further.

Activity: Each double-page spread contains an activity, or a short sequence of questions, to test your understanding and give you opportunities to apply your knowledge and skills.

@work: These activities help you to think about how your learning could be applied during your work placement.

Just checking: The most important points to understand, summarised so you can quickly refresh your knowledge.

Large case study: Some units contain a double-page spread case study to help you relate your learning to a real-life scenario.

Each chapter ends with assessment tips and an opportunity for you to check your skills and summarise what you've learned. You can also find help with technical terms in the glossary on page 235.

Assessment

This unit is assessed internally. This means that you will be set an assignment by your tutor, which should direct your work through a series of tasks connected to the running of a business related activity, so that you cover all of the learning outcomes for this unit. The work you submit for assessment must be original work, produced by yourself under controlled conditions – this will be arranged by your tutor. It will then be marked by your tutor and moderated by the awarding body.

You will be assessed on:

* your knowledge of how the principles of marketing are applied to the creation of the marketing mix and promotional materials

* your ability to carry out market research

* your understanding of how effective customer service is achieved

* your ability to handle customers effectively in a sales situation.

To aim for higher grades you should try to:

* think carefully about the product or service that you choose for this assignment (your tutor will help).

* produce promotional materials of a high standard that are suitable and appropriate for the product chosen, and consistent with the market research that you carry out

* include in your plan a clear and detailed description of how the four elements of the marketing mix have been used to position the product or service

* make sure that the data collected in your market research is sufficient in terms both of quality and quantity

* give a detailed description of typical customers of the organisation that you have studied, giving clear evidence to support your explanation

* display a positive attitude and demonstrate good communication skills

* assess your performance at different stages of the sales process, identifying specific things you could do differently next time, and give a clear explanation of the benefits.

148

We hope you enjoy using this book, and we wish you the very best for your Diploma course and your future career in Business, Administration and Finance.

Introduction

Every business that you have ever heard of was once someone's idea. Most of the products and services that you use every day started as ideas that were taken by business people and turned into successful, and often highly profitable, **enterprises**.

This unit will help you to think about the skills and qualities that many successful **entrepreneurs** have and be able to use your skills to come up with ideas for a product or service. It is your chance to learn the skills and techniques that will help you spot a gap in the market. You will do research to help you understand what makes businesses successful and be able to present your ideas. If you want to be a successful entrepreneur in the future, start reading now!

THINKING POINT

Think of every successful product or service that you have heard of and write them down. Why have you chosen these products or services? Did they make the most money, have the highest sales, or have the best reputation? Group them according to one of these categories or a different one of your own.

Case study: The Beautiful Vending Company

Neil Mackay and Richard Starrett realised that many women struggle with frizzy hair when they go out to venues like clubs or bars or even after visiting the gym. As a result, they decided to set up their own vending machine company. The company supplies hair straightening equipment for a small charge for around two minutes of use. The hair straightener vending machine has proved so popular they are now being installed in facilities, including shopping centres, up and down the country. Neil and Richard are continuing to expand their idea, and women are using the hairstyling equipment regularly.

To find out more visit www.beautifulvending.com.

1 What information did Neil and Richard use to come up with their idea?

2 List the personal characteristics you think Neil and Richard might have which have helped to make them successful.

Enterprise A business venture.
Entrepreneur Someone who looks for opportunities to set up a new business, and is prepared to take risks to make a profit.

How you will be assessed

This unit will be assessed through assignment work that shows you can work on your own and in a small group. You will need to provide work that shows your ideas, a written account of discussions, a presentation and your own contribution to the business plan. Your business plan will need to be very detailed and will include the start-up plans to help you launch the business, and also an implementation plan. Your assessor will also give a written statement describing how you have worked.

Personal, Learning and Thinking Skills

In this unit you will work in a group to think up, choose and develop and market a business idea. Working in a group will enable you to develop a range of skills – you will need to be creative, show that you can manage yourselves as a group and be an independent enquirer. By the end of the unit, you will have evidence of how these can be used as part of your assessment.

What you will learn in this unit

You will:

* know the features of entrepreneurship

* be able to generate and develop an idea for a viable product or service

* be able to present a business idea

* be able to plan a business enterprise.

1.1 What makes a successful entrepreneur?

An entrepreneur is someone who looks for opportunities to set up a new business, and who is prepared to take risks to make a profit. In this topic, you will learn about the different characteristics that successful entrepreneurs typically have.

Decision-makers and risk takers

Entrepreneurs tend to be people who make decisions that involve high elements of risk. They will spot an opportunity and then want to be part of it. They need to be determined and resilient.

Case study: King of Shaves

Will King set up the shaving and skincare brand 'King of Shaves' in 1992 with his girlfriend Ann. He developed his shaving products in a bedroom at home and sent them out to customers. He set up the business because he wanted to experience a better shaving experience for himself and others around him. In 2007 the sales of the business were worth more than £15 million and, in 2008, one product was sold every 3 seconds from more than 30,000 stores worldwide. In a relatively short time, Will has moved from being a very small entrepreneur to someone who is involved in a multi-million pound business.

To find out more visit www.shave.com.

In a small group, using the website above and thinking about other entrepreneurs that you have heard of, answer the following:

1 Why was decision-making so important to Will when he set up his business?

2 How has risk played a part in Will's success?

3 Some people say entrepreneurs are born, others say it is possible to learn how to be one – which do you think is right?

Motivated, self-reliance and dedicated

Having high levels of **motivation**, **self-reliance** and **dedication** are all important to be an entrepreneur.

Activity

Complete the assessment below to get yourself thinking about your own motivation, self-reliance and dedication levels.

Statement	Important	Not Important
Earning lots of money		
Time off for holidays		
Feeling secure in my finances		
Being paid when I am off sick		
Being in charge		
Looking after customers to very high levels		
Doing paperwork		
Going out and meeting people to make business contacts		
Dealing with banks or other agencies		
Being able to invest my own money		
Feeling responsible for everyone at work		
Spending money on fashion and going out		
Understanding and applying laws at work		
Getting up early or going to bed late for work		

Aware of changes

Entrepreneurs need to be aware of changes that are taking place around them – in technology, the **market**, fashion trends and competition – so they can spot new opportunities.

Hotlink

www.startups.co.uk includes profiles and useful information to help you to learn more about entrepreneurs. Carry out research on this website and find out as much information as you can!

Motivation The reason why someone does something and what makes them want to do it.

Self-reliance Not relying on others to help.

Dedication When you totally devote yourself to do something.

Market A specific group of customers that the business is aiming to attract.

Personal, Learning and Thinking Skills

To develop your skills, you will need to carry out an independent enquiry. As practice, find out the top five reasons why people choose to shop online. Make sure you note down where you have found your information and produce a **bibliography**.

Economy The wealth and resources of a country.

Bibliography A list of sources of information that you have used in your work. Make sure you quote other people's work that you have found on websites or in books.

Technology

Technology is changing rapidly and what was the most advanced piece of technology yesterday may already be out of date. Entrepreneurs use change to identify opportunities.

Market needs and fashion

When entrepreneurs think about the products or services that people want or need they consider what is happening in the market or what is fashionable. When the UK economy is booming, luxury products do well, but when the **economy** is suffering from a lack of credit, or things are more difficult, sales of cheaper goods tend to go up.

When unemployment is rising, or if people do not feel secure in their jobs, this will have an impact on the market for different goods. Other changes that affect the products and services that people buy include issues such as those relating to the environment, to changes in music and trends in how people like to spend their free time.

Competition

To be successful, an entrepreneur needs to offer something different from their **competitors** or be the only business that is offering that product or service in the area. By taking out a **patent**, a business can keep products and services as unique as possible and prevent others copying them.

Competitors can change what they are offering in many different ways:

* increasing or decreasing their prices
* giving special offers
* adding or taking away a product or service.

Case study: eBay

eBay has revolutionised the way that auctions are carried out. Started in 1998 in the USA, eBay was designed to bring together buyers and sellers in an online market place. Unlike traditional auctions, or garage sales, eBay directly evolved through changes in technology and access to the internet. Moving from traditional auctions to online access has resulted in changes to the way that buyers and sellers behave:

* Buyers and sellers can be in their own homes while trading.
* Trading can take place 24-hours a day, seven days a week.
* Trading can take place over a number of days, or weeks, rather than in a short timeframe, so providing the potential for increased interests and bids.
* Removal/distribution costs are reduced as the object for auction does not have to be transported to an auction room.
* Trading can be seen as fun, more like a hobby or interest.
* Extensive use of automated payments is made, potentially reducing costs.
* eBay attracts people of all ages.

eBay hasn't just stayed within the world of collectibles or items that are usually bought and sold second-hand but has always allowed people to trade new goods and for virtually anything to be traded online.

1 What difference has technology made to eBay and for new entrepreneurs?

2 Are there any other businesses or markets that have been revolutionised by technology?

Entrepreneurs aim to sell better products or services than their competitors.

Creative thinkers

Entrepreneurs need to think creatively when considering new ideas for products and services. You will need to do this for your assessment!

Different product or service

Entrepreneurs can use the differences in their products and services to promote themselves ahead of the competition.

Case study: Chilli flavoured ice cream

Purbeck Icecream is an award winning producer of ice creams, ranging from traditional flavours like Vanilla Bean to outlandish flavours such as Cracked Black Pepper or Chilli. Peter and Hazel Hartle who own the company suggest that one of the reasons it is so successful is because of the different products that it offers. This variety of products has helped Purbeck Icecream move from a small enterprise to one that now supplies supermarkets across Dorset, and even distributes its award winning products to wine bars and top hotels in London.

To find out more about Purbeck Icecream, visit their website www.purbeckicecream.co.uk

1 Why do you think Purbeck Icecream has been so successful over the past 20 years?

Did you know?

One of the best selling products in 2008 was the hot-water bottle. Due to difficult economic times, people chose to turn down their heating and instead use hot-water bottles to keep warm. In October 2008, the retailer John Lewis announced that sales of hot-water bottles had increased by 200 per cent.

Functional Skills

ICT

Bring your research ideas together using ICT. Produce a poster for display using images and text to explain how market needs and fashion trends affect businesses.

Competitors The other businesses which a company trades against.

Patent A business that is given the right to be the sole makers or sellers of a new product.

Hotlink

The Competition Commission is an independent organisation that checks that competition is as fair as possible. Visit their website www.competition-commission.org.uk for more details.

Better product or service

Entrepreneurs aim to sell better products or services than their competitors. They might point out the differences in:

* the quality of the product, e.g. its ingredients or materials

* the way the product is produced, perhaps in a greener way or from recycled materials

* the payment terms, e.g. it might only be necessary to pay for the product or service after six months or a year

* the reputation of the product or service

* its cheaper price – you may have noticed that identical products or services may be priced differently in shops and websites.

Activity

Use the table below to carry out research into where you can find the cheapest of the following products. Make sure you find the same or very similar products so that the comparison is fair. Think about the entrepreneurs who are running those businesses and what they have to offer.

Product or service	Name of company 1 and price	Name of company 2 and price	Name of company 3 and price
A flight from Gatwick to Ibiza			
A new 32" television (choose the same make and model)			
A one-night stay at the Ritz Hotel in London			
A year's car insurance for a 17-year-old male driver			

Flexible and able to adapt

Entrepreneurs need to be flexible and able to adapt quickly to make the most of new situations and opportunities to do business.

Case study: Lookalikes

You may have heard of Ugg® boots, which sold well across the world in 2008. Celebrities such as Oprah Winfrey and Britney Spears were seen wearing them at a cost of £180 upwards. In response, some entrepreneurs produced a similar looking boot, but at a much cheaper price – £9 and upwards. While entrepreneurs have to make sure they do not copy designs that belong to other organisations, if they can produce a similar product that costs less, they may be able to persuade customers to buy their product as an alternative.

Read about the story of Ugg® at www.uggaustralia.com by accessing the UK site and then looking at Ugg® Experience, History.

1 In a small group, discuss other products with cheaper alternatives.

Communicators

Entrepreneurs must be able to communicate their ideas to a range of audiences for different purposes, for example they might need to explain the importance of a new project or idea to their business partner, or to a bank to ask for a loan to expand their business. They will need to communicate online and in person with consumers to encourage them to buy products or use services.

Organisers and planners

'A business which fails to plan is one that plans to fail!' You will learn more about producing a plan later in this unit. Entrepreneurs must also be organised, which means that they need to take their businesses seriously and make sure that every last detail is accounted for. If businesses fail to do this, they may dissatisfy their customers which ultimately could lead to failure of their business.

The benefits of enterprise

There are lots of different benefits of having enterprising businesses in the UK and in the world. These are shown for you below.

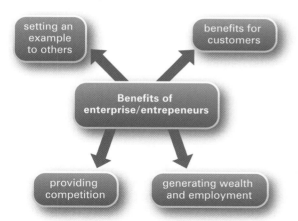

A business which fails to plan is one that plans to fail!

Having businesses in competition means that consumers have more choice, as they can choose different levels of quality for their purchases and also may be able to get goods cheaper. It also means that enterprises are more likely to be more careful about their customer service to make sure that customers return to them. New enterprise also creates jobs and wealth for individuals and the sectors they work in. Being an entrepreneur is something that many people aspire to. Famous entrepreneurs such as Richard Branson, Stelios Haji-Ioannou and James Dyson are admired, and looked up to, by many people as they have taken ideas that they believed in and have set an example for others to follow.

Just checking

* What is an entrepreneur?
* Name three skills that you would expect an entrepreneur to have.
* What is competition?
* How do competitors affect business?

1.2 Generating ideas for a product or service

A good entrepreneur needs to be able to spot opportunities, work out which ones are likely to be successful and then develop the one that they think is the best. Your work for this part of the unit will be completed in a group but you will need to show your individual contribution by writing up your notes.

Looking for opportunities

Entrepreneurs are usually good at working with people and resources to find out where the next opportunities are coming from.

Activity

Write a list of all the people that you know including family, friends, business people, and so on.

Work out how many of them are linked to businesses in their everyday lives.

How many of them run their own businesses or know people who do?

Activity

Now consider any business opportunities that you think might exist in your area.

✳ Have you ever been to a town or city, either in the UK or abroad, and found a product or service that you would love to have offered where you live?

✳ Are there any businesses that are always so busy it is hard to get into them, for example a restaurant, hairdressers or playzone for children?

Asking your business contacts for ideas is one way to start a business, but there other ways to look for opportunities. For example:

✳ look in the media, including magazines, journals and websites, for new possible ideas

✳ look at what is happening in other towns and cities and compare it with where you live – maybe they have businesses that would be good to bring to your neighbourhood

✳ look at trends in the type of goods and services that people are buying.

To find a good business opportunity, you will need to find a gap in your area, or in a particular market, for the product that you are offering. Is this product or service not being provided by anyone else? How? Why? Ask yourself: Could I do it as well?

Case study: The easyGroup companies

Stelios Haji-Ioannou is the founder of the easyGroup companies, which include some of the UK's greatest successes such as easyJet, easyCruise and easyCar. Stelios constantly looks for new ideas and then develops them. He does this by spotting opportunities to expand the easyGroup brand. For example, have you heard of easyBus that offers low-cost airport transfers, easyCinema where you can buy cheaper cinema tickets or easyPizza which is expanding across the country to deliver pizza to your door?

Stelios does not necessarily offer something new, compared with existing services or products that are on offer, but he adds the easyGroup brand and the low-cost approach, which attracts customers.

The easyGroup strategy involves building on its eight brand values: 'great value; taking on the big boys; for the many not the few; relentless innovation; keep it simple; entrepreneurial; making a difference in people's lives; honest, open, caring and fun' (www.easy.com).

1 In a small group, discuss the potential for a new easyGroup company. What would you suggest and why?

You should have started to think seriously about where some of the opportunities might come from for a business that you can work on for this unit. If not, don't worry there are some activities below to help you think of more ideas that you might want to use.

Mind mapping

Mind mapping helps you to think of different ideas that could be used for your business. Use the activities and the case studies that follow to help you think of ideas for your enterprise. Some possible ideas that you might want to consider are shown in the mind map below.

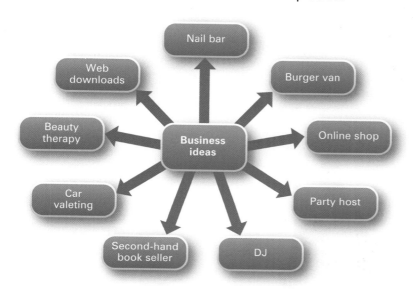

At this stage, you should start to be able to gather your thoughts together with other members of your class.

Case study: Minimum One

Minimum One is a very simple business idea that was thought of by Cheryl McAlpine before she was 19 years of age. She decided to set up her own T-shirt printing, online ordering service and now has expanded it to produce other products that can be produced individually.

To learn more about Minimum One, visit www.minimumone.com.

1 Are there any business ideas that you think might work by offering an online service or product?

Activity

* Think of a product that you have always wanted to eat but doesn't exist, such as a chocolate-flavoured burger or garlic chewing gum.

* Is there a service that would really help you in your everyday life such as someone who could clean your room or walk your dog?

* Are there any places for young people to go in your area, for example, a café or club?

* Do you have a skill or talent for something that could be shared with others?

Use websites to help you think of suitable ideas including www.talentedyoungpeople.com

Remember you must be able to choose an idea that you can put into practice so you will need to think carefully.

Activity

* Now, as part of a small group, discuss all the possible business ideas that you can think of that can be used for this unit. Produce a mind map of the ideas.

* For each idea that you have thought of write whether it is a new idea or whether it is an improvement to an existing product or service.

Just checking

* Where could an entrepreneur look for opportunities?
* Have you thought of business ideas that you will be able to put into practice?

1.3 Comparing ideas and making decisions

Once you've come up with a range of ideas, the next stage is to consider which of your ideas is most likely to be successful and make decisions about them. This topic will help you to choose your 'top three' ideas.

GREAT BUSINESS IDEAS

Dr Seuss, author of the famous *The Cat in the Hat* books, had his ideas rejected by lots of different publishers before he finally found a publisher who would use them. In your group, think of other business ideas that you have heard of that have been either very successful or unsuccessful. Discuss why you think this is.

Functional Skills

ICT

Using the work that you did for the mind mapping ideas activity in Unit 1.2, take your ideas and put them into a table in a word processing package. Add columns called '**Business idea**', '**What it is**' and '**Why it was chosen**'. For each idea add a description of the idea and why it was chosen.

Activity

Now think about your own business ideas so far – how likely are customers to buy them?

✱ How much would they cost to produce?

Time, money and resources

Sir Clive Sinclair with his invention the C5.

There have been some very famous business ideas that have gone very wrong. One example is the Sinclair C5. In the 1980s, Sir Clive Sinclair ran a very successful computer business. He then decided to branch out into different types of transport and came up with the idea for the Sinclair C5, an electric and people powered mode of transport. Unfortunately, it wasn't a success – the C5 did not go up and down hills well and gave 14-year-olds the opportunity to drive without a helmet or safety gear on main roads.

To assess an idea's potential for your Diploma, you will need to be realistic in terms of the time, money and resources available, your knowledge and skills and the possible market for your idea. This means that reinventing a major project, or coming up with a best-selling idea, may not be possible. What will be important will be to make sure that you have an appropriate budget available and members of your group that you can work with.

You will need to choose the best idea that you can think of from those selected. Think about the way that your ideas are affected by the next section and see if you can work out which one might be the best choice for you and your group.

Your knowledge and skills

When you are choosing a business idea that you are going to take forward you will need to have knowledge and skills that relate to the product or service, especially for this unit of the Diploma. You should try to choose a product or service that you know something about or that you know you could easily research within your time limits and budget.

If you have specific skills, or experience, that you have gained during work experience, or at a part-time job, make the most of these to help you. If you have a hobby or leisure activity that could be applied to the idea, make good use of your skills.

Activity

To help you choose the best idea to take forward and develop, do a knowledge and skills audit for three of your top business ideas. Copy and complete the table below with the details of everyone in your group by writing the knowledge and skills that the member of the group could bring to your idea. When everyone has added their knowledge and skills work out which idea is likely to suit your group best.

Name	Idea 1	Idea 2	Idea 3

A market for your idea

You might be thinking of an idea for a product or service that will be sold to people all year round. It is also possible to think of products or services that might be sold during religious festivals such as Christmas, Eid or Diwali.

You might consider seasonal goods for spring or summer rather than those that are sold in the autumn or winter. If you are going to sell your product or service for a short time, you will need to work out the size of the market for that period and check that you will make enough sales.

Functional Skills

Mathematics

Now roughly estimate the number of sales you think you would need to make to cover the costs of your business idea. How much budget do you have to start your business idea and buy your first resources?

Laws and regulations

You will need to consider all the laws and regulations that will affect your business idea. Some of the key ones are given in the table below.

Area of law or regulation	What you need to think about
UK law	Does your business idea have age-related restrictions that go with it? For example, you need to be 18 to consume alcohol or buy cigarettes, so you must ensure that your business complies with these laws. Also, your business must not deal with illegal goods.
Consumer protection	There are lots of laws including the Sale of Goods Act and Trades Descriptions Act that protect customers' rights when they are sold something.
Public liability	If you are going to have customers coming on to your premises or shop, you will need to think about insurance, including public liability insurance, to allow the public to enter your premises. You may also need additional insurance if you are offering services directly to people such as hairdressing or nails.
Health and safety	How can your product or service be offered safely in a way you that you and your customers are looked after?

Laws and regulations affecting business.

Functional Skills

ICT

To find out more information that is relevant to your business idea, visit the free business advice and support service website at www.businesslink.gov.uk.

Obstacles to overcome

You should also think about any obstacles that you might need to overcome. One of the biggest is usually financial and you will learn more about this when you start planning your business enterprise. The table below lists other potential obstacles and how you can plan to overcome them.

Potential obstacle	How you could get over it
Training in how to deliver the business idea	If you are providing a service, for example a nail bar, will you need training before you can carry it out? if yes, where can you get it from?
Experience of the business idea	Do you know local entrepreneurs offering a similar business to your business idea who would be willing to give you advice about how to take your idea forward?
Time	You will need to plan your time carefully and make sure that you can collect all the information that you will need for this unit.
Confidence	How confident are you about your business idea? Do you need to do more research to make sure that you know as much as possible about it?

Overcoming obstacles.

Just checking

* Where could you market your ideas?
* Which laws and regulations might affect the ideas you have chosen?
* What are the likely obstacles that you will need to overcome?

1.4 Choosing and developing the best idea

At this stage, you should know which of your ideas form your 'top three' – if you don't, go back and look at all of your ideas and put them into rank order, starting with the best one. You can then consider your final choice from the top three. You will need to have good reasons for your choice of final idea and how it compared to the others. This means that you will need to know what is good about the idea and any areas that might cause you problems. This topic will help you to choose, then develop the best idea.

Before making your final selection, in your group consider the strengths and weaknesses of each of your ideas to help you decide which the best one is. For each idea, identify its strengths and weaknesses, using a table like the one below.

Idea	Strengths	Weaknesses
To make and sell jewellery at local markets	Amel's aunty knows a supplier that might help us, etc.	The cost to buy the jewellery in the first place, etc.

Once you have made your final decision about which product or service to go for, you will then need to provide a detailed account of your idea.

What is it?

The first step is to describe your business idea and include lots of detail about it. Here are some questions to help you:

* What is your product or service? What is its name?
* Where will it be made/offered?
* How will it be made/offered?
* Where do the materials for it come from? How much do they cost?
* Who can help you with the idea?

Who is it for?

Next, think about exactly who the product or service is for. You have already learned about the concept of a specific market – that is, a group of customers that you are aiming to attract. Choosing the right market can mean success or failure for a business. Markets can be divided up in many different ways. By choosing the right **market segment**, it is possible to aim the product directly at those people.

Activity

Use the What is it? and Who is it for? questions opposite to help you in a group discussion. Make sure you write down your contribution to use as evidence for your coursework.

You will need to work out the right segment of the market for your product or service. Here are some questions to help you:

* Is it aimed at men/women or both?
* How old are the people who are likely to buy the product or service?
* How much money are they likely to have?
* How often might they buy it?
* What kind of lifestyle do they lead, e.g. healthy, sporty, vegetarian, etc.
* Where do they live?

Being clear about the reasons why someone might buy your product or use your service is also really important:

* Is this a product or service that will help them in their everyday lives?
* Is it convenient?
* Does it offer something that is not already available?

Is there any competition?

You should also think about any other businesses that are already offering your business idea. What do they offer, how are they priced? How many of them are there? You may wish to use a **market map** as shown below to help you to work out who your competitors are. The four different car washing businesses have been compared using quality and price and placed on the market map accordingly.

High quality

Shiny Motor	Individual Hand-washed motors
Cheap and Easy	
Self Service Wash	

Low price — High price

Low quality

Market map showing four different car washing businesses.

How could you sell it?

Finally, you will need to think about all the possible places and ways that your product or service could be sold, that is:

* direct to the consumer
* through a retail outlet
* through a wholesaler
* online.

Remember that the method of selling that you think would be the best for your business idea might have additional costs and resources.

1.5 Presenting a business idea

When you present your results and findings to potential investors it is important that you give a presentation that is as professional as possible. In this topic, you will learn how to prepare and make presentations, and the skills that you will need.

Preparing and making a presentation

You will be expected to give a group presentation to potential investors for your business idea. You will need to have enough notes and research to cover the following:

* What your original ideas were and careful explanation of them.

* The research that you carried out, including how it was done, to justify your business idea.

* Resource issues such as human, physical and financial – you will learn more about these on pages 19–21.

* Why you think it is an idea worth investing in – why it is viable.

* How you will know if it will be successful.

Your presentation should include graphs and charts.

To aim for top mark bands, you will need to produce evidence that covers all the main points that are shown in the presentation guide above.

Top tips for presenting data

* To aim for the higher marks you will probably want to produce a handout for the investors and show a PowerPoint presentation or other types of slide. You will also need to have your own notes to help you remember what you need to say.

* Make sure you don't include too much information on your slides – they can look too crowded and the investors won't be able to read them. Put the more detailed information on your handout.

* Always use a large font size – at least size 24 – to make sure everyone can see what you are presenting on your slides. Smaller text can be used in your handouts but make sure these are neatly presented.

* Make sure you include graphs, tables and charts for your data. You should also include images and video (if this is possible) to really impress investors.

* You might find it useful to include a questions and answers section in your handout and in your presentation where you write down every possible question that you think the investors might come up with. This should avoid you being asked any 'surprise' questions when you are being assessed.

I'D LIKE TO TELL YOU ABOUT ...

Prepare a two-minute talk to give to your group. Choose a topic about something that you enjoy such as a leisure activity. Take it in turns to make your talk. Other members of the group should then comment on different aspects of your presentation, e.g. did you speak with enthusiasm, did you fidget while you were talking? The aim of this activity is to help each other improve their presentation skills, so try to keep your comments helpful!

Did you know?

'If you don't know where you are going, you're probably not going to get there' (Forrest Gump) – think about your idea and where you are going and how you will know if you have been a success!

Good communication skills are important when making presentations.

An essential part of presenting your findings for this work is making sure that you show how your ideas have developed as clearly as possible and the reason why your idea is worth investing in.

Communication skills

You will need to make sure you practise your presentation skills carefully to give the best performance you can. You will need to think about:

* how you use your voice in the presentation, including the speed at which you talk (many people speak too quickly when they give presentations, do you?)

* how clearly you talk – can everyone understand what you are saying and how can you speak even more clearly?

* making eye contact and smiling at your audience – this will help to communicate that you are open and trustworthy

* shaking hands firmly with investors – this is also a way of showing that you are confident, but remember, being over confident is as bad as being shy and nervous because that may make the person viewing your presentation think you are big-headed

* during the presentation, make sure that while you are waiting to speak that you don't slouch or tap your feet as you may appear not to be interested in the idea.

Remember!

* When you are doing your presentation make sure you present your findings carefully and clearly.

* Speak to your audience rather than read from the presentation slides.

* Don't stand in front of the projector.

* Smile and try not to be nervous – be confident of your ideas, you have worked hard.

* Be prepared to answer questions.

Just checking

* Name three things that you will need to do when presenting data.
* List three important communication skills.

1.6 Planning a business enterprise

For your presentation, you will need to produce a business start-up and implementation plan. This will show the different aspects of a plan for your business enterprise, including the aims of that business and the resources that will help you to focus on what you are doing. In this topic, you will also look at the aims and objectives of businesses in the private, public and voluntary sectors.

Aims and objectives of businesses in different sectors

There are three different sectors that you should consider when planning for your enterprise:

* Private sector organisations provide goods or services for a profit. Their aims usually involve survival or growth.

* The public sector is funded by the state and provides services aimed at the community. Its aim is to improve service provision.

* The voluntary sector seeks to provide a service to a target group, to promote a cause, to survive or to make a **surplus** that can be invested for the future.

Activity

Complete the table below by thinking locally, nationally and internationally of businesses that you have heard of in each sector.

Sector	Businesses
Private	
Public	
Voluntary	

Now pick out for each sector, one business and look up its aims and objectives using books or through access to the internet.

Compare your answers with others in your class.

Business start-up and implementation plan

In your business start-up and implementation plan, you will need to include information on the areas described below.

What the business will do

This section should cover what the business does and its objectives. Objectives are the list of plans that a business uses to achieve its overall aims. They should be SMART, that is, Specific, Measurable, Agreed, Realistic and Time-constrained. This section should also include essential information about your product or service. You may wish to include diagrams or charts to help you.

WHAT MAKES A SUCCESSFUL PRODUCT?

Choose a popular product such as an iPod. In your group, discuss who the target market for the product is and how it is promoted and sold. What sorts of resources does the manufacturer need to make and market the product?

Surplus The money made by voluntary organisations, as opposed to profit made by commercial organisations.

The target market

The target market is the group of customers who you will be encouraging to buy your product or service. You will need to consider the age, gender, income or lifestyle of the customers that you want to attract to buy from you. This will help you to decide where you need to advertise and the type of pricing that you should go for. To make sure you have enough data, you might wish to use a questionnaire or interview to confirm your ideas.

Surveys/Questionnaires

If you use a survey or questionnaire for your research, you will need to consider how your questions are structured. Three different ways of asking questions are shown below.

* Questions that ask people to comment on how they feel about your product or service, for example:

I would pay £2.50 for a personalised greeting card:

Strongly agree   Agree   No opinion   Disagree   Strongly agree

* Questions that ask people to put a tick or cross in the box that is nearest to their views, e.g. asking people to rate a sample of fashion jewellery:

	1	2	3	4	5	6	7	8	
Fashionable									Not fashionable
Value for money									Expensive

* Interviews that ask different people for their thoughts about your product or service. You will need to come up with a set of questions to ask them. You might want to use specific questions by asking everyone the same question or you might want to allow people to give you feedback on your idea but without asking them specific questions. Suggested questions:

  * What do you think of this business idea?

  * How much would you be prepared to pay for it?

  * How often would you buy it?

  * What do you think of the name for our business idea?

Activity

Use the suggested questions above and others of your own to put together an interview. Make sure you test your questions on each other to work out the answers before you do your real interviews. If you don't get the answer that you expect, this will show if you are asking a question in a strange way!

How the product or service will be promoted and sold

You will also need to think about how you are going to promote and then sell your product or service. You started to think about this earlier when you considered how you could sell it, but now you will need to decide on the methods that you will use to actually promote and then sell the product or service. Are you going to use advertising to promote your idea? Are you going to give demonstrations and then sell? Review the ideas that you came up with on page 15 to help you decide.

Human resources

Your business idea will have implications for human resources. You will need to consider who is going to be responsible for which aspects of the business implementation. For example, if you are setting up a car washing business, who will buy the sponges, buckets and cleaning liquids? Who will wash the cars? Who will do the advertising? Who will collect the money? It is important that everyone knows what is involved and the jobs they are to do.

Physical resources

The physical resources are any premises, equipment or materials that you need to set up and keep the business running.

Case study: Lovefilm

The online DVD rental company Lovefilm's main resources are its website (www.lovefilm.com), a help centre where operators can respond to customers' queries by telephone and email, and a huge warehouse where the DVDs are stored. In May 2005, Lovefilm outgrew its warehouse and had to move to larger premises to cope with the demand for up to 80,000 DVDs that had to be distributed every day. Since then, the company has grown from strength to strength and has now expanded into retail and online downloads. In October 2008, they rented over 3 million DVDs per month from a catalogue of nearly 70,000 unique titles.

1 What premises, equipment and materials will you need for your business enterprise?

Financial resources

Financial resources are the amount of money that will be needed to set up the business, what the money will be spent on, and how the money will be raised.

You will need to provide a list of the costs for starting up the business. An example of start-up costs for the Clean House Cleaning Company is shown on page 20 to help you. You will need to make sure that you can show what the money will be spent on and why – you must be able to justify your choices with good research shown in your plan.

Start-up costs for the Clean House Cleaning Company.

Cost	£
Cleaning materials	200
Van	2,000
Overalls	200
Computer	1,500
Launch advertising	500
Website build and initial hosting	600
Mobile telephone	75
Total	**5,075**

Activity

Think of every single expense that must be paid for so you can operate your business idea, list them and then add them up to give you your overall start-up costs.

There are many different sources of finance that you could consider and these will need to be researched and written up in your plan.

Banks or building society loans	Banks and building societies are able to offer loans, business accounts and overdraft facilities based on the business plan. Interest is payable based on the predicted risk. Some security will need to be provided, e.g. assets such as a house.
Friends or family	Money from friends and family may either be invested in the business in exchange for shares or paid back as a loan, often at a lower rate than a bank loan.
Savings	Using your own savings in the bank/building society means that you don't have to pay any interest or pay back the money, but savings may take time to build up if you haven't got any already.
Government grants	These are available from the European Union, national government and local government. A grant is money that is given to an entrepreneur that doesn't have to be paid back and the amount of that money will depend on where it is coming from. For more information see www.businesslink.gov.uk.

Sources of finance.

Banks and building societies are able to offer financial help to businesses.

Prices and a simple cash budget

As part of your plan, you must provide a list of prices and a simple cash budget to show your estimated **income** and **expenses**.

Prices

When deciding on pricing, you will need to think about the following factors:

* The price must be high enough to cover your costs and/or make a profit depending on the type of business that you are.

* Customers will buy your product based on the price – too high and they may think it is not worth it (unless you have something unique), too low and they may not think it is of a high enough quality or you may have too many customers to handle.

* Will you set a price that appears to be cheaper, e.g. £9.99 instead of £10.00.

* Will you offer a low price to start with as your idea is new and then increase it after a while?

	October £	November £	December £
Cash opening balance	500	920	1,780
Revenue			
Sales	1,000	1,500	2,000
Total			
Costs			
Petrol	240	300	400
Van insurance	80	80	80
Cleaning materials	40	60	80
Personal insurance	40	40	40
Phone bill	40	40	40
Advertising	140	120	100
Total	580	640	740
Difference	420	860	1,260
Cash closing balance	920	1,780	3,040

A cash budget for the Clean House Cleaning Company.

Simple cash budget

A simple cash budget should show your estimated costs and revenues per month. It is usual to do a cash budget for at least three months, but you may wish to do it for six or twelve months in your plan. The cash budget opposite was produced for the Clean House Cleaning Company. Use it as an example to help you plan yours. When you are working out your cash budget, it is possible that at the end of the first few months you will find that you are paying out more than you might expect to come in while you establish your business. This would mean you have a cash deficit and you should show it in (brackets).

Just checking

* What types of information should be included in a start-up and implementation plan?
* What should a simple cash budget include?

Income Revenue generated by a business.

Expenses Costs accumulated by a business.

THINKING POINT

In a recent business survey, 72 per cent of people said that they had moved to a competitor after receiving poor service. Think of a time when you received poor service. Next time, did you choose a rival product or service?

The final part of your work for this unit will help you to put your plans into action and then adapt them as necessary. You will need to think about those plans, the materials you need, the law and regulations that ensure you run your business appropriately and the need to take into account environmental issues. Finally, you will measure the success of your business idea!

Putting plans into action and adapting where necessary

It is important to adapt your plans if you need to. When you worked out pricing, if you interviewed or surveyed potential customers and found that your price was too high or low, you would need to change your pricing and maybe some of your materials. For example, if you are setting up a greeting cards business and people say that they are willing to pay £1.50 but not £2.50 for a birthday card (as you had planned), you would need to change your business idea. You might need to decide how you can get different materials more cheaply. You will need to highlight these changes in your plan and presentation.

Promotional methods and materials

There are lots of different types of promotional methods and materials that you might use for your business idea. The type of activity will depend on the product or service and how and where you are going to let people know about it. Some useful methods that you might wish to consider are given below.

Demonstrations

If you are selling a service such as hair braiding or mendhi artwork, it might be useful to show your customers what customers look like after they have experienced the service.

Door-to-door sales

It might be appropriate for your group to promote the product, or service, in different places. In your school, or college, you might decide to go round to different classes. You might also visit other organisations to promote your product or service. Make sure you ask the permission of the teaching staff before you do this.

Advertising

If it isn't appropriate to let someone experience your service or to try your product, you might find advertising is better suited to your needs. With the permission of staff, you could place notices and leaflets around your school or college, or include advertising in a newsletter that is given out to other students or to their parents. You might be lucky enough to advertise online through a website or by email.

Functional Skills

English

When you are selling door-to-door you have a good opportunity to practise your functional skills of speaking and listening. This is because it is important that when you go round to different locations, you are as clear as possible when presenting your ideas. You will also need to listen to comments made by people hearing your ideas.

Order forms and advertising events

For demonstrations, you might want to advertise on a poster or notice or online about when the demonstration is going to take place. You will need members of your group to be ready to sell the product, or service, at the time of the demonstration and immediately after. If you are selling a product as part of a demonstration, for example cakes or biscuits, you might be able to take orders and then deliver the products later. If you do this, you will need to have an order form with prices to give out or have an online ordering system.

Leaflets

You might also decide to produce leaflets with all the relevant information on them which can be given out. Leaflets can be re-read so if someone forgets the information they can look at them again, but they can cause a problem with littering.

It might be useful to show your customers the service they are buying, such as Mendhi artwork.

Activity

1 Look at the advert below. What additional information should it include? How could it be improved?

Car Washing Service

Only £2.50

Available at lunchtimes every day from 12.30

Speak to Jason, Khalid or Sarah in Room 22 for more details.

2 Find two leaflets for local businesses. Think what is good about each one and how they could be improved. If you can't find any leaflets, go online and look at some examples to compare.

Functional Skills

ICT and English

Producing professional advertising materials, either on paper or online, means that you should use your ICT skills to bring information together and present it carefully. You will need to write your materials carefully and use formats that are appropriate for new customers. You will need to think about the type of language that you will use to persuade customers to use your product or service.

Top tips for designing leaflets and other promotional materials

* Make good use of white space.

* Use appropriate images.

* Make sure you check your spelling.

* Double check dates, times and room numbers – it is easy to make a mistake!

* Make sure your message is clear.

* Use a font that is easy to read.

* Make sure that the colours that you choose are appropriate for your message.

* Use the best paper or materials that are within your budget.

* Use phrases or words that will enable people to remember what you are selling.

Before your group starts its promotional activity, you will need to be sure that everyone understands the reasons for your choices, including alternatives that were considered, which jobs have been allocated to different people, where the activity will take place, how it will take place and what information is needed for the designs.

Complying with relevant law and regulations

As we saw earlier in this unit you will need to consider relevant laws and regulations that may affect your product or service.

Consumers are protected by legislation.

Consumer legislation

You need to include how your business idea is affected by the Trades Description Act, Sale of Goods Act, Supply of Goods and Services Act and Weights and Measures Act.

Record keeping

You need to make sure that you can show you are aware of laws relating to the keeping of records – this is so your business could pay taxes and other charges. You should also know about the Data Protection Act so that information about customers is stored safely and is not shared without the customer's permission.

Regulations

You have already learned about health and safety issues that you should consider as part of your plans, including the need to have insurance in place and to have procedures and equipment in place, for example planned escape routes in the event of a fire and an accident book at your premises.

Environmental issues

New entrepreneurs must take into account environmental issues when they are planning their businesses. It is very important that you think about waste/recycling of materials and ways to save energy.

Waste and recycling

Planning what your business is going to do with its waste is very important. All waste generated by businesses needs to be collected and disposed of. This costs businesses lots of money. Therefore, not only is it good for the business to keep its waste down but if it can reduce waste it will also save money. You should think about how your business could reduce waste at every stage of production. Consider how any materials that are left over could be recycled. Lord Chris Smith of the Environment Agency suggests that 'green business is good business' as it saves on materials and potentially leads to an increase in profits!

Energy saving

Entrepreneurs need to save energy for lots of different reasons. Like reducing waste and recycling, this can lead to greater savings and potentially higher profits, but there are other reasons why saving energy is good:

* to give the business a good reputation
* to keep the business ahead of laws and regulations
* to encourage people to come and buy from you.

Production and the importance of monitoring

Producing a good product or service is important, especially if the business is new or growing. This is because people tell their friends about your business and then you get new customers. It is important to monitor two particular aspects of how your business offers its products or services – the quantity and quality.

Quantity

Monitoring quantity means monitoring the physical numbers of products or services sold or given. It is important to measure any changes in numbers being sold and also the number of complaints, or positive comments, about what you are offering. Social networking sites like Bebo and Facebook often make recommendations between friends for different products and services. As a new entrepreneur, you need to check how your business idea is likely to be received and reviewed.

Quality

Quality means the physical attributes of the product that you have in your hand, for example you will need to ensure that if you are offering a product like a T-shirt or a birthday cake, you are able to offer the best quality that can be afforded for the price. The same is true of offering a service; you must make sure that you offer a good service so that customers want to come back and also that if something does go wrong, you put it right.

> **Did you know?**
>
> Some offices give their confidential waste paper that has been shredded to supply bedding for animals rather than having it wasted.

> **Did you know?**
>
> From October 2008, manufacturers have been able to measure the carbon footprint of their products. This is helping them to become more environmentally friendly by thinking of different ways to produce and distribute their products. For more information, visit the Department for Environment, Food and Rural Affairs at www.defra.gov.uk.

Case study: Wycombe Wanderers FC are the best!

Wycombe Wanderers Football Club won the award for Leisure and Tourism Customer Service Team of the Year 2008 for their high levels of customer service. This was the second award that they won in 2008 as they were voted Family Club of the Year 2008 as well.

Wycombe Wanderer's Managing Director Steve Hayes thinks that their service to fans is good because they always try their best. 'We are always trying to strive to make our customer service one of the best in the country, not just in football but in any industry.'

1 Why is customer service so important to a football club like Wycombe Wanderers?

2 What does winning two awards tell you about Wycombe Wanderers?

3 Can you name any other companies that you know of that have excellent customer service, and why?

@ Work

It is important that you give the best possible service that you can when you are at work. Researchers from the British Standards Institute asked customers about how satisfied they were with the service they were receiving:

* 64% believed that customer service in the UK is getting worse

* 72% moved to a competitor after receiving poor customer service

* 55% of customers are left unsatisfied by the handling of their complaint (BSI Customer Satisfaction Survey, March 2008)

1 Have you ever received poor or excellent customer service?

2 Why do you think it is so important to keep customers happy when you are offering a service?

3 Are there any services that you have received where you think you could do better? Is this a service that you could provide yourself?

Measuring success

The final part of your work for this unit is to measure the success (or failure!) of your business idea. When you give your presentation to potential investors you considered what would make the business a success, that is the potential number of customers and the number of sales that you might make.

Activity

Make notes in the boxes below for you then to write/type up. Remember the more detailed and careful your thinking and writing, the higher the marks you are likely to receive for this part of the Diploma.

Include:	Strengths (what was good)	Weaknesses (what was not so good)
How you decided to promote the business, and why?		
Copies of the promotional materials that you developed		
What did you do to put your idea into practice?		
My judgement of success		

If you want to move towards the higher marks, you may find it helpful to include a summary judgement at the end of your work that includes ways in which you would do things differently if you had to this project again!

Your final piece of evidence for Unit 1 is for you to write your own account of what you did to implement the business idea. Use your ideas from the PLTS activity opposite to help you complete the reflective activity.

Signs of a successful idea
The group felt that they had achieved progress towards the original aims and objectives of the business.
The group reached the number of sales that they expected to make.
The group made a profit/covered its costs.
The group worked well together.
The group felt that they had achieved everything they had set out to achieve.
The idea was popular with customers.
The target group of customers had heard of the business idea.
A certain number of hits had been received on the website (if using online methods).
A certain number of emails had been received expressing interest in the idea.
Customers were satisfied with the product or service.
There was good feedback from teaching staff/parents/neighbours/family.
The group felt they all gained new skills and knowledge about working as a team that they did not have before.

Signs of problems with the idea
There was lots of interest but very few sales.
Customers did not turn up at the right times or in the right place.
There were communication problems in the group and team members stopped working well together.
Customers were unhappy with the product or service and complained/asked for their money back.
There was lots of stock left over.
The enterprise lost money.
The activity was not finished or finished badly.

Personal, Learning and Thinking Skills

Throughout this project, you have worked as part of a team, been creative, have managed yourselves and been independent enquirers. Congratulations! You have used lots of personal, learning and thinking skills and will have evidence of how these can be used as part of your assessment. Reflecting on the work that you have done and making judgements about the success of the business idea is the last and very important stage of the process.

Use the **Signs of a successful idea** (opposite) and **Signs of problems** (opposite) **with the idea** lists to help you work out how the project went.

Just checking

* Why is it important to market a business idea using the right promotional materials?
* Why is it important to monitor the quantity and quality of a product or service?
* How will you measure your business idea's success?

Assessment

This unit is assessed internally. This means that you will be set an assignment by your consortium, which should direct your work through a series of tasks connected to the running of a business related activity, so that you cover all of the learning outcomes for this unit.

The work you submit for assessment must be original work, produced by yourself under controlled conditions – this will be arranged by your tutor. It will then be marked by your tutor and moderated by the awarding body.

To aim for higher grades you should try to:

* your knowledge of the features of entrepreneurship
* your ability to generate and develop an idea for a viable product or service
* your ability to present a business idea
* your ability to plan a business enterprise
* your ability to implement and review a business enterprise.

You will be assessed on:

* offer convincing examples to support your team's entrepreneurial activities
* produce a detailed and realistic plan for a business enterprise, showing how and why this has been adapted
* Provide a reflective account of what you lessons you have learnt, especially regarding what you would differently next time
* demonstrate good teamworking skills and a contribution when running the business, requiring only minimal support and guidance to achieve these
* give clear reasons why the final idea for a viable product or service was chosen, ensuring that the audience of 'potential investors' can fully understand the idea and why it should be worth investing in.

2 BUSINESS ADMINISTRATION

Introduction

Most jobs, even at senior level, require some administrative skills, and so learning about and improving these skills will provide a firm foundation for success in the workplace. Even basic administrative skills are transferable to a range of different jobs.

In this unit you will find out why good administration is so important and the different administrative tasks that businesses depend on. When working with other people you need to be able to manage your time and prioritise work to meet deadlines. Meetings are a core feature of the activities of a business and you will develop skills in organising and providing administrative support for them.

How you will be assessed

For this unit, you will be assessed by a single assignment connected to the running of a business-related activity. You will be required to plan the activities needed for a meeting and then organise and support the meeting using office equipment safely and creating an agenda, minutes and other business documents for the meeting. In addition, you will review administrative skills required in business, identify administrative processes that need to be carried out in organisations and who carries them out, and explain why effective administration is important.

WHAT SKILLS DO GOOD ADMINISTRATORS NEED?

Good administrators need to have a range of skills to make sure that tasks are completed properly and on time. In a small group, discuss the types of skills you think an administrator should have.

Case Study: Jo, experienced administrator

Jo has worked in administration since she left college in the 1980s after completing a secretarial course. She started as a junior secretary for the head of personnel of a small electronics company, while attending evening classes in business studies. Before she married and had a family, Jo had worked for an advertising agency, a firm of solicitors, and had progressed to deputy manager to the human resources manager for a national newspaper, with specific responsibility for staff development and training. While at home with her children, Jo used her administration skills to become treasurer for the play group which her children attended, and also voluntary work for a charity shop in town. To update her skills, she enrolled on an ICT refresher course and a teacher training course and now teaches business studies at the local secondary school.

1 Name the jobs where Jo has been able to use her administration skills.

2 What administration tasks do you think Jo undertook in each of the jobs?

What you will learn in this unit

You will:

* know the different administrative roles and processes in businesses
* understand the importance of effective administration
* be able to communicate effectively in writing
* be able to plan and carry out administrative work safely
* be able to organise and support a meeting.

2.1 Jobs that require administrative skills

In today's global business world, it sometimes seems that everything is rapidly changing making you feel that you're in a non-stop race to keep up with the processes or the technology. However, some things are constant and stable – such as the need for excellent administration to meet the demands of the challenging business environment. In this topic you will investigate a range of administrative job roles.

Roles in administration

All businesses whatever their size or location depend on administration in order to be successful and remain competitive. Learning good administration skills will provide you with the basis for progression to a whole variety of career pathways at different levels such as supervisory and management positions. Business and administrative skills are at the core of many roles across all industries and sectors – from office junior to senior manager – and the different roles within business environments vary enormously.

All businesses depend on good administration.

Administrative roles can often be found within an office environment and, in a large organisation, this may cover functions such as personnel, marketing, finance, research, production and other specialist areas. Job roles in these areas could be a receptionist, a marketing assistant, a finance officer, a customer services assistant, or a human resources assistant. The administrative role in a small business will be different as it may not have a separate administration department. It is important to be aware of different roles that you may be expected to undertake.

* **Receptionist:** duties can include greeting visitors, answering and forwarding telephone calls, handling enquiries, taking messages, arranging appointments, booking meeting rooms, dealing with the post, and general administration such as filing and word processing documents.

* **Marketing Assistant:** duties can include assisting with trade shows, exhibitions, events; creating or updating presentation software and marketing literature; tracking budgets and expenses; maintaining data systems of customer details and producing sales reports.

* **Finance Officer:** duties can include processing expenses; reconciling invoices against delivery notes; maintaining financial records and accounts and organising office supplies.

* **Customer Services Assistant:** duties can include dealing with customer enquiries either face-to-face, on the telephone, or through email.

* **Human Resources Assistant:** duties can include screening telephone enquiries for job applications; assisting with recruitment and selection; advertising vacancies; prepare contracts of employment and other documentation; collect data on staff absences and holidays and update training records.

Just checking

* Have you investigated a range of job roles in business, administration and finance?
* Do you understand the types of skills required for different job roles in business, administration and finance?

Case study: Amber's dream job

Amber is a conference organiser for a business advisory organisation. She plans and organises the venue, location and all resources including catering. Amber arranges the travel and accommodation for delegates as well as all the administrative aspects such as the distribution of documentation and follow-up activities after the conference.

Amber studied for an Advanced Diploma in Business Administration and Finance, followed by a degree in Tourism Management and was able to gain invaluable customer service and administrative work experience in different tourist attractions and theme parks. After graduating she was unable to immediately get her 'dream job' so joined an admin temping agency to pay her rent and further develop her organisational and planning skills. She gained her current role as a result of having a wide experience of undertaking different administrative tasks and excellent interpersonal skills.

1 How has temping helped Amber achieve her dream job?

2.2 Administrative tasks

Effective administration is the oil that lubricates the wheels of business. In this topic you will learn about different tasks, what they involve and how these are undertaken.

The range of tasks and responsibilities

Administrative tasks can be fun and challenging giving you opportunities for high reward. You may work with other people in a team, or for an individual, sometimes away from the office or attending meetings. Although the range of tasks will differ with each job role, you should be prepared to undertake any of the following:

* Receiving and welcoming visitors – it is important to present a positive image of the organisation and be able to deal with the requirements of different types of visitor. For example, a visitor where English is an additional language, or a visitor with hearing problems.

* Organising travel and accommodation – knowing the procedures for arranging travel and accommodation for business trips, preparing itineraries, knowing where to access information.

* Managing diary systems – being able to use both manual and electronic diaries for yourself and other people, and knowing the key features of these.

* Organising and supporting meetings – carrying out administrative tasks required, from organising a venue and refreshments to taking notes of decisions made, and preparing accurate records of the meeting.

As an administrator, it may be part of your role to receive and welcome visitors to the organisation.

* Producing documentation and managing manual and electronic information – it is important to know how to store and update records both in manual and electronic filing systems. Security of information is vital – a good administrator is aware of the consequences of security and confidentiality breaches.

* Using telephone systems to make, receive or transfer calls using an appropriate tone of voice to present a professional image.

* Providing information to internal and external customers, such as requests for reports, updates, company literature, or progress chasing in a timely fashion.

* Undertaking financial transactions such as processing invoices, orders, or expenses for colleagues.

Skills

Whatever tasks you undertake you will have to use a range of practical and **interpersonal skills**. These include communication skills such as listening and questioning, presenting a positive image, time management and planning skills, problem-solving and using technology. For example, when answering the telephone to a potential customer, you will need to:

* answer according to the organisation's procedures, such as before the third ring

* use a tone of voice to present a courteous and professional image

* obtain the name of the caller and listen to what they want

* take accurate messages

* read the message back to the caller to check that you have understood exactly what they have said.

@ Work

Try to find job descriptions of two different administration job roles. List the similarities and differences in terms of tasks, responsibilities, and salary.

Functional Skills

English

Use your speaking and listening skills in order to contribute successfully to group discussions.

Interpersonal skills Used when interacting with others in different situations; often referred to as communication skills or people skills.

Job description Document informing an employee what their job title is, their duties and responsibilities, who they will be working with, and the terms and conditions of the job.

Activity

Collect **job descriptions** from a newspaper, or the internet, for two different administrative roles, one related to working in finance and the other in customer services. Which interpersonal skills are needed? Why are these important? Compare and discuss the differences in the roles.

Just checking

* Name five different administrative tasks.
* Have you examined the job descriptions for two different roles?
* Do you know what interpersonal skills are needed to carry out different administrative tasks?

2.3 The importance of effective administration

Regardless of the size of the organisation, administration is vital to the effective operation of the business. A core administrative function will ensure a consistent approach for all staff and customers across different departments.

Functional areas

Functional areas ensure that all important business activities are carried out. Often these are separate departments in a business, although they could be carried out by a single function in a small business.

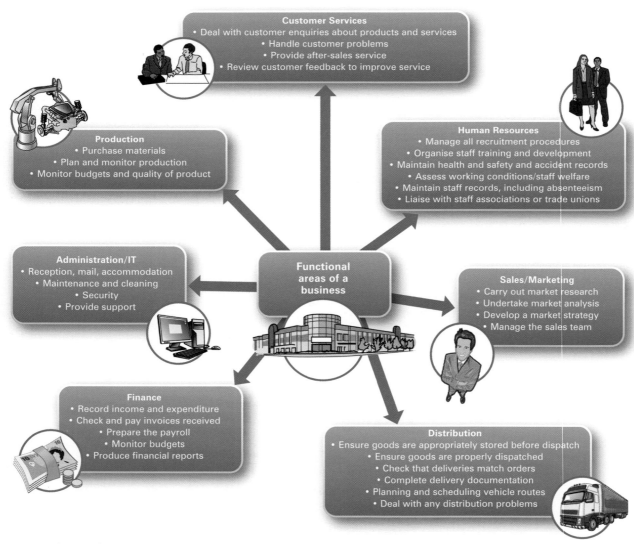

Customer Services
- Deal with customer enquiries about products and services
- Handle customer problems
- Provide after-sales service
- Review customer feedback to improve service

Production
- Purchase materials
- Plan and monitor production
- Monitor budgets and quality of product

Human Resources
- Manage all recruitment procedures
- Organise staff training and development
- Maintain health and safety and accident records
- Assess working conditions/staff welfare
- Maintain staff records, including absenteeism
- Liaise with staff associations or trade unions

Administration/IT
- Reception, mail, accommodation
- Maintenance and cleaning
- Security
- Provide support

Functional areas of a business

Sales/Marketing
- Carry out market research
- Undertake market analysis
- Develop a market strategy
- Manage the sales team

Finance
- Record income and expenditure
- Check and pay invoices received
- Prepare the payroll
- Monitor budgets
- Produce financial reports

Distribution
- Ensure goods are appropriately stored before dispatch
- Ensure goods are properly dispatched
- Check that deliveries match orders
- Complete delivery documentation
- Planning and scheduling vehicle routes
- Deal with any distribution problems

Functional areas of a business.

Activity

Departmental links are important to meet the aims and objectives of the business. Suggest several reasons why.

* Finance would need to link to Human Resources
* Sales/Marketing would need to link to Production
* Customer Services would need to link to Sales/Marketing.

@ Work

Investigate the different functional areas in the organisation. Make notes of these functional areas and check with a supervisor how administrative support is provided to other functional areas.

Activity

In a small group, list the functional areas of two different businesses, preferably a large national business and a small local business. There may be ones that you can visit such as a local business or even your school or college, or they could be researched using the internet. For each business, identify the following:

* the administrative tasks undertaken in each functional area
* how administrative tasks contribute to the processes
* the administrative tasks that contribute to the effective operation of the business.

Prepare a short presentation to deliver to the rest of the class.

Functional area A person, area or department, which carries out a specific business function, for example customer service, human resources, or production.

Functional Skills

English

Use your speaking and listening skills in order to contribute successfully to discussions with others.

ICT

Use your ICT skills to bring together information to suit content and purpose. You will also use ICT skills to enter, develop and format information when delivering an electronic or PowerPoint presentation.

Customer services are an important function in any business

Just checking

* List at least five functional areas in a business.
* What are the links and interactions with other functional areas?
* What is the importance of the administrative functional area for business success?

COMMUNICATION POINT

Think about the last three times you communicated with a business either on the phone, in person or in writing. What was the purpose of the communication. What format did it take? Discuss with a partner.

2.4 What is business communication?

Communication is a method of sending a message from one person to another. Businesses need to communicate to receive or pass on information to others involved, or connected, to the business such as employees, customers, suppliers, shareholders, tax authorities, etc. You need to learn about the importance of effective communication, the different methods used for communicating information and the advantages and disadvantages of each of these.

The communication process

As can be seen from the diagram, most communications are two-way requiring some feedback or response from the receiver.

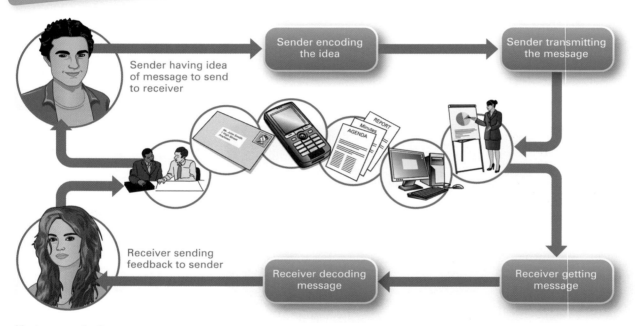

Most communications are two-way.

Channels of communication

There are three main channels communication: spoken, written and electronic. These channels can be **formal** or **informal**. The choice of channel will depend on various factors, including:

* the importance and urgency of the communication

* whether the information in the communication is confidential

* whether a record is needed

* whether any costs are involved

* who the receiver is such as a close colleague, a supervisor or manager or a customer

* the purpose of the communication – to give information, or instructions, to obtain information, to persuade or to sell.

Advantages and disadvantages

A range of methods may be used for each of the three channels, as shown in the table below.

Method	Advantages	Disadvantages
Spoken, e.g. face-to-face meetings, seminars, briefings, appraisals, grapevine, telephone conversations	Provides instant feedback Opportunity for discussions	No permanent record Can be time wasting and costly
Written, e.g. letters, memos, reports, agendas, notices, minutes, messages/notes, presentations	Permanent record Used for both simple and complex messages	Often takes some time for message to arrive Slow or no feedback
Electronic, e.g. email, telephone	Speed Convenience (sending, storage) Cost Resourcing/environmental benefits	Information overload Technological and computer literacy requirements for users Risk of sending information to the wrong person Hidden costs, e.g. data storage

The advantages and disadvantages of communication methods.

Why do communications fail?

Communications can fail for a variety of reasons. How many times have you heard someone say 'I thought what you meant was…' or 'I assumed you were referring to…' Effective business communication depends on each step in the communication process being successful and the correct channel being used.

The cause of failure may be the fault of the sender as the message may not be clear or simple enough to be understood by the receiver. Alternatively, it may be too complicated, or badly presented, so that it does not hold the receiver's attention. The receiver may be unreceptive because they are too busy or distracted, or the choice of channel is incorrect. For example, discussing a complicated report on the telephone will only be productive if the receiver has a written copy of the report to refer to.

Formal channels Based on the organisation's needs; the systems are normally planned by the organisation.

Informal channels Based on the needs of individuals and groups; these can be designed to meet organisational objectives or satisfy social needs, and usually develop spontaneously such as the office grapevine (where staff discuss news, gossip and rumour).

Activity

Nominate one member of the class to convey a message to another member of the class without anyone else hearing. This can then be passed on to another class member and so on until the message has been passed to everyone. What was the end message? What has happened in the communication process?

In a small group, discuss reasons why businesses need to communicate and how communications can fail. See if you can add to the list of advantages and disadvantages of using different methods.

Just checking

＊What are the different communication channels used by businesses?

＊Draw a simple communication process.

＊Give three reasons why business communications can fail.

2.5 How to present business letters

Being able to write effective business communications is an important skill for an administrator to develop. If, during a conversation, you hear something you don't understand, you can ask the person to explain what they mean. You can also check that the verbal message has been received. However, when the message is written, you don't have the same opportunities to check that the meaning has got across.

Business letters

Letters are used in business to communicate with other businesses such as customers or suppliers, or formally with employees such as employment contracts, notices of promotion or **disciplinary matters**. Sometimes a business may want to send the same letter to a large number of people, and using a mail merge feature on the word processor, a standard letter can be produced whilst keeping it personalised to the individual recipient. Business letters are also used to explain complex matters that need careful consideration.

THINKING POINT

Think about different types of written communication you have received in the last month from any business. In a small group, discuss how effectively the message has been communicated and why.

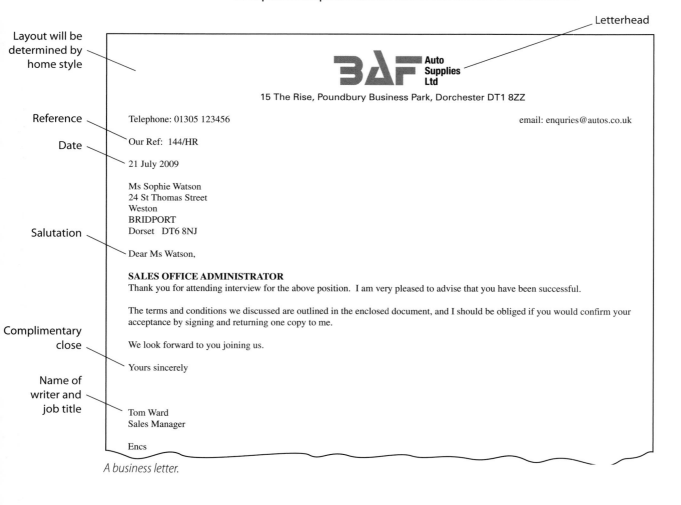

Layout will be determined by home style

Reference

Date

Salutation

Complimentary close

Name of writer and job title

Letterhead

BAF Auto Supplies Ltd

15 The Rise, Poundbury Business Park, Dorchester DT1 8ZZ

Telephone: 01305 123456   email: enquries@autos.co.uk

Our Ref: 144/HR

21 July 2009

Ms Sophie Watson
24 St Thomas Street
Weston
BRIDPORT
Dorset   DT6 8NJ

Dear Ms Watson,

SALES OFFICE ADMINISTRATOR
Thank you for attending interview for the above position. I am very pleased to advise that you have been successful.

The terms and conditions we discussed are outlined in the enclosed document, and I should be obliged if you would confirm your acceptance by signing and returning one copy to me.

We look forward to you joining us.

Yours sincerely

Tom Ward
Sales Manager

Encs

A business letter.

The presentation of any written communication is important to get the message across. As a letter often presents a first impression of the company to a customer, it is vital that the communication is displayed correctly, the content is accurate and grammatically correct, with no misspellings.

Accepted conventions

For formal letters, a business would use its own letter headed paper, which often includes the logo and other information such as quality accreditations. The font and way documents are organised are very important to create a positive image of the company, and layout is usually determined by house style.

There are some accepted business conventions:

* Text in capitals is much harder to read than upper/lower-case text. Although house style will determine fonts and sizes, don't use a font smaller than 10pt if you want people to read more than a few lines of text. Extra space between lines will always increase readability.

* Language is formal and you must take care to ensure that the letter has been checked for accuracy, spelling and grammar, otherwise it will appear unprofessional. Tone is important too. A letter to a friend would be much less formal than a letter to the tax authorities.

* Avoid **jargon** – only use technical language if it is appropriate and you are certain the reader will understand it.

* If the letter starts with 'Dear Sir' or 'Dear Madam', then the close should be 'Yours faithfully'. If the letter uses the person's name, e.g. 'Dear Mr Andrews', the close should be 'Yours sincerely'.

@ Work

Examine the organisation's letter-head and find out the house style used for layout, fonts and sizes.

Disciplinary matters

Unacceptable behaviour on the part of employees which has to be handled according to the organisation's procedures in line with employment law.

Jargon Technical words, often buzzwords, which relates to specific activities or groups and can be used to show you are a member of a group or an outsider. It is a barrier to effective communication.

Functional Skills

English

Use your reading skills to compare, select, read and understand texts.

ICT

Use your ICT skills when using software applications and entering and formatting information. Remember to apply editing techniques when producing information that is fit for purpose and using accepted layouts and conventions as appropriate.

Activity

Draft a letter to a customer who has asked you for more information on the tariffs for a new mobile phone package. Use a word processor and a letterhead template provided by your tutor to create the letter. Check for accuracy, spelling and grammar, and then check your partner's letter.

Just checking

* Name three uses for business letters.
* Are you able to draft a layout?
* Do you understand the importance of checking spelling, accuracy and grammar?

2.6 Looking at other written business communications

There are other methods of written communication a business can use, both internally and externally, which also have their own conventions in terms of layout. This topic will help you explore these further.

Memos

Although emails have largely superseded memos, many businesses still use the memo for internal communication. They are mostly used for making arrangements or requesting information. As with letters, memos have a typical layout and must be accurate, grammatically correct, and without misspellings – but the language used is often informal. Although memos are a simple communication tool, there is no proof of receipt or immediate feedback.

MEMO

TO: Jack Smith, Service Manager

FROM: Natasha Patel

DATE: 30 July 2009

SUBJECT: NEW SALES OFFICE ADMINISTRATOR

Just to advise you that Sophie Watson will be joining the company on 10 August. Sophie is well qualified to do the job and has previous experience in the auto industry.

A memo.

Activity

Using a memo template, or creating your own, word process a memo to your tutor listing the advantages and disadvantages of using different types of written business communications.

Reports

These are widely used in business to present and interpret information, record facts, and include recommendations. A detailed report giving information on a research activity is likely to include visual aids such as charts, diagrams or photographs. The language used is formal and written in the third person. If the report does not have a clear structured format, it can be difficult to understand and important detail may be overlooked.

Table of contents

The contents page from a report.

Notices

These are a good way to communicate the same information to a large group of people, although they must be placed so that people will see them and – more importantly – read them! Often they are displayed on a general noticeboard such as in a staff canteen or rest room, and as a result these might get damaged if not laminated or covered. Examples of notices could be to inform staff of a social event. Some notices are required by law such as health and safety notices and warning signs.

There is no formal layout for a notice and these can be created in an eye-catching way using clip art and headings. The language should be clear and simple and the message should be as short as possible to encourage people to read it. See if you can find an example of a notice in your centre.

Functional Skills

ICT

When using software applications and entering and formatting information you will be using ICT skills. Remember to apply editing techniques when producing information that is fit for purpose and using accepted layouts and conventions as appropriate.

Just checking

* List the uses for memos, reports and notices.
* Why is it important to use correct language and tone?
* List three advantages and disadvantages of using different written methods.

2.7 Oral communications in business

Effective interpersonal communications play an important role in developing good working relationships. In administration, you will use oral communications in different situations such as face-to-face discussions, on the telephone, at meetings, and through presentations.

Face-to-face discussions

At work, these will usually involve one-to-one discussions, such as an appraisal or performance review, or group discussions, such as a team meeting. Discussions are useful for instant feedback, and they also allow you to observe non-verbal communication, known as body language.

The signs of non-verbal communication can include facial expression, eye contact, gestures, posture and proximity.

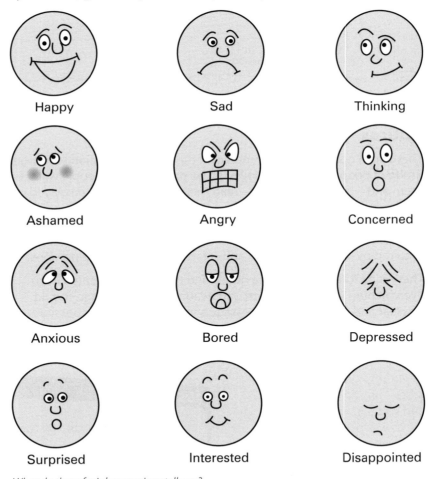

Happy	Sad	Thinking
Ashamed	Angry	Concerned
Anxious	Bored	Depressed
Surprised	Interested	Disappointed

What do these facial expressions tell you?

When taking part in a discussion, body language can show whether someone is anxious and can be used to put someone at ease. Active listening involves using both non-verbal and verbal techniques – it is not a passive activity. An active listener is always focused upon the speaker, listening and observing, encouraging and then checking that they have understood correctly.

Good listeners use a variety of techniques to demonstrate that they are taking in what is being said. It is important to look at the person who is speaking to you. This shows that you are interested in what they are saying, and allows you to pick up meanings. It is important to smile when listening – this indicates that you are open to hearing what is being said, and using facial expressions shows that you are reacting to the emotional content of what the other person is saying. If you mirror the other person's face, this can show that the message is getting across.

Activity

Practise body language with a partner. Taking turns at both listening and speaking and using both verbal and non-verbal signals, indicate you are:

* interested in what the other person is saying
* very bored listening to them
* ready to move on to another topic.

Make notes on how it felt to be on the receiving end of these signals. Which techniques were the most effective, and which techniques did you feel most comfortable using?

@ Work

Observe the body language of those people around you. Without listening to what they are saying can you see how well the conversation is going? How can you tell they are really communicating?

There are many cultural variations to be aware of in non-verbal communication, especially in personal space and body language. For example, simple hand gestures can have various interpretations in different cultures and could be regarded as offensive. Touching, or being too close to someone can also have a negative effect.

Telephone discussions

Body language cannot be seen on the telephone, unless you are using video phones or video conferencing, as you can't see the person you are talking to. Therefore, you are often unable to tell how the other person is reacting to what you are saying. However, you can gain a lot of information from the tone and volume of the person's voice.

Making and taking calls

In order to convey a professional impression when you make a telephone call, prepare a list of questions you want to ask and have the relevant information to hand before you make or return a call. When you make a call, state your purpose as soon as possible and, if the other person is unable to have the conversation now, arrange a time when you will ring back. Speak clearly; make sure your language, tone and volume of voice are appropriate. If you sit up straight, or stand up, as well as smiling as if meeting the person face-to-face, this will be reflected in your tone of voice. Check understanding by asking questions, repeating what you hear, taking notes of important points. Listen and try not to interrupt.

Functional Skills

English
Use your speaking and listening skills to practise body language activities and be able to contribute successfully to group discussions.

Personal, Learning and Thinking Skills

Asking questions when answering the telephone and in discussions with others will help you become an independent enquirer.

Just checking

* Identify different oral communications in the workplace.
* What verbal and non-verbal techniques can be used to show you are listening to the other person?
* How can you create a professional image when making or taking telephone calls?

2.8 Managing your time

When working in business you need to develop and maintain good working relationships. It is essential to be able to plan work with others to meet deadlines. Time management is about making the best use of time and through this topic you will explore several techniques which will help you to use time effectively.

Use of time

Time cannot be stored up or replaced; it is a limited resource, so you need to use it wisely. Good time management will help you achieve more goals, produce better results, gain more job satisfaction, have more time to think and more leisure time.

In order to improve how you manage time, you need to understand how you use it at the moment. The best way to do this is to record your activities using a time log, completing timesheets, or making notes of what you do and for how long over a period of time and then analyse the results.

MAKING GOOD USE OF YOUR TIME

How effectively are you using your time? Are there things you want to achieve but do not have time for at the moment? Write a list of the things you want to achieve.

Week Commencing:			
Activity	**Number of Hours**		
	Daily	**Weekly**	**% of 168**
Sleeping			
Travelling			
Eating			
Time spent studying			
Time with family and friends			
Time on your own			
Outdoor activities			
Domestic activities			
Job/profession			
Interests, hobbies/sports			
Others			
Total			

A time log.

Time stealers

Everyone wastes time to some degree, and although sometimes it is not within your control, such as prolonged meetings, some time stealers are down to you. One of these is procrastination (putting things off until later) – maybe it is a difficult piece of work or a problem phone call. One way of dealing with procrastination is recognising that you do this and then consciously doing something about it, such as doing difficult tasks in the morning rather completing the easier tasks first. This way you be will motivated to tackle work that you would normally put off.

Interruptions are another time stealer. However well intentioned these are – they could be from colleagues or supervisors – you can use techniques to help prevent them or minimise the damage they can do. These include being assertive and politely saying 'No', telling the other person you can't talk now but arrange a time when it would be suitable for both of you.

Other time stealers include idle conversations or a cluttered desk where you can't find anything, which may cause frustration.

Activity

Think about your own performance in your personal and work life. Do you recognise any of the above time stealers? Which areas could you improve on? Make notes of actions you could take to improve your time management.

@ Work

Keep a time diary for one week – analysing it will help you see how you actually spend your time. You may be very surprised! You can then identify what changes you want to make, with the reason why.

Using the Daily Time Log produce a log of all activities carried out in the workplace (e.g. Monday to Friday). Select a typical one week period, which avoids public holidays, sickness periods or leave periods and record your daily activities. You will need to be fairly disciplined about this and include every time you change activities, even opening mail, making a cup of coffee, chatting with colleagues.

Prioritise each activity using a grading system **A, B, C, X**

A = very important tasks – **must-do** tasks that you should either finish or make progress on during the day. These contribute significantly to your work goals.

B = important but non-urgent – **should do** tasks, but the time element is less important. You may need to make progress but not complete them.

C = routine, non-essential tasks – **would like to do** tasks, which have a minor effect on the company's performance and your job, and can be delegated, put off or handled at a low priority time.

X = non-scheduled tasks (emergencies, interruptions, demands from more senior personnel, etc.).

Note the difference between urgency and importance. It is often assumed that urgent and important are the same. They are not: urgency implies a timescale; important implies something that affects the business.

You may wish to use codes to save time, e.g. M = meetings, P = phone calls, I = Interruptions, etc.

Analyse your week of recordings using an analysis sheet and comment on your analysis, e.g. do you spend time on planning and scheduling? Are you doing work that could be delegated? Try the same exercise to prioritise the list of things you would like to do.

Personal, Learning and Thinking Skills

When you evaluate how you spend time you are being a reflective learner. This will help you when you are planning your time in the future.

Just checking

* Have you recorded and analysed your activities for a weekly period?
* List the differences between urgent and important tasks.
* Have you identified your time stealers?

2.9 How to plan work

Making full use of your time will depend on your individual energy cycle. Everyone is different – some people are at their best in the morning, others in the afternoon. Here you will learn how to make the most productive use of your time through planning.

Daily planning

Now that you have some idea of when you perform at your best, you can start to plan your work. If you aim to list things that you need to achieve in the next month, then you can make a plan for the week. From this you can compile a daily plan which should cover only those things that you're going to do today – it could be divided into 'Must do', 'Should do' and 'Could do'.

It's important you write the plan the night before; otherwise, if you leave it until the morning, you might get too busy and lose control of the day. You need to start by setting SMART objectives, that is they should be:

Specific

Measurable

Achievable

Realistic

Timely.

A SMART objective would be 'Complete documentation needed for sales meeting to be held next Monday 28th by 1230 hrs on Friday the 25th'.

Things to do TODAY Date:		
Must do	**Should do**	**Could do**

A daily planner.

Planning aids

All businesses need to plan. Good planning is essential for the smooth running of the office operations. Administrative systems such as staff or holiday rotas rely on planning aids. A basic list can be used to prepare daily, weekly or monthly activities, although individual sheets of paper may get lost, so a wall planner could be used instead. These are especially useful for tasks that can be planned on a yearly basis such as an annual general meeting, financial activities relating to year-end or dates of quarterly reports.

Planners can also be used for tasks that can be planned on a monthly basis, such as team briefings or monthly reports.

@ Work

Try to find examples of paper-based and electronic planning aids. What are they used for? How effective are they? Make notes on what they are used for, what works well, and what could be improved.

Case study: Setting objectives

Roseanna is helping the Sales Manager to plan the launch of a new skincare range. The launch is next month, and there are various work activities that need to be completed. Roseanna lists the objectives of these:

Launch of new skincare range

Objectives

* Book venue and organise refreshments which need confirming five days prior to the event (Day 1–5).
* Invite people (Day 5).
* Advertise in appropriate media (Day 5).
* Organise brochures for printing – need 10 days (Day 21).
* Arrange for samples to be ready one week before launch (Day 24).
* Chase up numbers attending (Day 24–25).
* Confirm numbers for venue (Day 26).

1 How has scheduling her work helped Roseanna?

2 How are the objectives SMART?

3 Do you think the schedule could be improved? If so, how?

Electronic organisers are useful for reminders of appointments, to block out time for completing priority tasks and as memory joggers. They can give access to work colleagues' diaries to make arranging meetings easier.

Just checking

* Try to set a SMART objective.
* List two purposes of planning aids.
* How can electronic organisers be used for planning work?

2.10 Using office equipment safely

Alexa has just started working as assistant to John Sheridan, Facilities Manager for a leisure centre. She knows the importance of using office equipment correctly and has just completed health and safety training as part of her induction. Her job role includes ordering stock, monitoring maintenance contracts and producing monthly building maintenance reports. She is expected to use a range of office equipment, including a computer, printer, photocopier and telephone.

Using the computer

When using the computer Alexa ensures she:

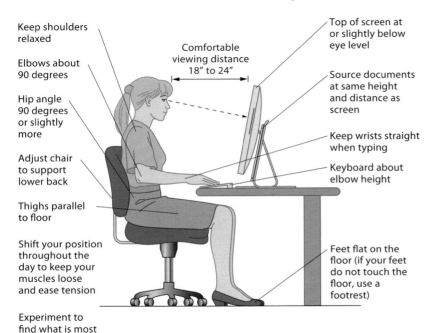

Keep shoulders relaxed

Elbows about 90 degrees

Hip angle 90 degrees or slightly more

Adjust chair to support lower back

Thighs parallel to floor

Shift your position throughout the day to keep your muscles loose and ease tension

Experiment to find what is most comfortable

Comfortable viewing distance 18" to 24"

Top of screen at or slightly below eye level

Source documents at same height and distance as screen

Keep wrists straight when typing

Keyboard about elbow height

Feet flat on the floor (if your feet do not touch the floor, use a footrest)

How to maintain a correct posture at the computer.

* maintains a good posture
* has an adjustable chair that is comfortable and allows her to keep her feet flat on the floor (if this is not possible, then she would use a foot rest to reduce the problem)
* has suitable lighting and checks that the monitor, keyboard, mouse and documents are correctly positioned to avoid strain or glare
* keeps her wrists straight when using the keyboard
* does not grip the mouse too tightly
* keeps the monitor at eye level to avoid neck injury.

Alexa knows that it is important when using a computer to avoid spending hours looking at the screen without a break as this can cause tired eyes and discomfort. Ideally, she tries to take a break away from the screen every hour.

The printer

Before using the printer, Alexa familiarised herself with the user guide. Her colleague also showed Alexa how to use it and explained how to deal with common problems such as printer offline, a paper jam, printer out of paper, toner or ink. In an office environment, printers are often shared between several users, which can have disadvantages if you are waiting for someone else's document to print and your document is urgently required.

Laser printers are often positioned near a work station, but as they can produce ozone, it is advised they should be sited at least one metre away from where a person is sitting, and the printer's filters should be checked regularly.

Alexa also understands that using a printer safely means ensuring you don't print off any personal information that could contravene the Data Protection Act.

The photocopier

Where possible, photocopiers should be installed in a well-ventilated area because of the chemical vapours given off. If they are in an enclosed room, then the room must have mechanical ventilation. They should be regularly maintained and located away from work stations to reduce noise.

When Alexa used the photocopier for the first time she saw there were lots of features, such as double-sided copying, collation of pages and stapling, so she read the user guide and asked a colleague to demonstrate how to use it. As part of her training, Alexa had been shown how to lift heavy boxes of paper safely to avoid injury.

The telephone

Alexa has to use the telephone to contact suppliers and contractors. Using telephones safely involves making sure there are no wire trip hazards around the work station area. Alexa needed to learn the functions of the telephone such as redial, how to forward calls, how to set for messages, etc., so it was essential to use instruction manuals, and ask someone to show her.

Functional Skills

English
Use your reading and writing skills to proofread your documents for spelling and grammar.

Activity

John has asked Alexa to help him prepare material for a staff training day on health and safety in the leisure centre. Alexa has produced a couple of scenarios showing typical health and safety issues in an admin office and a works canteen.

1   In a small group, complete a five-stage risk assessment for the above scenarios (visit the HSE website to help you).

2   Research the Data Protection Act and Human Rights Act and summarise how these can affect the printing of documents.

Safety hazards at work.

Just checking

✳ Have you checked user guides before using office equipment?

✳ Do you always check your posture is correct when using a computer?

✳ Can you follow instructions to transfer a telephone call?

2.11 Types of meeting

Meetings are an important communication method in everyday business. They are used to exchange information, put ideas forward for discussion, solve problems and take decisions. Here you will look at different types of meeting and what steps to take when organising one.

Formal and informal meetings

Not all meetings are necessary. In fact, you have probably attended a few of these where all you gained was information that could have been emailed or posted to you, where there was no need for you to be there, nothing of importance was decided upon, or they were poorly conducted with lots of disruptions. Understanding reasons why meetings can be unsuccessful will help you organise meetings that will achieve their objectives.

In business, there are two different types of meetings that you need to be familiar with: formal and informal.

Type of meeting	Example
Formal – this would normally have a set of procedures and terms of reference that states how they must be run (see the case study on Lowtown College)	* *Annual General Meeting (AGM)* – generally held every year to inform members and shareholders of previous and future activities, and is often the forum for electing directors and officers for the company. * *Extraordinary General Meeting (EGM)* – a meeting called to vote on a major company issue such as a take-over or major acquisition. * *Board of Directors* – establishes broad policies and objectives for the day-to-day running of the business. * *Committee and sub-committee meetings* – have the power to make a decision binding on the organisation, giving advice or making recommendations.
Informal	* Weekly or monthly team meetings * Briefing meetings * Staff training * Project progress meetings

Formal and informal meetings.

WHY HAVE MEETINGS?

In small groups, discuss the benefits of having a meeting. Think about any recent meetings you have attended, either in school or college, at work, or elsewhere. Were they useful? Did they achieve the objectives? Discuss and compare your experiences.

@ Work

Find out the types of meeting that are run at the organisation. Check what policies and procedures there are for these meetings, the purpose of the meeting and what documentation is normally required. Make notes about the types of meeting and their purpose.

Case study: Lowtown College

Health and Safety Standing Committee for Lowtown College

Membership

Chairperson: Each committee meeting must be chaired by the Principal or their nominee of a senior standing. The Principal must attend at least one meeting a year.

Members: Heads of Faculty or their senior nominees   Student representatives

Heads of Administration Departments   Specialist advisers if needed

Trade Union representatives

Frequency of meetings: At least three times a year

Terms of reference:

✻ To monitor the day-to-day implementation of the health and safety policy in their area

✻ To deal with unresolved health and safety issues

✻ To make recommendations about health and safety practices and training

✻ To consider any recommendations from staff or students

✻ To produce an annual report for the Senior Management Team.

What other procedures do you think should be included for a formal meeting?

An informal meeting.

External meetings

Not every meeting will be held in the company's offices. In business, many meetings take place with suppliers or customers at their premises. For example, a customer may need a project progress update for a new product design and it may be more convenient or a requirement of a contract to attend a meeting at their place of work; or it might be easier for a supplier to demonstrate the technical features of a prototype at their premises. Very often, you may be expected to attend external meetings to provide administrative support for your manager.

Functional Skills

English

You will need to record your notes of types of meetings at the workplace, so think about presenting the information clearly and concisely.

Just checking

✻ Give examples of five formal and two informal types of meeting.

✻ Do you know which types of meeting are held externally?

2.12 Organising meetings

As an administrator, you will play a very important role in helping organise and run successful business meetings. It is important that certain steps are followed, whether they are formal or informal, at meetings. Here you will examine the activities for which you will be expected to provide support for, including preparing documentation for the meeting.

Preparing for a meeting

Preparing for a meeting is a very important task for an administrator. Firstly, as you will need to prepare the agenda, you will need to get a clear brief from the chairperson of the date and time of the meeting and what items are needed on the agenda. You might find it helpful to read the minutes and agenda of the previous meeting, if these are available.

BEFORE THE MEETING

Imagine you have been asked to organise a meeting for your boss to be held at the company's premises next week. Six people are to be invited; two of them have to travel a long distance. Think about what you would need to do to prepare for the meeting. Discuss in your group.

Lowtown College
Health and Safety Committee

AGENDA

Meeting to be held in the Conference Room at 11 am on Wednesday 21 January 2009

1. Apologies for absence

2. Minutes of the previous meeting

3. Matters arising

4. Correspondence

5. Revised staff rotas

6. Revised safety procedures

7. Any other business

8. Date and time of next meeting

An agenda must clearly state the time and place of the meeting.

In addition, you will need to find out who will attend, the venue, resources, including catering requirements, whether you are expected to attend to take notes, and any meeting papers that will be needed. Whether the meeting you are arranging is at the company premises or an external venue, you should find it helpful to draw up a checklist which may cover the following:

* Prepare and circulate all relevant documents (agenda, minutes of previous meeting, any supplementary documents).

* Book the venue – is the size suitable? Is there wheelchair access? Are there adequate electrical sockets? What are the emergency procedures? Is the location suitable, e.g. near motorway or train station?

* Check car parking – is it sufficient? Are there any public car parks nearby? What are the charges? What public transport is available?

* Confirm arrangements with reception and the switchboard.

* Check whether any equipment is required such as audio-visual, flipchart, OHP, computer, etc. Is it included in the cost, is it working?

* Check on refreshments, any specific dietary needs, and what arrangements there are for teas/coffees.

* Keep a record of apologies and confirmations of attendance received.

* Where relevant, prepare a seating plan.

* Check on car parking arrangements.

If the meeting is to be held in an internal venue, then most organisations have allocated meeting or conference rooms. You need to make sure an appropriate room is booked through the correct procedures. If the venue is external, more planning is required and you may have to check whether you need to work to a budget, if any people require overnight accommodation and car parking. You should also provide details of how to get the venue.

Functional Skills

ICT
Use word processing skills to prepare an agenda applying appropriate formatting techniques.

English
You will need to prepare the agenda according to business conventions so make sure you think about the appropriate style and tone for communicating effectively.

Personal, Learning and Thinking Skills

As a self-manager, you need to organise time and resources when preparing for meetings. For example, you should prioritise the checklist of tasks to be completed.

Activity

Sometimes things do not run as smoothly as you would like. With your tutor's support, arrange a half hour meeting with a suitable person who has responsibility for facilities in a local business to discuss potential problems and suitable solutions for them. Prepare an agenda for the meeting using accepted conventions.

Just checking

* What is the difference between internal and external venues?
* Do you know how to prepare an agenda?
* List the steps to follow when preparing for a meeting.

2.13 Providing support at meetings

Providing administrative support at meetings usually involves ensuring that all arrangements are met, and accurate records of the meeting are taken. In this topic you will gain a full understanding of the support you would be expected to provide.

Before the meeting starts

One of the first tasks an administrator will do is check that the room is fully prepared, and that all the equipment is tested and working. The layout of the room is important and you should ensure that all relevant paperwork is ready, taking a few additional copies of documentation to the meeting in case anyone needs them. You will probably want to meet with the chairperson beforehand to talk through the arrangements; you should also take the attendance list with you.

You may be expected to welcome the participants, check their names against the attendees' list, hand out any name badges and additional documentation, and direct them to facilities, such as a cloakroom, if required.

Usually refreshments are available when people arrive, especially if they have travelled long distances to attend. It is important to confirm with the caterer the times for refreshments on the day of the meeting.

Health, safety and security issues are very important when supporting meetings. For example, you will need to ensure the security of material and equipment, especially those relating to confidentiality of information. You may need to check the ventilation and heating levels in the room and know how to adjust the settings to ensure that everyone is comfortable. When checking audio-visual equipment is working you must ensure there are no trailing wires or cables to cause a hazard, as well as checking the height is correct so that everyone will be able to see any presentation.

Delegates at the meeting may need familiarising with the venue's emergency procedures. You should check if a fire drill is planned at the time of the meeting so you can advise attendees where fire exits are located. Also, make sure you familiarise yourself with the emergency procedures.

Registration at a meeting.

Records of meetings

Most meetings have a written record of the proceedings, whether a few handwritten notes in a meetings book or a full set of formal **minutes**. Summarising a meeting in this way should contain certain essential information and be a clear and accurate record of the meeting in a specified format. It should include:

* a list of the people who attended

* any apologies and absences.

You will need to listen carefully to the discussions and make notes of actions to be taken. This may sound daunting, but it is a skill that needs to be developed. Don't worry, it is not necessary to write down every word that is spoken, and the chair may summarise what has been agreed at the end of each agenda item. It is good practice to write up the records of the meeting as soon as possible after the meeting whilst it is still fresh in your mind.

> **Minutes** The written record of all the decisions made at a meeting.

Activity

Watch a TV programme that has lively debate, such as BBC Question Time. Take notes of the important points made by panel members for three of the topics discussed. Summarise your notes and record these in a business meeting format.

Did you know?

Some of the common terminology used at formal meetings:

* Address the chair – speak directly to the chairperson.

* Quorum – the minimum number of people who must be in attendance before the meeting is official.

* Motion – this is a proposal that is officially put before a meeting and has to be accepted or defeated. It must be recorded in the minutes.

* Proposer – this is the person who moves the motion.

* Seconder – a person who supports the motion.

* Resolution – the name given to a motion once it has been agreed by the meeting.

* Casting vote – the chairperson has a second or deciding vote when votes are equally divided for and against the motion.

* Unanimous – no one objects to the motion.

Functional Skills

English

You will need to use your listening, writing and reading skills to take accurate notes. Make sure you listen carefully and write the notes concisely and clearly.

Just checking

* Do you understand how to welcome meeting delegates?
* What type of support would an administrator be expected to provide during a meeting?
* Can you take accurate records of discussions?

WHAT HAPPENS NEXT?

Imagine you have supported a meeting for your manager. In your group, discuss what activities an administrator is likely to have to do when the meeting ends.

After a meeting, there are important administrative tasks that have to be completed. This topic will help you understand the importance of preparing accurate records of the decisions taken, as well as making these available to all relevant people.

After the meeting

Administrators may get involved in helping clear the meeting room. This may involve tidying up any crockery, turning off electrical equipment and arranging for it to be returned if it came from elsewhere, making sure that all unused documentation is collected and disposed of according to the organisation's procedures, and, if required, that the room is locked after everyone has left.

The records of the meeting should be written up as soon as possible after the meeting using the accepted house style of the organisation, and checked with the chairperson for accuracy. A small meeting with just a couple of people may only require a list of action points. A more formal meeting, such as a committee meeting, will usually have a standard format and require a formal set of minutes.

Preparing minutes of meetings

Lowtown College

MINUTES OF THE HEALTH AND SAFETY COMMITTEE

Held in the Conference Room, 11 am on Wednesday 21 January 2009

Present:
Mr R Stone (Chairperson)
Mr N Singh (Health and Safety Officer)
Miss J Kail
Mr L Cross
Miss R Summers (Secretary)

ACTION

Apologies for absence:
Apologies were received from Mr M Slater.

Matters arising:
Mr Singh (NS) reported that the new vending machines had been installed two days ago and trials were currently underway. Feedback from the trials would be reported at the next meeting.

Any other business:
Miss Kail expressed concern that spaces allocated for visitors, car parking were often used by staff instead, causing problems when clients visited. NS was asked to investigate this and report back to the next meeting.

Date and time of next meeting:
Thursday 25 February at 11 am in the Conference Room.

Minutes of a meeting.

Usually, minutes are structured as follows: the type of meeting, place, date and time of meeting, a list of those present, sometimes with job titles alongside. Usually the name of the chairperson is first, others are put in order of seniority or alphabetically, and finally the name of the meeting secretary. Apologies for absence should be recorded next.

Headings are used to separate different agenda items, and notes of what has been discussed and/or decisions taken. The minutes should be dated with the date they were prepared, and space should be left for the signature of the chairperson.

Ensuring people receive accurate records of meetings

When the records of the meeting have been approved they should be circulated to all attendees, usually within a defined timescale, making sure the correct date for the next meeting is included. Usually you will have to send copies to people who did not attend, including those who did not send apologies for absence.

Why is it important to circulate the minutes as soon as possible? Well, there may be actions agreed that affect people who did not attend. For example, a decision might have been taken to close the canteen for a day whilst maintenance to the refrigerators is carried out. This would mean that other people who use the facility have to be informed.

Confidentiality

As an administrator attending meetings, you will often hear confidential and sensitive matters being discussed, sometimes relating to staffing issues. This information must not be discussed by you with anyone outside the meeting. It is essential that you do not breach confidentiality, even accidentally. Keep all confidential documents you are working on securely locked away, and when word processing the minutes make sure your screen is not in view of others. Log off your computer when you leave your work station.

Functional Skills

ICT

Use word processing skills to prepare records of a meeting applying appropriate formatting techniques.

English

You will need to prepare the minutes according to business conventions so make sure you think about the appropriate style and tone for communicating effectively.

Activity

You work as personal assistant to the Sales Manager of a busy sports and leisurewear retailer. Your company is expanding into Europe and you have been asked to organise and support meetings in different venues. Your boss thinks you will need some additional administrative help, so suggests you prepare guidance notes for new staff on the administrative tasks that need to be undertaken at meetings.

Just checking

* Identify the different administrative tasks which need to be completed after a meeting.
* Can you prepare accurate minutes of meetings?
* Why is it important to ensure confidentiality of documents when preparing records of meetings?

Assessment

This unit is assessed internally. This means that you will be set an assignment by your consortium, which should direct your work through a series of tasks connected to the running of a business related activity, so that you cover all of the learning outcomes for this unit.

The work you submit for assessment must be original work, produced by yourself under controlled conditions – this will be arranged by your tutor. It will then be marked by your tutor and moderated by the awarding body.

You will be assessed on:

* your knowledge of the different administrative roles and processes in business
* your understanding of the importance of effective administration
* your ability to communicate effectively in writing, plan and carry out administrative work safely
* your ability to organise and support a meeting.

To aim for higher grades you should try to:

* offer explanations of what is involved in the activities when carrying out administrative roles
* think carefully about the importance of effective administration for both the staff and the organisation
* produce documents which conform to standard document conventions, have a clear message, few language errors, and create a positive impression on the reader
* demonstrate good organisational skills when organising and supporting a meeting through planning your work, prioritising whether tasks are important or urgent, and producing and distributing any meetings documentation within agreed timescales
* use office equipment in a safe manner without difficulty, particularly when sitting at a computer.

3 PERSONAL FINANCE AND FINANCIAL SERVICES

Introduction

Personal finance involves learning how to manage your money wisely. It is a skill that you will work to perfect all your life. One benefit of learning about personal finance is that it can make you wealthier through helping you to make educated choices about your money.

One of the best ways of managing your money is by gathering as much information as possible. If you are aware of the financial services and products available to you, then you will be able to plan your own finances wisely.

How you will be assessed

This unit will be assessed by a short written examination lasting one hour. It will contain a range of questions based on personal finance and financial services.

What you will learn in this unit

You will:

* know the main types, features and sources of money
* understand how sources of financial information and advice differ
* know how to plan and manage personal finances
* understand the main features of common financial products and services.

THINKING POINT

In small groups, discuss what information you need to know about personal finance. Where would you get the information and advice?

Case study: Loan choices

Rizwan is interested in buying a car. The manager at the local car showroom has offered him a loan through them over 5 years with an interest rate of 14.9%.

1 Do you think Rizwan has enough information?

2 What other details do you think he needs?

Natalia is hoping to open her first bank account. She is 14 and her mum has suggested that she should open the account at the branch she banks at. Natalia has seen some advertisements for another branch that is offering an MP3 player for opening an account.

1 Which bank do you think she should open an account with?

2 Do you think she needs more information?

Personal, Learning and Thinking Skills

This unit will ask you to use a variety of skills that will be vital to you in the world of work, from reading your payslip to how much tax you should be paying.

3.1 What is money?

'Money is anything that is widely used for making payments and accounting for **debits** and **credits**.' (Glyn Davis, *A History of Money*, 2002*)*

Legal tender

Legal tender is a payment that, by law, cannot be refused in settlement of a debt. The status of **legal tender** is given to certain types of money. In the UK, this is set out in the Coinage Act 1971, which states that 20p and 50p pieces are legal tender, but only in amounts up to £10; 5p and 10p pieces are legal tender up to amounts of £5; and 1p and 2p pieces are legal tender up to amounts of 20 pence; £2 and £1 coins are legal tender up to any amount anywhere in the UK. Bank notes are legal tender in any amount of value, but they are only legal tender in England and Wales as Scotland prints its own banknotes.

The difference between paying a debt and paying for a service not yet received

If you are paying a debt, that is, paying for something you have already bought or used, then whoever you are paying must accept legal tender. If you are paying for a service which you have not yet used, then the trader may choose to accept only certain types of payment.

Activity

Which of the following transactions cannot be refused?

1. Tom buys a chocolate bar for 34p and pays in 1p pieces.
2. Aaisha, who lives in Newcastle, buys a motorbike on eBay for £500. She is going to pick it up in Scotland where she'll pay in £50 notes.
3. Jenny borrows £10 from Adam. When she pays it back she offers it to him in 20p pieces.
4. Yanne buys a can of coke for 60p, and pays with a £10 note.
5. Nina stays overnight in a hotel in Northern Ireland. The bill comes to £28 and she pays with £2 coins.
6. Ben has his hair cut, which costs £6, and pays in 10p pieces.

Types of money

Cash

Cash is the most common type of money in the UK. It is available in a variety of different **denominations**: £50, £20, £10 and £5 notes and £2, £1, 50p, 20p, 10p, 5p, 2p, and 1p coins.

Cheque

A cheque is a form of money, but it is a payment method and not legal tender. It is a written order from one bank account holder instructing their bank to pay a certain sum of money to another bank account holder. Cheques are no longer as popular as they once were – many shops and traders are no longer accepting them, preferring to be paid for goods and services electronically by debit and credit cards or in cash.

Debit cards

This is another type of payment method. In effect, it is an electronic cheque. Instead of the bank account holder writing a cheque, the debit card is optically read by a machine, and the money is transferred electronically from one account to another.

Credit cards

This is similar to a debit card. In this case, the credit card company pays businesses directly for goods and services purchased by the credit card holder. The credit card company then bills the credit card holder for payment at a later date.

Using a debit card.

Debits Money that you owe.

Credits Money that is owed to you.

Legal tender Payment that, by law, cannot be refused in settlement of a debt.

Denomination A unit of measure, especially in monetary value. The different amounts coins and notes come in are known as denominations.

Hotlink

Learn more about UK coinage by visiting the Royal Mint, where all of our coins are made: www.royalmint.gov.uk

The Bank of England has been issuing banknotes for over 300 years. For more information and the latest designs, visit: www.bankofengland.co.uk

Just checking

✳ What is considered to be legal tender in England and Wales?

✳ What are the four types of money?

3.2 Properties of money and 'near money'

Direct exchange or **barter** is where you swap goods with another person. This is good if both parties want what the other has. For example, if you wanted to swap five chickens for a pig, the person owning the pig must want five chickens. This system would be difficult today and has been replaced by money. If you offer money for something that someone is selling, they will accept it, because they know that they can exchange money for what they want, whenever they want it. This topic looks at the properties of money and 'near money'

Cowrie Shells were one of the first types of money used in 1200BC in China.

Properties of money

Easily recognisable

Money must retain its value for it to be thought of as money. If you look carefully at a bank note, you will see the words 'I promise to pay the bearer on demand the sum of …'. This was originally printed on the notes so that the person holding the note could go to the Bank of England and withdraw the note's value in gold.

Easy to carry around

In the past, some types of money, like stones, were not easy to carry. Some of the larger 'money' stones were 1.8 metres across! Money must be easy to carry around and store. In 2008, people in Zimbabwe had to take suitcases of money to the shop just to buy a loaf of bread.

Available in different denominations

One of the features of money is that it must be divisible, for example £1 is worth 100 pence. Also, it must be able to pay for small items, so it wouldn't work if our smallest coin was £1 – how would we pay for penny sweets?

> **Did you know?**
>
> Amber, animal skins, axes, barley, beads, blankets, bronze bracelets, cattle, cigarettes, corn, cowrie shells, drums, eggs, feathers, grains, gongs, hoes, ivory, kettles, jade, leather, mats, nails, oxen, pigs, quarts, rice, salt, stones, tea leaves, thimbles, tobacco, tools, vodka, volcanic rock, yarn and whales teeth have ALL been used as money!

Case study: Small change

In 1992, the Australian government started to take 1 cent and 2 cent coins out of circulation. It decided to do this as as the coins were not worth very much (1 cent is worth about ¼ of 1p) and the little coins were not needed. The 1 and 2 cent coins are still legal tender, but they are not considered currency and are no longer released for circulation, so you can take them to the bank and change them for currency of the same face value.

1 How do you think this affected the prices charged in shops in Australia?

2 Do you think the UK should copy Australia and get rid of 1p and 2p coins?

Hard wearing

Money must last a long time as it is expensive to make. Some of the oldest types of money were not very durable, for example grains, eggs and barley can rot and animals can die suddenly, so it wouldn't help to have a large store of these things.

Worth the same amount

Money must be worth the same amount day after day. There is usually a reduction in the value of a currency over time (this is called inflation), but this should be minimal.

Same basic features

This means that the same denomination coins and notes should have the same dimensions and basic features, for example the monarch's head on one side and the denomination of the coin on the other.

Rare

If there was an abundance of money and it could be found anywhere, you would need a lot of it to be worth anything. Money must be rare – sand wouldn't be a good idea for money, but diamonds would be sensible as they are rare.

Barter Swapping goods to pay for things, not using money at all.

Activity

Using the table below, work out which of the following are money:

	Cattle	Stones	Grain	Cheques	Whale Teeth
Recognisable					
Easy to carry					
Available in several denominations					
Hardwearing					
Worth the same					
Similar features					
Rare					

'Near money'

The items below can be used like money, and are referred to as 'near money'.

Loyalty cards

Some shops, particularly supermarkets and department stores, issue loyalty cards to their customers. Whenever the customer shops at the store, they receive points in relation to the amount of money they spend. The loyalty card points can then be exchanged for goods or services. This means that they are not widely accepted apart from in the stores or chains of stores that they are linked to.

Vouchers

Money-off vouchers are issued by manufacturers and supermarkets to encourage shoppers to buy certain products. Although these are not money, they do have a cash value (usually found on the back of the voucher), which is usually about 0.0003 pence. They are only redeemable against a certain product, or in a certain shop, and are not widely accepted enough to be money.

There has been a growth in the use of gift cards as presents. These are plastic cards that have an amount of money put on them for the customer to use in the store that the gift card is from.

Travellers' cheques

Another type of payment method, travellers' cheques are similar to cheques, except that they are expressed in a foreign currency. They are issued by banks, building societies, travel agencies and foreign exchange bureaux and can be used in the same way as cash by people travelling outside the UK. They are safer to carry than cash as they can be cancelled if stolen.

E-money

Electronic money is only available virtually – there is no physical money to hold. E-money can be used to pay for things on the internet. It is a method of payment transfer. The money is held by the company who issues the e-money until it is spent. Customers can prepay money into their account or build up money by selling items on auction sites such as eBay. Paypal is an example of e-money.

Rail cards, season tickets and pre-paid tickets

These are types of pre-payment for journeys. You pay for trips in advance and the card is proof that you have paid.

Savings stamps

These are another form of pre-payment. The stamps are issued by one shop (usually supermarkets) to help people save up money to pay for big bills, for example at Christmas.

Just checking

* What are the properties of money?
* What is the difference between money and 'near money'?
* What would be a good type of money that has not been covered, and why?

To identify money you have to know its features. To describe a face someone may say that it has two eyes, a nose and a mouth. These are all features of a face that people can recognise. The features of money are less obvious, but once you know them, it is easier to understand the differences between money and 'near money'.

Security features

Banknotes are printed on special paper which gives them their unique feel. The new style £20 note, first issued in 2007, has the most advanced security features of any UK banknote. They include:

* **Raised print** – you can feel this on some parts of the note, for example on the front, the words 'Bank of England' and 'Twenty Pounds'.

* **Metallic thread** – the thread is embedded in the paper in every banknote. This appears as silver dashes on the back of the note. If you hold the note up to the light, the metallic thread appears as a continuous dark line.

* **Watermark** – by holding the note up to the light, in the clear area on the left, you will see an image of the Queen's portrait together with a bright £20. This can also be viewed from the back of the note.

* **Quality of printing** – the printed lines and colours are sharp, clear and free from smudges or blurred edges.

* **Holographic strip** – this appears in the same position on the front of every note and runs from top to bottom. It contains a number of foil patches with alternating holographic images. The positioning of the patches varies along the strip. When the note is tilted, one hologram shows a multi-coloured image of Adam Smith (Scottish economist), the other changes between a multi-coloured pound sign and the figure 20. The figure 20 is also embossed on the strip, and is positioned in the same place on every note – just to the right of the signature of the Chief Cashier.

* **Micro lettering** – below the Queen's portrait the value of the note is written in small letters and numerals – 'TWENTY' and '20' (you might need a magnifying glass to see this clearly).

* **See-through register** – by holding the note up to the light, you will see coloured irregular shapes printed on the front and back which combine to form the pound sterling symbol. This feature is unique to the new-style £20 note.

* **Signature** – the signature of Andrew Bailey, chief cashier, appears on the left-hand side of the front of the note. He signs the note on behalf of the Governor and Company of the Bank of England.

CAN YOU DESCRIBE A £5 NOTE?

In pairs without looking at an actual note, try to recreate a £5 on a sheet of paper, adding as much detail as possible. When you have completed it compare your picture with another pair. What do you agree on? Now look at a real note. What did you get correct? Why do you think it is such a hard task?

Design features

The new style £20 note, with a profile of Adam Smith on the back, is the second highest denomination note in value and the second largest in size (approx. 149 mm x 80 mm).

The new style £20 note.

Its design features include:

* **Denomination numeral** – a large pound sign and the number 20 appear in the top left-hand corner of the front of the note to enable easy recognition of its value; this means that a special symbol for the partially sighted is not required. A slightly smaller value figure appears in the top and bottom right-hand corners of the front of the note. 'Twenty Pounds' and '£20' are also printed on the back of the note.

* **Unique number** – each note has its own serial number which is printed horizontally and vertically on the back of the note. The horizontal number is in the bottom right-hand corner and consists of multi-coloured letters and numbers of graduating height. The vertical number runs down the left-hand edge and the letters and numbers are the same height and colour.

* **Copyright symbols** – the international copyright symbol is printed to the left of the holographic strip on the front of the note and under the words 'Bank of England' on the back.

* **Historical character** – an image of Adam Smith (1723–90), one of the fathers of modern economics, appears on the back of the note. In one of his great works, *An Inquiry into the Nature and Causes of the Wealth of Nations*, Smith famously used the example of workers in a pin factory to describe the benefits created by the division of labour, and, as explained on the note, 'the great increase in the quantity of work that results'.

Counterfeit notes are most often found by banks when they are sorting genuine bank notes. The Bank of England records how many forgeries are found by banks.

Counterfeit and genuine Bank of England Banknotes in 2007 (numbers of notes)		
Denomination	Counterfeit banknotes taken out of circulation (rounded to nearest 1000)	Genuine banknotes in circulation (averaged for the year rounded to nearest 1mn)
£5.00	4,000	235,000,000
£10.00	6,000	608,000,000
£20.00	276,000	1,234,000,000
£50.00	4,000	141,000,000
Total	290,000	2,218,000,000

1 Which is the most copied bank note? Why do you think this is?
2 Do you think these figures include all of the counterfeit bank notes in circulation?
3 Did you think there would be more or fewer forged notes found by the Bank of England? Why did you think this?
4 Why is it important to remove counterfeit notes from circulation?

Hotlink

Go to www.bankofengland.co.uk and look at Banknotes, Security Features. Make sure you know how to check that a banknote is genuine and check out the other features on different bank notes.

1 How many bank notes has the Bank of England produced in the last three years?
2 What happens to the old notes when a new design is introduced?

Just checking

* The new £20 note is the most advanced banknote in circulation in the UK. Why do you think this is?
* Identify at least five security features on a new style £20 note?
* What are the reasons for having a large denomination numeral on the note?

3.4 Sources of money

All of the money in your purse or wallet came from somewhere. A business might need to get a large amount of money quickly. It has to know where it can get money from and how much it will cost in total.

Banks and other lenders

Where do people get money to start a business? The table below shows you some of the most common sources of money.

Source of money	Advantages	Disadvantages
Own savings	Does not have to be repaid Does not give ownership of the business to anybody else	Risk of losing own money May not have enough savings to start business
Bank loan	Can raise a large amount of money quite quickly	Must be repaid Must pay **interest**
Commercial mortgage (a long-term loan over many years, e.g. up to 35 years)	Can raise a larger amount of money quite quickly Long period in which to repay	Must pay interest on the mortgage, which can be considerably more the original loan A long-term commitment
Profit retained in the business (this can only be used once the business has been set up)	Maintain control of the business Does not need to be repaid	Must be making a regular profit

Common sources of money.

You could use all or any of these sources of money to start a business, but what if you want money to buy a large item such as a car? The obvious place to start is a bank or building society, but there are other types of lenders.

Doorstep lenders

These are businesses which generally provide small loans (of around £50 to £500) and come to your door to set up and collect payments. The loans are usually for a short period of time (usually weeks), the **interest** rates are very high (sometimes as much as £60 charged for every £100 borrowed) as the people who borrow are considered high risk.

State benefits

State benefits are a form of financial support paid by the government to help a range of people. For example:

* Jobseeker's Allowance – paid to unemployed people seeking work.

* Employment and Support Allowance (replaced Incapacity Benefit and Income Support for new claimants from October 2008) – paid to disabled people unable to work.

WHERE DOES YOUR MONEY COME FROM?

Where did the money in your pocket come from? If you needed £100, where would you be able get it? There are many places where you could borrow the money if you are over 18. Using the internet, look for a range of places where you could borrow £100 pounds.

Activity

Visit the Department for Work and Pensions website (www.dwp.gov.uk) to find the current average amounts paid for at least five different state benefits.

* Child benefit – paid to a parent or care giver of every child under 16 years, and up to 18 if the child is in education or further training.
* Education Maintenance Allowance (EMA) – paid to students aged 16–19 who qualify for extra help while learning/training.

All of these benefits have to be applied for, but they do not have to be paid back to the government.

Personal sources of money

Earned income

This is commonly known as earnings. It is the amount you are paid as a wage or salary before tax and other deductions.

Inheritance

When people die everything they own is usually passed on to their heirs, normally their next of kin, that is their spouse or children. If a person has made a **will**, it will state who will receive what when they die.

Selling

Once you have decided that you no longer need something, you can sell it to raise money for something else. There are different groups of people that you can sell things to.

You can sell an item to any of the groups. Internet auction sites such as eBay have made it possible for people to sell items to anyone in the world; the only limitation is the cost of postage.

Borrowing

In order to buy things that they could not otherwise afford, some people borrow the money they require. There are a number of sources from which you can borrow money:

* Parents or family – a very good method of borrowing, as your family will usually ask for little interest to be paid on the loan.
* Bank overdraft – if you have a bank account, the bank may allow you to use this facility. For a small charge, you will be able to withdraw more money than is in your account. The bank will set a limit to the amount available; if you go over the limit, there will be a charge.
* Bank loan – this is a fixed amount of money that the bank agrees to lend. The borrower then pays it back, with interest, over an agreed period of time. The bank pays out the full amount at the beginning of the loan.

Using savings

Some people save money every month for a rainy day or for a large item that they would like to buy. If they put the money in a bank or building society, they may receive interest. They will not have to pay back more than they have spent.

Interest The sum that you are charged for borrowing money from a bank or other lender.

Will A legal document declaring a person's wishes regarding the disposal of their money and possessions when they die.

Just checking

* There are different sources that people can get money from. How many can you name? (without peeking at the contents above!)
* Which of the sources of money for a business do you think is the best, and why?
* Which of the sources of money would be your least favourite choice? Why?
* Name five types of benefit which you qualify for if you have a change in circumstances.

3.5 Sources of financial information

There are many places where people can get help and information about the many different methods of raising money. Some may offer impartial free advice, some may offer only their own products and some will make charges for their financial advice.

SEARCHING FOR ADVICE

If you were looking to purchase a large item (e.g. car or house), who would you ask for advice? Copy out and fill in the table below:

Advice from	Positives	Negatives	Bias?
Sales person	They'll know all about the products they offer and what you are likely to be accepted for.	They are trying to make a sale. They will only offer the products they sell, and may try to lend you the maximum amount you can borrow.	Probably biased towards the products which give them the most commission (a fee the business will get for selling the product).
Family member			
Friends			
Bank manager			
Parents			

Where can you get advice?

People use different sources of information according to the financial advice they need and their ability to find information. The following are the most common places to find information:

* **Citizens Advice service** – this provides free and impartial financial information and advice to any individuals who require it, especially those in financial difficulties. It also helps anyone who wishes to appeal against council tax payments or if they disagree with their state benefit entitlement.

* **Banks and building societies** – these provide advice on their own products and services.

* **Independent financial advisers** –these are independent professionals who give advice on products from a range of providers. They are either paid by the customer or by the company whose products they sell.

* **Debt counsellors and Individual Voluntary Arrangements (IVAs)** – these provide advice and agreements on how large debts can be repaid. Very often IVAs can be used by those in serious debt to save them from declaring **bankruptcy**.

* **Department for Work and Pensions** – this government department offers free advice on state benefits and entitlements and how individuals may claim them.

* **HM Revenue and Customs** – this government department offers advice on personal taxes and what should be paid by employees and businesses.

* **Financial Services Authority (FSA)** – the UK's financial watchdog provides facts about financial products and services to consumers on its 'Money made clear' website.

Case study: Seeking financial advice

* Moira is a single mother who has built up a large amount of debt on credit cards. She is looking for advice to help her sort out her financial situation.

* Paul has just started a new job. He has received his first wage slip and is very confused as the company has given him the tax code BR, which is different from the code he had at his last job. Also, the amount of tax he is paying seems to be much more than before.

* Doreen has just retired. She does not receive a company pension, and needs to know what she is entitled to in her retirement.

1 Where should Moira, Paul and Doreen look for advice? (There may be more than one place.)

2 Where could they look for information using the internet?

Which advice to choose?

You now know where information can be found, but the same type of information can be found in many different places. How do you know which one to choose? The main things to consider are the objectivity, quality and degree of detail of the advice. Banks usually only tell you about their products, which means that their advice may not be impartial as it will not consider the whole market.

Just checking

* Why can financial information be found in many different places?

* Any financial information should be carefully considered. Why will some advice not be objective?

* Why does the Department for Work and Pensions provide lots of information and forms on its website?

Functional Skills

ICT

You will be able to demonstrate the skill of finding and selecting information by evaluating the types of financial information available on the internet and considering whether the websites are fit for purpose.

3.6 Planning personal expenditure

Once you gain your financial independence, going into debt is the one risk associated with personal finance. You must be able to plan financially, including taking into account your income and basic tax liabilities. This topic looks at the benefits of planning personal expenditure.

Avoiding getting into debt

Below are some tips to help you avoid getting into debt:

* Pay with cash whenever possible – that way you will never spend more than you have.

* Avoid impulse purchases – always consider whether it's something you really need.

* Avoid 'buy now, pay later', 'interest-free financing' and similar offers that simply postpone debt.

* Compare prices before making major purchases.

* Avoid borrowing to finance essential purchases.

* If you cannot avoid borrowing, use the lender that offers the lowest interest rate.

* Avoid bank overdraft charges by keeping a close check on your bank balance.

* Always pay more than the minimum payment on credit card bills, if possible.

* Avoid applying for more than one or two credit cards at a time.

Credits cards are one of the easiest ways people get into debt.

Controlling costs

Part of your income will be used to pay for living expenses, such as gas, electricity, insurance, food and rent. These costs tend to increase year-on-year. Shopping around to find the lowest prices can save money. There are many price comparison sites on the internet which give the consumer the opportunity to reduce their costs or at least keep them the same.

Avoiding legal action and repossession

You may have heard in the news about people losing their homes because they haven't been able to keep up with mortgage repayments. When this happens, the lender will take back the property and sell it to recover the money they are owed. This is known as repossession. It is not only your home that can be repossessed but anything that was used as **collateral** for a loan. If you do not keep up with the repayments on a car, for example, the company who lent you the money can repossess the car.

When considering making a large purchase, to avoid the possibility of legal action and repossession in the future, it's wise to ask whether you can really afford it. The person borrowing the money needs to think how they would pay back the money if their circumstances suddenly changed, for example they lost their job.

Collateral A security pledged for the repayment of a loan.

Maintaining a good credit rating

When a company considers an individual for a loan, it will check their credit history, which is information held on computer by credit reference agencies such as Experian about a person's past borrowing and their ability to repay. If you borrow money, ensuring that you pay it back promptly with interest, will help to ensure that you maintain a good credit rating. A poor credit rating may prevent you from getting a loan.

Just checking

* Suggest six ways to avoid getting into debt.
* What is repossession?
* What is the importance of a good credit rating?

3.7 Case study: Phil's finances

Managing your expenses and considering new purchases carefully can really help you avoid getting into debt. When you first move away from home, for example when you go to university, you should consider creating a personal budget. This topic looks at how one student, Phil, managed his finances.

YOUR BUDGET

Draw up a list of your monthly income and outgoings (expenditure).

Activity

Phil is about to start his first term at university. During his first year, he will be living in student accommodation and has decided to get a part-time job to help to fund his socialising. He receives a student loan and his parents have agreed to give him an allowance every month.

Income	Budgeted (£)	Actual (£)
Student loan		
Money from parents		
Part-time job		
Total Income		
Expenditure	**Budgeted (£)**	**Actual (£)**
University fees		
Accommodation		
Travel		
Food		
Clubs/societies		
Clothing		
Nights out		
Total expenditure		
Overall	**Budgeted (£)**	**Actual (£)**
Credit/debt		

Part 1: Drawing up the budget

Using the following information, draw up Phil's budget. Enter all of the figures below in the 'Budgeted (£)' column. Total up his income and expenditure, then subtract one from the other to work out if he will be free of debt.

Planned income

* Phil receives a student loan of £2,000.

* His parents give him £60 per month.

* Phil has had two job offers. Choose from either: (a) Student tutoring, which pays £10 per hour. Phil will work 30 hours in his first year; (b) Candy's Canine services is a dog walking company which will pay Phil £6 an hour and he will complete 70 hours in his first year.

Planned expenditure

* University fees are £1,000.

* Student accommodation costs £1,600.

* Phil travels to university either on the bus or on his bike. Going by bike is free; a yearly bus pass is £50.

* Food can be either eaten at university – £300; self-catered – £200; or takeaways – £500.

* The money left over has to be split between clothing, club and societies and nights out.

Part 2: What actually happened

Record what actually happened to Phil in the 'Actual (£)' column based on the following information:

* Phil's student loan was £2,000.

* Both the accommodation charge and the university fees were as expected.

* Phil's uncle has given him an extra £20 per month on top of his parents' contribution.

* Candy's Canine Services only offers Phil 55 hours of work over the year.

* The hourly rate for student tutors has risen this year to £15 and he works 30 hours.

* Bus passes are 50 per cent cheaper for students.

* Phil discovered many coupons and offers and his takeaways only cost £350.

* University food prices remained the same.

* The local supermarket is more expensive than expected, and the self-catering budget is £100 more than expected.

* All students have overspent on their nights out budget by 15 per cent.

* The clubs and societies are as expected.

* Phil spends 5 per cent less on clothing than he thought.

1 Based on your choices how well do you think Phil planned for university?

2 How well did his budget work based on the 'Actual' column?

3 Did Phil have any money left over or did he go into debt? How might this affect his second year at university?

> **Income** All money received by an individual.
>
> **Expenditure** All money spent by an individual.
>
> **Contingency** An emergency or unexpected expense that must be prepared for.

Student life is very exciting. Planning your expenditure will reduce your chance of getting into debt.

Activity

In his second year at university, Phil records his weekly **income** and **expenditure** in a diary. He has an allotted amount to spend each month, and records all of the bills he receives as well as his current balance of account. At the end of each week, he notes down how much he has left to spend.

1 Do you think Phil's idea is a good one?

2 What problems might there be with his system?

3 If Phil has a large unexpected item of expenditure, he should consider having a contingency plan. This is a plan in case things go wrong. What could Phil have as a **contingency plan**? (It could involve keeping some emergency money or saving some money for a rainy day.)

Personal, Learning and Thinking Skills

Budgeting is a life skill that you will use for the rest of your life. It is important to learn now as mistakes made now are likely to be for smaller amounts

Just checking

* Record all of your income and expenditure for a week. Create a budget for the next week using this information.

* Some expenditure is regular and can be deducted week on week (e.g. contract mobile phone bills); some are irregular and cannot be spread round the year (e.g. birthday presents). Make a list of both irregular and regular payments that you have made recently.

* What is an expenditure diary and why is it used?

3.8 Personal taxes

There are many different types of taxes ranging from indirect taxes such as VAT, vehicle tax to personal income tax which is a direct tax on your income. This topic looks at the different types of taxes that you may come across when you begin earning.

Income tax

This is a tax collected by the government from people's income, which includes any money they earn. The government uses the money to pay for services that people in the UK need such as education, health care, the police and other emergency services, the army, navy and air force. Income tax benefits the country and people who are less well off who would not be able to afford services like hospitals if they were not free.

Everyone who pays income tax will have a Personal Allowance, which is an amount of money they may earn that is not taxed. In 2008–09, the Personal Allowance for people under the age of 64 was £6,035. The Personal Allowance is first deducted from a person's income, and then earnings over this amount are divided into tax bands and a different percentage of tax is charged on each band – see the table of income tax bands and rates below.

The tax year, which runs from 6 April to 5 April the following year, is used to calculate how much someone should pay.

Income tax bands*	Income tax rates
£0–34,800	Basic rate: 20%
More than £34,800	Higher rate: 40%

Income tax bands and rates for the year 2008–09.

* Personal Allowance of £6,035 has been deducted

Case study: Javeria's income tax

Javeria has just got a part-time job at the local GPs' practice. As a receptionist, she earns £10,000 per year. How much tax should she be paying in the tax year 2008–09?

She will pay no tax on the first £6,035 of her earnings, which means that she must pay tax at 20 per cent on the remaining £3,965. This works out at £793.

1 Javeria gets a pay rise and now earns £14,000 a year. How much tax will she pay now?

2 Dr Whyte, who also works at the practice, earns £82,000 a year. How much tax will she pay? (Remember, she will pay tax at both basic and higher rates.)

Full amount earned per week	Class 1 NICs
Up to £105 (the 'earnings threshold')	0
£105 to £770	11%
More than £770	1%

National Insurance contributions for employees for the tax year 2008–09.

National Insurance

In addition to income tax, people aged over 16 who are in work must pay National Insurance contributions (NICs). Paying NICs helps people to build up their entitlement to certain benefits, including the state pension. The amount of NICs people pay depends on how much they earn and whether they are employed or self-employed. You stop paying NICs when you reach state pension age.

Just like income tax, people only need to start paying National Insurance when they have earned a certain amount of money. The contributions vary, but we will find out about NICs paid by employees, known as Class 1 contributions.

Case Study: Javeria's National Insurance contributions

Javeria originally earned £10,000 per year. To work out how much she earns per week, we need to divide her salary by 52. £10,000 ÷ 52 = £192.31 per week.

On the first £105, she will not have to pay any NICs. On the remaining £87.31, she must pay NICs at 11%, which is £9.60 per week.

1 How much will Javeria's NICs be when her salary rises to £14,000?

2 What will Dr Whyte's NICs be? (Remember, her annual salary is £82,000.)

Buttershaw Health Centre				Date: 02/01/2009		
Payment Period 02/12/08 – 01/01/09				**Payment Method** Credit Transfer		
Tax Code 603L		**Employee Number** 0025		**Employee Name** Javeria Khan		**N.I Number** RT875432H
PAYMENTS				**DEDUCTIONS**		
Description	**Hours**	**Rate**	**Amount**	**Description**	**Amount**	
Basic Pay T			833.33	PAYE Tax	66.08	
				N.I.	41.60	
Gross Pay 833.33 **Net Pay 725.65**				Total Deductions 107.68		
Taxable pay to date 8,333.30				Tax paid to date 660.80 N.I. paid to date 416.00		
T = Taxable						

Javeria's payslip.

Tax code

All employees have a tax code. This is used by the employer to work out the amount of tax to deduct from an individual's pay. The numbers in the tax code are the first three numbers in the employee's Personal Allowance. For example, Javeria has the tax code 603L. To work out her personal allowance you remove the letter and add a zero (603L = 6030). Not all tax codes start with 603 as they differ based on people's circumstances.

Just checking

* What does NIC stand for?
* What is the Personal Allowance? How much is the Personal Allowance for 2008–09?
* What is bought with income tax contributions by the government?

3.9 Personal and cultural attitudes

Everyone has a different attitude to money – if you gave 100 people £100 each, they would probably do 100 different things with the money. Some people would save it, some might use it to try to make more money (for example, buy 100 lottery tickets) and others would spend it on a variety of goods and services. There are reasons behind people's personal consumer behaviours which we'll look at in this topic.

Personal circumstances

The way you spend your money will depend on, your age, whether you are employed or perhaps dependent on benefits, your personal responsibilities or the financial commitments you may have.

Personal attitudes towards risk and reward

Each of us will have different attitudes to risk and reward. When you decide to invest money, even in a savings account, there is a certain amount of risk involved. The bank may go bust or your account may be defrauded. A bank is a very safe place for your savings to be kept, but the reward (the amount your money increases) is very little. If you were to risk £20 on a bet on a flip of a coin (heads you win and double your money, tails you lose), you have a 50% chance of doubling your money and a 50% chance of losing it completely. This would be an investment with a very high level of risk.

Other factors may also affect how you view risk and reward, including ethical beliefs and cultural factors.

Ethical beliefs

Some people believe that they should invest only in businesses that are socially and environmentally responsible, so that their investment is not used to harm the natural environment or exploit people who make, or provide, goods or services. Ethical banks – also known as social or sustainable banks – are concerned with the social use of their investments and loans. They share a common set of principles, the main one being the social or environmental aims of the projects they finance.

Cultural factors

Different cultures have very different views on borrowing money, for example Shariat law forbids Muslims from lending and borrowing of money for interest. Some banks have encouraged Muslim savers by giving them the option to donate interest to Zakat, which is an obligation on Muslims to pay part of their income to specified charities.

3.10 Storing versus saving money

When people earn more money than they need for their daily living they often want to be sure that this extra money is stored safely for future use. There is a difference between saving money by putting it a bank or investing it and storing the money by putting it somewhere safe such as under the bed!

At home

Some people, particularly those from an older generation, prefer to keep their money at home. This is often based on mistrust of banks and a lack of understanding about saving and investments. Over the years, the value of this money will decrease in line with inflation, for example £10 today may buy less in 5 years' time. However, the money will be relatively safe and will not decrease in balance.

In a bank or building society

The most common place to save money is in a bank or building society, usually in a savings account. This type of account pays the account holder a sum of money – interest – for keeping their money with that bank. The balance of the money will therefore increase by a small percentage of the balance of the account, which may keep up with the rate of inflation. This money is fairly safe as the government guarantees all savings in each bank up to £50,000, so if the bank goes bust savers get their money back (unless they have more than £50,000). A saver can put as much or as little money as a they wish into a bank. Some accounts have limits as to the amount you can save and when you can withdraw your savings. Most people use a current account for everyday living costs. Often these pay little or no interest and are not the same as savings accounts.

Investing money

In property

Until recently, buying a property in order to rent it – known as 'buy to let' – was a popular way for people to invest their money. With property prices rising year-on-year, people could get a very good return on their investment, but when property prices started to fall in 2008, many 'buy to let' investors found that they had lost money. Another way to get money out of a property is to sell it, but this may not be the best option if you only need a small amount.

In valuables

Some people store their money in valuables, such as gold and jewellery, which makes the money portable – and you could even wear the jewellery! This is a storage method as the prices of gold and precious gems are unstable, and may go up or down. Also, the price of second-hand jewellery or scrap value may be lower than the original cost of the jewellery.

CHOOSING A BANK

Most people do all of their banking through one bank. There are many in banks that trade in the UK – currently, the British Bankers' Association has 203 member banks. Which bank do you use? (If you do not have a bank account, which bank would you choose?) Why did you choose that bank?

Activity

There are many other sorts of products in which to save and store money, such as stocks, shares, gilts, bonds, wine, paintings, gold, antiques, foreign currency. Using an internet search engine, find out about at least three of these. Which are high risk? How easy is it to withdraw your money?

Just checking

* How many banks can you name that trade in your town?
* Which of the methods mentioned above has the most risk associated with it?
* What is the main difference between a savings and a current account?
* What problems can you think of with keeping your money in gold or valuables?

3.11 Current and savings accounts

Most people use businesses such as high street banks and building societies to help them store and control their money. Over the next four topics, you will learn about the financial services they offer to the public. This topic looks at opening and managing a bank account.

Opening a bank account

In order to open a bank account, you will be asked to:

* prove who you are
* prove where you live
* prove student status (if applying for a student account)
* fill in an application form
* in most cases, pay money into the account.

Why do I have to prove who I am?

Proving your identity helps the bank fight against money laundering. This is where criminals open bank accounts in false names to hide the proceeds of illegal activities. It is a legal requirement for banks to check their customers' identity before allowing them to open an account or buy financial goods and services.

High street banks offer business services to help them store and control their money.

Features, rewards and benefits

Current account

This allows you to manage your money on a daily basis. For example, you can pay cash or cheques into your current account – your employer may also pay your salary directly into it. You will be given a cheque book and cheque guarantee card or debit card so that you can withdraw cash and pay bills. You can also set up direct debits and standing orders to make regular payments (see below). Some banks may allow you to have an overdraft (see Unit 3.4).

A current account may also offer interest on your money. The bank may also provide other special services such as sending money abroad or cashing foreign cheques for which there will be a charge.

Savings accounts

These give you interest on your money and are deposit-based, so for every £1 you save, you will usually get £1 back plus some interest (see Unit 3.10 for more on savings accounts). Savers may be given a savings book or card which they can use to deposit or withdraw money from the account. Some savings accounts are telephone or internet based.

Types of savings accounts and interest rates

Most banks and building societies offer a choice of five main types of savings accounts, as shown in the table.

Type of account	Description	Notice needed?	Limit	Interest rate
Easy access accounts	Gives instant access to savings	None – no penalty and no lost interest	None	Slightly lower than most saving accounts
Notice accounts	The bank/building society needs to be told in advance when you would like to withdraw money	Yes – also, there may be a penalty of lost interest for withdrawing funds	None	Usually higher rate – the longer the notice needed, the higher the rate
Bonds	A high interest savings account which offers the highest rates of interest	Yes – money cannot be withdrawn until the bond matures	None – but you cannot add any extra money to the bond once it has started	The highest available at the bank
Regular savings accounts	Aimed at people who want to save an amount each month. Every month a payment is made into the account and at the end of the term (usually a year), a lump sum is paid out with interest added	Yes – money cannot be withdrawn. If it is, the account is closed and the money paid back to the customer with the interest added	None	Usually good rates of interest
Cash ISAs (Individual Savings Accounts)	An account which is free from tax. You are only allowed to invest in one ISA in any financial year	No – but once the maximum allowed investment is reached, no more can be added	Maximum investment in any tax year is £3,600	Slightly lower, but they are tax free so this means they are very competitive

Types of bank/building society savings accounts.

Calculating interest and borrowing charges

Interest is a fee, paid on money that you borrow. Interest can be thought of as 'rent on money'. For example, if you want to borrow money from the bank, there is a certain rate you have to pay according to how much you want to borrow.

The fee is compensation to the lender for not being able to choose other investments that could have been made with the money. This is known as the **opportunity cost**.

The money is given to the borrower to purchase the item, the money must be repaid over time and the total is divided by the amount of months they have chosen to repay. The borrower pays a percentage of the total as a fee to the lender. This is called the interest rate.

Calculating simple interest

Interest is quoted as a percentage rate that is the amount to be paid per year per £100. For example, James pays 7 per cent interest on his bank loan. This means for every £100 he has borrowed, he will pay £7 in interest per year.

Opportunity cost The value of the next best option that is given up when making an investment.

Paying and/or withdrawing money

There are many different ways to deposit and withdraw money from a bank account.

At the counter

This is the traditional method of withdrawing money from your bank account and paying bills.

It is fairly secure as you go into a branch with your **debit card** or cheque book. There will be a video taken of the people entering and leaving the bank and if an unlawful transaction takes place there will be some evidence of it.

Direct debits

People no longer need to go to the bank to pay all their regular household bills such as electricity or council tax.

A direct debit is a payment system that allows an organisation to collect varying amounts of money directly from a customer's bank account, using **electronic funds transfer**. The customer authorises the organisation to collect the agreed amount from their bank account at regular intervals.

Direct debits are set up with the customer's authority, but the amount taken out can vary for utility bills, for example, which leaves this method open to misuse even if by accident. A direct debit can be cancelled by the customer at any time and is a fairly secure method of payment.

Standing orders

A standing order is an instruction a bank account holder gives to their bank to pay a set amount at regular intervals to another account.

They are typically used to pay rent, mortgage or other fixed regular payments. Because the amounts paid are fixed, a standing order is not usually suitable for paying variable bills such as credit card, or gas and electricity bills.

BACS

The Bankers' Automated Clearing System (BACS) is an industry body which enables organisations of all sizes to make payments by electronic transfer directly into a bank or building society account. For many businesses, this is the preferred way to pay employees' salaries.

ATMs

ATMs or automatic teller machines were a breakthrough in 1967 as they allowed people to withdraw money from the bank outside of banking hours. Today, the Link cash machine network has over 65,000 ATMs in the UK. This allows you to withdraw money from your account at any of their machines.

To use an ATM, you must have a bank card and a Personal Identification Number (PIN) number, which is a four-digit code that allows you access to your bank account. Most ATMs have cameras fitted inside them so

> **Electronic funds transfer**
> The transfer of money electronically from one bank account to another.
>
> **Debit card** A card which can be used to take money from a person's bank account.

any cases of money being illegally taken from the account should have photographic evidence.

Telephone banking

Telephone banking is a service provided by banks that allows its customers to perform transactions over the telephone. Most telephone banking services use an automated phone answering system with phone keypad response or voice recognition capability. Instead of a PIN, the customer must first authenticate through a numeric or verbal password or through security questions asked by a bank employee at its call centre. You can complete most transactions over the telephone, except withdrawing or depositing cash.

This method of banking is open to people fraudulently obtaining details of accounts from bank customers – there will be no evidence other than a recording of the person's voice who ordered the transactions.

Internet banking

Internet banking, sometimes called online banking, allows customers to conduct financial transactions on a secure website operated by their bank. It enables access from anywhere there is an internet connection. This huge benefit also has a major drawback as computers can be the targets of hackers who try to gain illegal access. This sort of illegal activity leaves very little evidence.

Postal banking

This is not banking by post, but banking through the Post Office. In the UK this is offered though National Savings and Investments (NS&I). This operates in the same way as a bank or building society. Each Post Office branch allows you to withdraw money, pay bills, etc. This means that customers have access to all 12,000 branches which is more than any high street bank. This method of banking has the same drawbacks as paying at a counter.

Just checking

* What do the acronyms BACS, PIN and ATM stand for?
* Which type of banking do you think is the safest?
* Which type of banking is the quickest to do?
* What are the main differences between a direct debit and a standing order?

3.12 Financial products: rewards and risks

If you want a reward for investing your cash, then there is a risk. The greater the reward, the bigger the risk of losing the money invested. There is no risk to savings of up to £50,000 kept in a UK bank, as the government guarantees these. Money kept there can be expected to increase by a small percentage each year. On the other hand, if you invested £50,000 in a new business, while you could double your money, you could also lose it all if the business does badly and goes bust. This topic looks at the rewards and risks associated with financial products and services.

Main providers of financial products and services

Mortgage specialists

These are companies that specialise in finding a mortgage to suit a person's requirements. The mortgage adviser will explain to the client the different options they have available to them. The client then makes a decision based on the information given. The reward is the amount of money that can be saved by a customer being advised well. The risk involves trusting another person to help you make possibly the biggest investment of your life. The FSA (Financial Services Authority) regulates the financial service industry in the UK which helps minimise the risk to customers.

Retailers

Store cards work in a similar way to credit cards but can usually only be used in the store or chain of stores that issues them. The 'reward' for taking out a store card is usually an offer like 10 per cent off your first transaction. Store cards usually charge quite a high interest rate, such as 29.9 per cent, which means they are expensive and people can run up a large debt quite quickly.

Loans

Although personal loans can be expensive, their interest rates can be in single figures, for example 9 per cent, which is much less than a credit or store card. Loans are a good way of raising money quickly to buy a large item. The risks are different depending on whether the loan is secured (on a large asset such as a house), which is a major risk if the loan is unpaid. An unsecured loan is usually for a smaller amount. In this case, the bank accepts the risk that it may not be repaid and it will have to take that as a loss.

Judging the risk

When you try to increase your money by investing it, there is an amount of risk. You hope for a favourable outcome, that is, an increase in the value of your investment, but it is a gamble and you will need to assess the risk very carefully. Investors use a risk/reward ratio to compare the expected returns of an investment – the profit or reward – with the amount of risk taken to get those returns. This ratio is calculated mathematically by dividing the amount of profit the investor expects to make by the amount they stand to lose if the value of the investment falls (that is, the risk).

BANK'S LENDING DECISIONS

In a small group, imagine that you work in a bank and have £250,000 to use for loans for customers. You want to make the most money for the bank. Discuss and decide on which type of customers would you lend to and the questions you would ask on loan application forms. What products will you offer?

Did you know?

If a person had invested in 10,000 35-cent Wal-mart shares when they were floated on the New York stock exchange in 1972 and kept hold of them till 2008 they would now be worth $6.2 million!

Premium Bonds

This is a government savings scheme operated through National Savings and Investments (NS&I) which gives you the chance to win a large amount of money. The minimum stake is £100 and you can redeem your £100 at any time. Each £1 Premium Bond has a number (so if you purchase the minimum of £100, you will have 100 separate numbers). Each month a draw takes place and numbers are randomly chosen. There are two top prizes of £1 million plus over a million smaller prizes. The system works on a prize fund (similar to the National Lottery), where the more bonds there are in the draw, the more prizes there are on offer. The odds for each £1 bond winning are currently 36,000–1 (which is better than the National Lottery which has odds of 1 in nearly 14 million!).

Choice of interest rates

When you take out any financial product, you have a choice of different types of interest rates such as fixed, variable or tiered. If you want a guaranteed payment, then a fixed rate of interest is for you. If you want to bet on the Bank of England base rate decreasing, then a variable rate would suit you better but be a little more risky as the rate could rise and become more expensive.

Non-interest based investments

People can invest their money by buying shares in a company. If the company makes a profit, they will receive a dividend (sum of money) per share, and the value of their shares may also go up. The risk is that the value of shares may also go down if the company performs poorly or makes a loss. If the business goes bust, shareholders are unlikely to get their money back.

Other forms of investment include property, which is generally regarded as a good investment as it does not devalue when second-hand, and valuables such as jewellery and paintings, although these can go in and out of fashion which makes their value variable.

3.13 Obtaining foreign currency

Going to a foreign country can be confusing, particularly if you don't understand the language or the customs. For some people, the most confusing aspect is using the local currency. Working out the real cost of items is often quite difficult, especially if it is not a simple calculation.

GOING ON HOLIDAY

You're going on holiday and want to get £100 in the local currency. Which of the institutions below would you use?

ACME Bank	XYZ Bank	Bloggs Bank
Exchange rate £1 = 0.5 units of currency	Exchange rate £1 = 0.45 units of currency	Exchange rate £1 = 0.35 units of currency
Commission charged at £10 per transaction	Commission charged at 1% of amount changed	No commission
	Any leftover currency in note form exchanged at the original rate	

Dominant currencies

Some currencies are more trusted than others. This is because they are more stable and do not tend to fluctuate as wildly as other currencies. The most dominant currency at present is the US dollar closely followed by the Euro. The Euro, which is the currency of the European Union, was introduced on 1 January 1999 as an electronic currency. On 1 January 2002, the first notes and coins were released.

Did you know?

Not all EU countries use the Euro: the 16 who do are: Germany, France, Italy, Spain, Portugal, Belgium, Luxembourg, the Netherlands, Austria, Finland, Greece, Ireland, Cyprus, Malta, Slovenia and Slovakia.

Exchange rates and their effects

An exchange rate is the price of one currency in terms of another. For example, in early January 2009, the sterling/dollar exchange rate was £1:$1.49. This means for each pound you exchange, you would receive $1.49, so if you changed £40 into dollars you would receive $59.60.

Different currencies take some getting used to when on holiday.

Ways to obtain foreign currency

Cash

You can buy notes in foreign currency from a bank or main post office. Some smaller branches of banks may not hold stock of currencies but could order them for you. Cash is very flexible as you can spend it straightaway, but it cannot be replaced easily if stolen, so carrying too much money with you could be unsafe.

Travellers cheques

Travellers cheques are special cheques that are either in the local currency or in **sterling**. They are issued in your name and each has its own serial number. For security purposes, when buying the cheques you sign them all – when you cash a cheque you sign it again, and the two signatures are compared. Travellers cheques are not as flexible as cash, but if you lose them or if they are stolen, you can be issued with new cheques.

Using a debit or credit card

When you are abroad, you can use your bank debit card to get money out of an ATM. You can also pay for goods or services in a shop (as long as they accept your card). You can use your credit card in the same way, but it will be more expensive to withdraw cash from an ATM.

Commission

Banks usually charge a **commission** when you change currencies (both when you buy them and, if you have any left over, when you sell them back). This reduces the amount of money that you get. In the example above where we changed £40 into dollars, the bank might take 2% commission on the transaction. This would be 2% of the $59.60, which is $1.19, so you will only get $58.41. When you are abroad, you should be careful of **Bureau de Change** and **Cambio** kiosks, as they usually charge a high commission and have a high minimum fee.

> **Sterling** The currency of the UK – the pound.
>
> **Commission** A charge for changing money from one currency to another.
>
> **Bureau de Change** French for 'currency exchange'.
>
> **Cambio** A currency exchange bureau, from the Spanish word for 'change'.

Just checking

- ✱ Which method of holding foreign currency is the riskiest in large amounts?
- ✱ Which is the most flexible way of holding foreign currency?
- ✱ What is the symbol for the dollar, euro and yen?
- ✱ How many countries use the euro as legal tender?

Assessment

This unit is assessed externally. This means that you will be set an external assessment, a 60-minute examination under controlled conditions, based on a series of questions that will test your knowledge and understanding of the learning outcomes for this unit. This will be marked by the awarding body. The mark you receive will be based on how well you answer the questions, and based on a mark scheme that will have been developed specifically for the paper set in each examination series.

You will be assessed on:

* your knowledge of the main types, features and sources of money
* your understanding of how sources of financial information and advice differ
* your knowledge of how to plan and manage personal finances
* your understanding of the main features of common financial products and services.

To aim for higher grades you should try to:

* use past papers to study the structure of the question paper and the types of question that are used
* review the content and approach of the mark schemes produced for past papers
* make sure that you are familiar with the basic terminology used in the learning outcomes and assessment criteria in the unit specification
* make sure that you are familiar with the command words used in the questions; this will help identify the kind of answer that is required. Command words are usually at the start of a question, for example:
  * assess: judge the extent or degree of something
  * calculate: manipulate numbers, quantities or values to provide information or solve a problem
  * choose: to select from a range, make a decision based on what is considered to be the most appropriate
  * compare: to show the similarities and differences, or advantages and disadvantages between two or more things
  * construct: present values or information to create records of financial products and services, such as budgets etc.
  * describe: provide information so that the reader can understand what it is that you are describing
  * explain: give a summary of the main points/features; to give reasons and/or the procedure for how or why something occurs
  * identify: name, mention, select or list key elements, facts, features, etc. as appropriate from information given
  * outline: provide reasons for a decision, a procedure, etc.

4 BUSINESS FINANCE AND ACCOUNTING

Introduction

Money is the lifeblood of a business. Without money flowing into a business from selling products and services, there would be no money for it to pay for supplies of materials needed or even employees' wages. This unit will introduce you to the roles and responsibilities of people who work in finance and accounting. It looks at the type of financial information they keep and how that information is used to make financial decisions. You'll also look at key financial documents that help businesses to report on their financial performance.

What are business finance and accounting?

For a business to be successful, its owners or managers need to be skilled in managing the business's money and be good decision makers. This will ensure that the business continues to trade and makes a profit.

Accounting involves recording a business's **financial transactions**. The records can then be used to create key financial statements that provide information on how a business is performing financially and what a business is worth.

How you will be assessed

This unit will be assessed by an assignment based around a new product or service that a business wants to start selling. The business you use could be your own business enterprise, or a case study based on a real or imaginary business. This will involve planning for the selling of a new product or service; managing transactions and reporting on financial performance.

What you will learn in this unit

You will:

∗ know the nature of business finance and accounting

∗ be able to budget for a product or service

∗ be able to manage transactions

∗ be able to report on financial performance.

HOW ENTERPRISING ARE YOU?

In Unit 1 you looked at what it takes to be an entrepreneur. In a small group, discuss (if you are to make your first million) what financial information is essential to a new business owner and why?

There's no getting away from it – finance is all about money.

Financial transactions
Selling products and services for money.

4.1 Working in finance and accounting

A business cannot run unless it has finance to purchase equipment and materials, and pay rent, wages and bills. As finance is central to the success of any business, in medium to large businesses there are finance and accounting staff whose job it is to ensure money goes into and out of the business efficiently and that important financial information is provided to business managers so that the right business decisions are made.

Job roles

Director of finance

The role and responsibilities of a director of finance will vary depending on the size of business. The larger the business, the more likely they are to oversee the functioning of the finance department. They are responsible for the following financial and legal duties:

* Obtaining finance (money) such as bank loans to be invested in the business, e.g. in new machinery.

* Ensuring that accurate records of all business **transactions** are kept. This makes it easy to find out what money is owed to and by the business. It also aids the production of key financial statements such as profit and loss accounts and balance sheets. By law, businesses that have a **'limited' status** are required to send a copy of their accounts to **Companies House**. The records and financial statements are also used to calculate how much tax needs to be paid to the government.

* Managing business finances (cash). This involves ensuring that all money owed to the business is paid promptly. Without this money, the business will not be able to purchase materials to make new products or provide services, or to pay bills.

* Supervising the production of **budgets** for all departments and reviewing spending.

* Reviewing and analysing financial statements and budgets against actual financial performance.

Cashier

To most people, cashiers are the people behind the till in retail businesses such as supermarkets. In finance and accounting, cashiers oversee all the business's bank accounts. They usually bank the cash and cheque payments received by the business every day. Much of their time will be spent carrying out **bank reconciliations**.

Financial accountant

The financial accountant supports the director of finance, and is responsible for the smooth running of the business. They do some or all of the following tasks:

* Ensure record keeping is accurate so that financial statements correctly show the business's performance.

DECISIONS, DECISIONS, DECISIONS ...

Imagine you work as a sales manager for a chocolate manufacturer. You supervise 40 members of sales staff whose job is to contact existing and new customers to sell a range of chocolate-based products. What information do you think the finance and accounting department will provide you with, and why would it be useful to you in your role and also to the business?

Activity

In a small group, list the personal characteristics and qualities you would expect a director of finance to have.

Activity

How does the work of cashiers in finance and accounting contribute to the director of finance's responsibilities as listed below?

* Record keeping and production of financial statements
* Managing business finances (cash)
* Analysis and communication of financial information to aid decision making

* Liaise with all relevant government agencies in the payment of taxes.

* Prepare regular financial reports.

* Produce financial statements and send them to Companies House.

* Analyse financial performance and recommend how financial performance could be improved.

* Track money owed by customers and chase up **debts**.

Management accountant

Management accountants are responsible to the director of finance. They provide information to the business's managers which helps them in their decision making. Management accountants do some or all of the following tasks:

* Help managers create budgets for their departments.

* Provide monthly financial reports that highlight where departments have gone over or under budget.

* Work with managers to give advice and identify opportunities for making more income or reducing costs.

* Review the cost of materials and supplies.

Accounts clerk or finance clerk

Accounts clerks, also known as finance clerks, are responsible for maintaining the business's accounting records, which enables the accountants to prepare financial statements and reports. Their duties typically include:

* inputting sales invoices, receipts and payments on to computerised financial accounting systems

* checking that inputs into the accounts system are accurate and correcting any errors

* providing administrative support to the accountants.

Transactions The sale and purchase of goods or services for money.

'Limited' status Privately and publicly owned companies which are registered at Companies House.

Companies House The government department responsible for the registration of privately and publicly owned companies in the UK.

Budgets The amount of money each department is given to run the business.

Bank reconciliations Checking transactions shown on a bank statement match with the records held by a business.

Debts Money owed to a business.

Activity

How does the work of the accountants contribute to the director of finance's responsibilities as listed below?

* Obtaining finance
* Record keeping and production of financial statements
* Managing business finances (cash)
* Analysis and communication of financial information to aid decision making

Just checking

* Name three responsibilities of a director of finance.
* What does a cashier do?
* Name and describe two responsibilities of a financial accountant.
* Name and describe two responsibilities of a management accountant.

4.2 Purposes and use of financial information

Finance and accounting staff generate a lot of valuable financial information. In this topic, you will explore the main purposes and uses of financial information.

Forecasting

Forecasting is one of the main uses of financial information in business. Financial information can be used to make decisions about what happens or what is predicted to happen in the business. For example, most manufacturing companies will attempt to forecast what sales they are expecting in the next year in order to decide how many products they will need to make and therefore what quantity of supplies or materials they will need and how many members of staff they will require. Forecasting often involves looking at the past year's data. This is particularly useful when sales are not even throughout the year; they are seasonal, for example manufacturers of sunglasses or ice-cream would expect sales to be much higher in the summer months than during winter. This is known as seasonal variance.

Activity

Different businesses have different busy seasons. In pairs, for the businesses listed below, decide when their busy seasons will be and when their sales are expected to slow down. Some businesses have more than one busy time. Explain your reasoning.

* Ice-cream manufacturer
* Travel agent
* Umbrella manufacturer
* Garden centre
* DIY shops
* Pub/bar

Financial reporting

Companies that are listed on the London Stock Exchange are required by law to report their company's results to Companies House. Their financial statements are published and shared with the general public, regardless of how well they did. This information can be used by potential investors or lenders (for example, banks) to decide whether they wish to invest in a specific company or not.

Activity

Look at the following list of typical users of financial statements and information. Working in a small group or pairs, produce a poster identifying the users of financial statements in your chosen business and their need for such financial information. If you have access to computers and printers you may wish to make your poster eye-catching enough to be displayed in your teaching room.

* Present investors/shareholders
* Potential investors
* Owners
* Managers
* Employees
* Lenders
* Suppliers
* Customers
* Government

Interpreting profitability and liquidity

When a business prepares its results it works out the amount of **profit** or loss it has made. This can be done either daily, weekly, monthly or annually, and allows the business to take decisions based on its profits, for example whether to purchase new equipment or new premises. Quite often, profitability ratios are used to calculate how profitable a business is. This compares the amount of profit made to the total amount of sales. For example, a business which makes £25 profit on every £100 of sales is more profitable than a business which makes £2 on every £100 of sales. We will look at ways of measuring a business's **profitability** later in this unit.

Financial statements can also be used to calculate the level of **liquidity** in the business. A business must have enough cash to pay for all of its day-to-day activities. It must be able to pay its wages and its bills. We say this cash is in 'liquid' form because it is not invested and is therefore easy to get hold of and spend. There must be enough cash to cover the everyday costs but not too much as this could be invested and earn the company interest.

Meeting legal requirements

The Companies Act 1989 requires the directors of all limited companies to produce financial statements. Some of the requirements of the act are:

* A company has a duty to keep accounting records.

* A company has a duty to prepare company accounts.

* Financial statements are required to give a true and fair view of the profit or loss for the financial year.

Saving costs and investment

As mentioned earlier, financial information can be used by managers to investigate the costs and incomes of a business. They can use the information to identify possible sources of wastage, overspending and poor sales. Managers can then make decisions such as trying to source cheaper supplies to reduce costs or reducing product prices to increase sales income. Also, businesses can see the success of its investments and make decisions about what investments to make or which investments to keep.

Profit The amount of money left over in the business for its owners or shareholders after costs and expenses have been deducted from the income of a business.

Profitability A measure of how profitable a business is.

Liquidity A measure of how easily a business can pay its debts. The more liquid a business is, the more cash it has available to pay debts such as wages and bills.

Just checking

* What does seasonal variance mean?
* Which law covers who must produce financial accounts?
* What is the difference between profit and profitability?

4.3 Calculating the cost of a product or service

Businesses rarely sell the same products and services year in and year out. They are always looking for new products and services to offer their customers and fight off competitors. However, designing a product or service that customers then don't buy could end up being a costly mistake. This is why businesses carry out research and forecast, based on their findings, what the likely sales and costs of a new product or service are likely to be in the first few months or year after its launch. This information allows managers to identify how many of a particular product or service needs to be sold to cover its costs.

Indirect and direct costs

It is quite likely that for this unit you will be asked to calculate the cost of a new product or service for the business your assignment is based upon. When working out how much a new product or service is going to cost you will need to consider two main categories of cost: indirect and direct costs.

Indirect costs (overheads)

Indirect costs are generally the costs of making a product, or providing a service, which are not influenced by the amount, or volume of items produced or services provided. For example, a business that makes plant pots and pays £1,000 rent a month for premises will have to pay £1,000 whether it makes one pot or 10,000 pots. Other examples of indirect costs include:

* insurance costs

* administration costs – the cost of the paperwork associated with running the business.

* rates – all businesses have to pay business rates; the payments help fund local services provided by local authorities

* wages and salaries

* equipment and machinery rental.

Therefore, indirect costs are those costs that cannot be directly attributed to a unit of production, or service, provided to a customer but have to be apportioned (shared out) across the total number of products or services provided. For example, if a plant pot making business pays £1,000 rent a month but makes 10,000 pots a month we would attribute £1,000/10,000 of indirect rental cost to each pot made, and this would be £0.10 for each pot.

Direct costs

These are costs which can be easily attributed to each unit of production, or each service, provided to a customer, for example raw material costs and some labour and energy. The total amount of direct costs incurred by a business over a period of time will therefore depend on the number of units of production or the amount of services provided, for example, take a business that makes fresh ready made meals in sealed containers. The containers cost 3p each and can be directly attributed to each ready meal made. Therefore, packaging represents a direct cost of 3p per meal produced. If the business makes 10 meals the cost of containers will be 30p and if they make 500 meals it will be £15. As you can see, the total direct cost incurred by a business varies depending on how many meals are being produced.

Activity

Imagine you are a window cleaner. You have a car, ladders, bucket and other items needed for cleaning windows. What are the indirect and direct costs that you will have to incur? Explain how you might work out the direct costs of detergents used per window, or house, so you can work out how much it costs to provide window cleaning services to your customers.

Total cost

Once you understand the difference between indirect and direct costs you should be able to work out the total cost of making a certain item. We can use the following formula:

$$\text{Total cost (TC) per item} = \frac{\text{Total fixed costs (FC)} + \text{Total variable costs (VC)}}{\text{Number of items manufactured}}$$

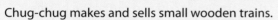

Case study: Making a profit at Chug-chug

Chug-chug makes and sells small wooden trains.
Using the information below, answer the questions on costs.

Chug-chug manufactures 1,000 trains a month. Each train uses woods costing approximately £2. The wheels cost 25p each and there are six on each train. To paint each train costs 20p in paint materials. Employees are paid £4 for each train they make. To protect the finish of the trains, they are packaged in special wooden boxes that cost 30p each. The rent for the workshop is £12,000 per year. The manager's salary is £18,000 per year. The business's insurance is £1,200 per year. The equipment for making the wooden train shells costs £2,000 per month to rent and can make up to 3,000 trains a month. Heating, water and lighting are £500 per month. The administration cost of the business is currently £100 per month and business rates are £500 per month.

1 Work out the total indirect costs for one year of manufacturing.

2 Work out the direct costs per train. Work out the current total costs for the year if the company makes 3,000 trains per month.

3 What is the total cost per train?

4 The train currently sells for £20. Based on your answers to 1–4, do you think this is a sensible price? Explain your answer.

Just checking

* Which of the following are direct or indirect costs: raw materials, wages and salaries, rent of factory, heating, administration.
* Write a definition in your words describing the difference between indirect and direct costs.

4.4 Introducing budgets

Budgeting is a vital part of being in business and staying in business. A budget is a detailed plan of future financial activity, covering a business's costs and revenues (what it earns from sales). Each department will have its own budget, usually agreed to by its manager who will work very hard not to exceed budgeted costs or fall below expected and budgeted incomes (sales).

The purpose of budgeting

To plan

A business that budgets generally knows how much money it will have to spend. This is because it will have a forecast of what income it is expected to make from sales. Having an estimate of income (from sales) makes it easier to plan the amount of money needed by each department. For example, if a garden pot manufacturing company knows it will sell 5,000 pots in April, it will be able to estimate how much material and the number of staff that will be needed by the production department that month.

To control

Budgets also help the managers of a business to control spending. For example, if the garden pot production department was budgeted £2,000 for materials in April, it will need to try not to spend more than this. The manager may have to find cheaper materials if it looks as though the budgeted figure might be exceeded. Budgets therefore help a business monitor the cash flowing in and out of the business overall and what money is available for each department for planned expenditure.

To motivate

A budget can provide managers responsible for meeting them with a focus and discipline. Some companies use their budgets to evaluate how effectively a manager runs their department and use this to motivate staff by offering bonuses or rewards for not exceeding budgets or finding ways of not spending all the money allocated to them.

Types of budgets

Budgets can be set for many different areas of business.

Sales budgets

The sales budget is possibly one of the most important budgets set by a business. It forecasts the amount of expected sales so that the revenue or income of the business can be predicted. Sales are estimated in units of production and their cash values. The simple example below shows a sales budget for the garden pot manufacturing business.

	Jan	Feb	Mar	Apr	May	Jun
Budgeted units						
Green pots	250	375	750	1,250	1,500	1,750
Total units	250	375	750	1,250	1,500	1,750
Budgeted sales (£1.50 per pot)						
Green pots (£1.50 x units)	£375.00	£562.50	£1,125.00	£1,875.00	£2,250.00	£2,625.00
Total sales (£)	£375.00	£562.50	£1,125.00	£1,875.00	£2,250.00	£2,625.00

Garden pot sales budget for six months from January to June.

Sales budgets are forecast using some of the following methods:

* Analysis of sales from previous years. This involves calculating average sales based on past sales to identify trends that can be projected into the future.

* Surveying customers. The business can survey its current customers to see if they will buy again. They may also approach people who have shown an interest in becoming customers.

* Market research carried out by a professional market research company.

Production budgets

The production budget is prepared and based on the predictions of the sales budget. The production budget takes the predicted number of sales and uses them to calculate what needs to be manufactured and when. Usually, a production department will try to make enough products to satisfy up and coming sales. For instance, in some manufacturing businesses, they aim to manufacture enough in January to satisfy orders that are expected in February. As the example of the garden pot company is a seasonal business, it is highly likely that the production department will slowly **stockpile** pots over the quieter winter and autumn months to satisfy high sales in the busier spring and summer months. Look at the example below. You will see that the garden pot business can only make a maximum of 5,000 pots a month, so it has to slowly stockpile to ensure it has enough pots in its warehouse when sales reach 7,000 pots and above.

	Jan	Feb	Mar	Apr	May	Jun
Budgeted units						
Green pots (units)	1,000	1,125	1,000	1,250	1,250	1,250
Blue pots (units)	1,600	1,800	1,600	2,000	2,000	2,000
Red pots (units)	1,400	1,575	1,400	1,750	1,750	1,750
Total units	4,000	4,500	4,000	5,000	5,000	5,000
Stock remaining at end of month		2,500	4,000	3,000	2,000	0

Garden pot production budget for six months from January to June.

> ## Activity
>
> In July green pot sales are forecast to be 1,900. The business plans to increase the price per pot to £1.60. Calculate the budget sales for July.

> **Stockpile** Make more of a product than is needed at the time and store them for future sales.

> There are 2,500 pots in stock from February and 4,500 pots were also made in February. In March, 3,000 pots were sold, which means that there are now 4,000 pots in the warehouse.

> This is calculated by finding the difference between what was made in January and what was sold of it in February. At the end of February, there are 2,500 pots unsold and in the warehouse.

101

You will see that by working in this way the production from one month to the next does not vary too much. This is good for planning staff requirements. In the example above, it is likely that the business will employ the same number of staff all year round. During the less busy months of January to February, it might use staff with free time to carry out maintenance in the factory or do other jobs.

Materials budgets

This budget covers the direct material costs involved in each production item so that overall direct costs can be calculated and predicted. It helps the business work out how much material it will need to order and when. At this stage, it will be clear to finance and accounting staff where material costs may be too high. This means that sometimes a cheaper material might be sourced and used in order to reduce the cost of producing each item.

Below is an example of a materials budget for the garden pot manufacturing company. Its pots are simple and uniform. It manufactures only one size of pot. Each pot consists of 1 kg of clay and 0.5 litre of glaze. Clay costs 10p per kilogram; and green glaze costs 5p per 500 ml.

	Jan	Feb	Mar	Apr	May	Jun
Expected production						
Green pots (units)	1,000	1,125	1,000	1,250	1,250	1,250
Total units	1,000	1,125	1,000	1,250	1,250	1,250
Budgeted material needs						
Clay (kg)	4,000	4,500	4,000	5,000	5,000	5,000
Green pots – glaze (litres)	500	562.5	500	625	625	625
Budgeted material costs (£)						
Clay (10p per kg)	400	450	400	500	500	500
Green pots – glaze (10p per l)	50	56.25	50	62.50	62.50	62.50
Total material cost	450.00	506.25	450.00	562.50	562.50	562.50

Garden pot material budget for six months from January to June.

Labour budgets

The **labour budget** is prepared when the sales and production budgets have been completed and when a business knows just how many products it is to make and when. If the business was a retail outlet, it would want to plan how many members of staff it would employ each day (probably more on a Saturday) and work out how much it is likely to cost (most likely an hourly rate).

An example of a labour budget for the garden pot business example is shown below. For each pot made, a production worker is paid £0.75. Workers can make approximately 1,000–1,500 pots a month. If the factory can produce a maximum of 5,000 pots a month, this would suggest that it should employ about four production workers.

Labour budget Forecast of monthly staff needs.

	Jan	Feb	Mar	Apr	May	Jun
Labour budget (£)						
Green pots	£750.00	£843.75	£750.00	£937.50	£937.50	£937.50
Blue pots	£1,200.00	£1,350.00	£1,200.00	£1,500.00	£1,500.00	£1,500.00
Red pots	£1,050.00	£1,181.25	£1,050.00	£1,312.50	£1,312.50	£1,312.50
Total labour costs	£3,000.00	£3,375.00	£3,000.00	£3,750.00	£3,750.00	£3,750.00

Garden pot labour cost budget for six months from January to June.

Overhead budgets

Overheads are all the other costs of doing business not directly connected to the production of goods or provision of services but necessary to the running of the business. This budget can be set using last year's costs for expenses such as insurance, administration, rent, rates, salaries, equipment and machinery and advertising and promotion. If any changes need to be made because of the amount of products to be produced, these may have to be new estimates or quotes.

Master budget

The master budget contains all the other budgets and shows the overall expected financial position or performance of a business at the end of a period of time. The diagram below illustrates the relationships between the master budget and all the other budgets created. For example, we can't work out the production budget until the sales budget is created. Material usage and labour can't be worked out until we know what will be produced, when, and so on.

Activity

The cost of electricity for the garden pots business, which includes the cost of running the one kiln used in the production area, is treated as an overhead (fixed cost). Why do you think this is?

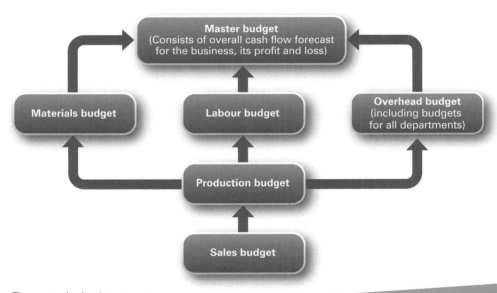

The master budgeting process.

Just checking

✱ Why is it useful to produce budgets?

✱ What information might a business collect to help it produce its sales budget?

✱ An increase in the sales budget would affect which types of budgets?

4.5 Budgeting techniques

In the last topic, we learned how to go about constructing simple budgets, but what do we do with them then? In this section, we'll look at the technique of variance analysis which allows businesses to highlight where actual income and costs don't agree with what was anticipated or budgeted.

Variance analysis

Budgets are monitored by a process called '**variance analysis**'. Daily, weekly, or monthly actual performance figures are compared with budgeted performance figures. For example, a mobile phone company would continuously monitor the budgeted or anticipated amount of phone contracts it had forecast to sell against actual contracts sold. If contracts sold are less than budgeted, we would say there is an *adverse* or *unfavourable* variance. The company would investigate the reasons for such a poor performance, for example better contract deals being offered by a competitor, and make decisions on how the negative variance could be addressed, for example offer a free games console with every contract. Simply put, variance analysis is the process of working out the difference between budgeted and actual figures (sales and costs) to aid understanding of what is happening in the business and enable better, well informed decision making. The formula we use is:

Variance = Budgeted amount – Actual figure

Some variances will be *favourable*, which means that either costs were less than what was budgeted or sales were higher than expected. A variance of zero means the actual cost or income is the same as the budgeted one; this is arguably the best situation to be in and shows that the budgeting process has been an accurate and well-planned one.

A VARIED APPROACH!

Why do you think it would be useful for all people, not just businesses, to compare on a regular basis what their planned expenditure was compared to their actual expenditure? In a small group, suggest ways of doing this.

Variance analysis The analysis of differences between predicted costs and actual costs.

Case study: Variance analysis at Crucial plc

Crucial plc is a company that manufactures films on DVD. The company budgets costs and sales for each film produced basing predictions of sales on the number of people who went to see the film at the cinema. Every month the finance and accounting team performs variance analysis. In March, they had anticipated or budgeted sales of £200,000, wage costs of £55,000, total overheads of £28,000, DVD production of 20,000 units and material costs of £30,000.

The actual figures were wages £62,000, sales £180,000, overheads £28,000, materials £33,000 and production units of 22,000.

1 Perform variance analysis using the data provided in the case study.

2 Which of the variances are 'unfavourable' or 'adverse' for the company?

3 Which variances were 'favourable' for Crucial?

Reasons for variances

There are many reasons why budgeted and actual figures for costs and sales vary. The sales budgeted can quickly become inaccurate because of unexpected changes in demand for a particular product or service. For example, ice-cream is much more popular in warm weather; a typical British rainy summer can change the demand for ice-cream dramatically.

If products are not being made quickly enough or in big enough quantities, it is likely that a business may have to pay its staff overtime to make sure enough of the product demanded reaches shelves in time to satisfy customer needs. This would cause labour costs to increase above what was budgeted. The labour budget is, in fact, very difficult to predict accurately. Staff absences can be costly as either more staff need to be employed or existing staff have to be paid overtime to cover the absent person's duties.

Activity

1 In what ways are the production and materials budgets of a business linked to its sales budget?

2 If predictions of sales were to increase, which of a business's budgets would be affected?

3 In what circumstances might there be a favourable variance in a business's materials budget?

4 What is meant by the terms 'favourable' and 'unfavourable' variance? Provide at least one illustration of each based on either your Unit 1 enterprise business or the business in your Unit 4 assignment brief.

5 'Budgets aren't always 100 per cent accurate.' Explain this statement giving illustrations where you can.

Just checking

* When discussing budgets what does 'variance' mean?
* Give two examples of favourable and unfavourable variances?
* How are variances used by a business's managers and financial staff?

4.6 Internal sources of finance

A business can obtain finance from a variety of sources. The most common sources are shown in the diagram below. Over the next two topics we'll look at internal and external sources of finance.

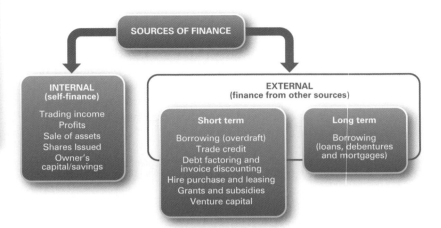

Sources of business finance.

Internal sources

Trading income

Trading income is the income received from a trade or profession. For example, it is the money you might earn from working as a Saturday assistant in a shop which you might then invest in a business opportunity.

Profits

A business may receive money or income from selling goods or services. Any money that remains after paying the costs and expenses of selling those goods or services is 'profit'. Profit is the reward to owners of a company for risking money and time in their business. Some business owners retain their profits, reinvesting them in the business to finance the purchase of more assets so that it can grow and sell more goods or offer more services in the future. Profits are also sometimes retained if the owners of the business think that they may have difficulties in the near future such as a downturn in the economy.

Sale of assets

Businesses that own high-value property, equipment or machinery may release cash for the organisation by selling these assets to a buyer, and then either leasing them back or hiring or renting them from other suppliers. It makes sense to have access to thousands and maybe even millions of pounds to invest in the business rather than having the money tied up in assets. However, this source of finance has its disadvantages: by selling assets a business's worth or value will be reduced, and by renting assets instead it may mean a business becomes locked into a long-term lease agreement, during which time machinery or equipment may become obsolete.

Case study: Leeds United

After failed attempts to attract investors in the football club, in November 2004, Leeds United took the decision to sell the club's Elland Road stadium on a 'sale and lease back' deal. The chairman of the club said the deal would mean that they had money to invest in the club now with the option to buy back the stadium at a later time.

1 Leeds United obviously needed money to invest in its club if it was to continue to exist. What other sources of finance do you think the club might have tried to access first?

2 What are the pros and cons of the lease-back deal the club agreed with the person who bought the stadium?

3 What advantages would there be for an investor to purchase a stadium when the club could buy it back whenever it wanted?

Shares issued

Small businesses wishing to grow may choose to become private limited companies. Shares in the company may be sold to specific people, such as family and friends. In this way, the company is able to raise money to invest in the business.

Larger companies may choose to become public limited companies (plc) and **float** their businesses on the stock exchange. By selling shares in its business to the general public and other investors, the company will be able to raise large amounts of finance for investment and further growth of the business.

Owner's capital or savings

New businesses find it very difficult to access sources of finance because it is regarded as very risky to invest in new businesses or new business ideas due to their high chance of failure. The most common source of capital for new businesses is therefore from the savings of their owners. Many new businesses are started up using inheritance or redundancy money. A recent example is Jamie Oliver, the television chef. He financed his new restaurant, 'Fifteen', using 15 raw recruits to the catering trade and a large amount (£500,000) of his own cash.

> **Float** The process whereby a company offers its shares to the public and lists itself on the stock exchange.

Just checking

* What is the difference between internal and external sources of finance?
* List three examples of internal sources of finance?
* For what reasons would a business sell its assets?

PUT IT ON THE TAB!

We often hear the phrase, 'Put it on my tab'. In business, it means the person saying it has opened an account with the trader, purchased some items, and would like to be billed at the end of the week or month for it. In a small group, discuss the benefits of this?

We have investigated the sources of finance that a business can produce itself. In this topic, we'll look at the sources available from outside the business.

Borrowing

Borrowing refers to all the sources of money a business can obtain from a lender (usually a bank).

Overdrafts

All businesses have bank accounts through which the payments made by and to the company will be made. Most banks offer businesses an overdraft facility, which allows a business to borrow more money than it actually has in its account. The advantages of overdrafts are that money can be borrowed only when it is needed and interest is only charged for the time it is used. However, there are drawbacks to this source in that overdrafts are usually charged at very high rates of **interest** and banks could, with very little notice, request an overdraft to be paid back, which could possibly bankrupt the business.

Loans

These are formal arrangements between a business and its bank, which agrees to loan an amount of money at a rate of interest. Loans are used for financing expensive items like property, machinery and equipment. Mortgages and debentures are types of loans but are usually for very large amounts, such as the purchase of land or premises, and can take up to 25 years to repay.

Loans are often quick to obtain and repayments can be easily planned for by the business. On the downside, loans can take a long time to pay off and can be costly in terms of interest. Quite often, banks will secure loans on a business's property, which means that if the business does not make its repayments, the bank can seize and sell the business's property in order to get its money back.

Trade credit

This is an arrangement between businesses and their suppliers to buy goods or services on account. This means they can receive goods and services but do not have to pay for them for an agreed period of time, which can be anything between four and twelve weeks. This allows organisations the time to make sales *and* collect payments from their own customers. The advantages of this are that goods and services are provided free for a period of time while they can be used to make money for the company. It is a temporary way of increasing the cash available to the company. However, suppliers may give companies that pay quickly good discounts on their purchases, so trade credit could actually cost the businesses that use it. Businesses must remember, if they owe too much or have reached their trade credit limit, suppliers may refuse to supply any more goods or services until a payment has been made.

Interest A sum of money that the business pays to a lender in return for the use of their money as a loan. Interest is usually a percentage of the loan.

Debt factoring and invoice discounting

Debt factoring and invoice discounting enable businesses to 'sell' their invoices (the money they are owed by customers) to a third party – known as a factor – in order to obtain a source of finance. It turns sales for which a business has not actually received payment into cash. This can be important to smaller companies that need money quickly so they can afford to purchase and pay for materials, labour and other costs of running a business. The factor will give them the value of what is outstanding less a percentage charge. The factoring company then has the responsibility of actually collecting the debt that it has bought. A drawback of factoring is that businesses may pay a high percentage of their sales to factors and so it can be a very expensive way of getting finance into the business.

Hire purchase

A hire purchase agreement allows the business sole use of an asset, such as an item of equipment, for a set amount of time, after which the business has the right to buy the asset for a small amount. The benefit of this source of finance is that businesses gain immediate use of an asset without having to find the finance to pay for it. It also allows them to spread the cost of purchase. The one drawback is that the business may still be paying for a piece of equipment that is out of date or obsolete.

Leasing

Leasing companies buy and own assets, such as machinery, that are required by businesses. They then rent the asset over a set period of time. This saves businesses taking out expensive loans or using their own sources of finance. Leased equipment is maintained by the leasing company and the business has the option to update on a regular basis the machinery or equipment they are leasing. On the downside, the business never owns the machinery and so if the business was ever struggling they would not have it as an asset to sell.

Grants and subsidies

This is a source of finance which does not need to be repaid. There are many different types of grant available. Setting up a new business in a poorer area may qualify the company for grants. Subsidies are similar to grants in that they are money from the government or local council to add to the income from a product.

Venture capital

Venture capital is finance contributed at an early stage in the development of a new enterprise. The businesses invested in are usually risky and may fail but may also make a lot of money if successful. The five venture capitalists on the BBC's 'Dragons' Den' give out finance for a share in any business they see promise in.

Activity

In a small group, use the internet to research grants, subsidies and other forms of government support for new businesses or businesses with a new product or service idea. You might find the grants and government support information on the Business Link website, www.businesslink. gov.uk, useful. Produce an eye-catching poster aimed at new businesses that explains:

* what grants and subsidies are
* the types of grants and subsidies available
* where to find help and support if you are a new business or a business developing a new product or service idea.

Just checking

* List three examples of external sources of finance.
* What is trade credit and why is it a useful source of finance.
* What is the difference between leasing and hire purchase?

4.8 Transactions and financial documents

A key task in finance and accounting is the recording of all business transactions. This information is then used by accounting staff to create accurate documents that will be sent to or shared with customers or suppliers. This topic investigates the many documents produced when recording the different transactions that take place between businesses, their suppliers and customers.

What are financial transactions?

The buying and selling of goods, materials and services between businesses, their suppliers and customers are known as transactions. Transactions are events where money changes hands and, in general, are recorded in a range of different financial documents. Businesses may conduct thousands of transactions a day, week or month, which means they need a way of recording where goods or services are going to or have come from, how much was charged and whether or not they have been paid for.

Financial documents

Financial documents provide records of the details of each financial transaction, and are sent in a particular order – known as the 'flow of financial documents'. The most commonly used documents are described below.

Enquiry

This document is sent from a buyer wishing to purchase goods, materials or services to a potential supplier (seller). They will be 'enquiring' about the following things:

* Can they supply a list of the features of the goods/services required?

* What price will they charge?

* Can they deliver by the date required?

Quotation

This document is sent by the supplier to the buyer in response to an enquiry. The quotation contains all the information requested by the business wanting to make a purchase. A quotation will be very detailed, giving the following information:

* prices of goods/services requested

* delivery conditions

* special conditions requested by the customer, e.g. changing a feature of the product

* any discounts that may be offered.

Purchase order

This document is sent by the company wishing to make a purchase to the supplier. Orders form the basis of all business transactions whether they are in writing or simply verbal (spoken) arrangements between buyers and sellers. Orders communicate clearly what the transaction consists of so that it can be carried out accurately and so that buyers are satisfied with their purchases. An example of a purchase order is shown below.

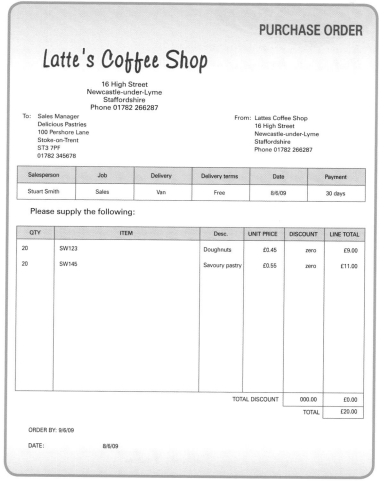

A purchase order.

Activity

Look at the example of the purchase order from Latte's Coffee Shop and answer the following:

1 Who is the purchaser that placed the order?

2 What goods have been requested (type, quantity, price per item and item code)?

3 What is the order reference number?

4 What was the reference number of the original quotation?

5 How will the goods be delivered and how much will it cost the purchaser?

6 What are the payment terms for this transaction? Explain clearly what you mean.

Delivery note and goods received note

This is a document from the supplier that accompanies the ordered goods when they are delivered. The goods from the supplier will arrive with a delivery note that includes the following information:

* order number

* number of packages sent

* description of the goods sent

* quantity of goods sent.

The buyer will check that they have received everything that is listed on the delivery note and when they are satisfied they will sign a duplicate copy of the delivery note to confirm to the supplier that the goods have been received and that the order has been satisfied in full. The delivery note is sent to the accounts department to confirm that the goods were actually received. At this point it becomes a goods received note.

Account balance The amount of money that a customer owes for goods or services supplied by another business.

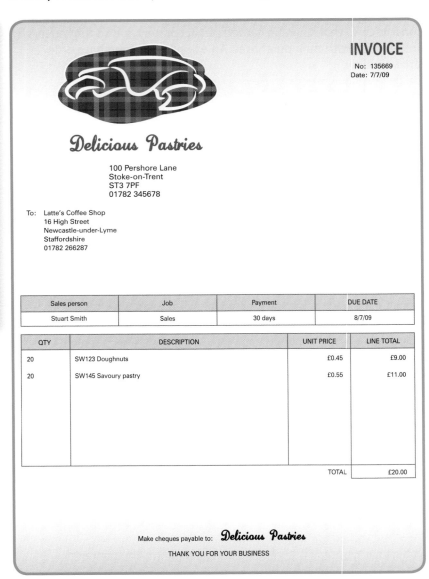

An invoice.

Invoice

This document is sent from the supplier to the buyer as a request for payment. The supplier may ask for payment to be made immediately or, if trade credit terms have been agreed, at a later time. An example of an invoice is shown below.

The buyer will always check that what has been invoiced for actually agrees with what was received. They can do this by comparing the delivery note they kept when the goods were received with the invoice. If there are any mistakes on the invoice, for example they have been charged for too many of one product, then the buyer can request a correct invoice be sent to them before actually paying for it.

Statement of account

This document is sent to the purchaser and shows the total amount of money owed to the supplier. A buyer may have several transactions with the same seller over a period of time, a month for example. They will receive many invoices during that month and instead of paying each one individually, the purchaser may pay all of them together at the end of the month as shown in the **account balance** on the statement. Every month, the purchaser will receive a new statement of account from the supplier listing all the transactions that have taken place during that month. An example is shown below.

Cheques

A cheque is a written instruction, which tells a bank to transfer the amount stated on it into another business's account. The counterfoil is the part of the cheque, which stays in the cheque book to remind you to whom each cheque was paid, the date, why the money was paid and the amount. The counterfoil can be used to check the bank statement.

STATEMENT OF ACCOUNT

No: 237
Date: 20/07/09

Delicious Pastries

100 Pershore Lane
Stoke-on-Trent
ST3 7PF
01782 345678

To: Latte's Coffee Shop
       16 High Street
       Newcastle-under-Lyme
       Staffordshire
       01782 266287

Sales person	Job	Payment	DUE DATE
Stuart Smith	Sales	30 days	8/7/09

QTY	DESCRIPTION	UNIT PRICE	LINE TOTAL
20		£0.45	£9.00
20		£0.55	£11.00
		TOTAL	£20.00

Make cheques payable to: *Delicious Pastries*

THANK YOU FOR YOUR BUSINESS

A statement of account.

Remittance advice slips, receipts and credit notes

When a cheque for payment is sent to a supplier it is common for a remittance advice slip to be included with it. This lists which invoices the cheque payment relates to.

A receipt is used as evidence that a cash payment, as opposed to a trade credit transaction, took place. They are sometimes referred to as proofs of purchase.

A credit note is the opposite of an invoice. It confirms the amount to be deducted from a customer's bill due to faulty, damaged or undelivered goods or services.

The flow of documents

The flow of documents shows the sequence of ordering, receiving and paying for goods and services from the viewpoint of the buyer; or the sequence of receiving an order, sending goods or services and receiving payment for them from the viewpoint of a seller.

Just checking

* What is a purchase order?
* Why is it important that calculations are checked on documents such as quotations and invoices?
* What is a statement of account?
* Why do customers return a remittance advice slip with a cheque payment to a supplier?
* What is the flow of documents?

4.9 Cash and trade discounts and VAT

Just to make things more complicated, when invoicing customers for goods or services purchased, businesses will often have to add VAT to the total owed. They may also offer discounts as a means of encouraging customers to pay their bills on time (cash discounts) and remain loyal to them as their suppliers (trade discounts).

Cash (settlement) discount

Money moves through a business. It comes in when customers pay for goods or services they have received. It leaves when the business makes payments to its suppliers of goods and services and when other bills, including employees' wages and the running costs of the business, need to be paid. So, you can see that money is the lifeblood of all businesses. Without a healthy flow of money, some businesses will fail to survive. Businesses may try to encourage their buyers to make prompt payments or even pay in cash for their goods and services by offering them **cash discounts**. For example, Mr Ling bought £10,000 worth of furniture from a furniture wholesaler. The wholesaler put a 5 per cent cash discount on the invoice. But Mr Ling would receive the discount only if he paid the invoice within four weeks. The cash discount is calculated like this:

$$\text{Cash discount} = \text{Invoice value} \times \frac{\text{Cash discount}}{100}$$

$$= £10,000 \times \frac{5}{100}$$

$$= £500$$

Activity

Your college or school has just purchased 30 desks for its new computer room. Each desk cost £99. The supplier has offered a 3% cash discount if the desks are paid for by the end of the month.

1 What would the total value of the invoice be?

2 What cash discount would the school/college get by paying on time?

3 How much could the desks possibly cost your school/college?

4 Why would the supplier offer 3% discount?

Trade discount

Trade discount is different from cash discount. It is deducted from the amount invoiced for goods. The discount rate will vary depending on who the buyer is, how long they have been dealing with the company and the value of goods bought.

Here is an example of how trade discount works: Princess Toy Shop has been a trusted customer of a toy wholesaler for six years. It usually buys about £1000 of goods a month. The wholesaler gives Princess Toy Shop 8 per cent trade discount and 5 per cent cash discount to encourage the owners to keep trading with them and to pay within an agreed period of time (known as terms of payment). The trade discount is calculated like this:

Trade discount $= \text{Value of invoice} \times \dfrac{\text{Trade discount}}{100}$

$= £1000 \times \dfrac{8}{100}$

$= \underline{£80}$

Cash discount $= \text{Invoice value} \times \dfrac{\text{Cash discount}}{100}$
(after trade discount)

$= (£1,000 - £80) \times \dfrac{5}{100}$

$= £46$

The cost to Princess Toy Shop if it pays within 28 days (one month) will be:

Price paid = Value of invoice – Trade discount – Cash discount

$= 1000 - 80 - 46$

$= £874$

Activity

A wholesaler offers one retailer customer 5 per cent trade discount and another 3 per cent trade discount.

1 Each retailer purchased £3,500 of stock from a wholesaler in January 2009. What trade discount would each receive?

2 Suggest one reason for the difference in trade discount.

Standard VAT

Standard VAT is added on top of the price of many goods. From December 2008, the rate of VAT was reduced from 17.5 per cent to 15 per cent. To calculate VAT, you simply add the percentage of VAT to the total invoice value.

Activity

The toy wholesaler is registered for VAT. VAT is calculated after trade and cash discounts are deducted. Bearing this in mind, what would be the new invoice total for the Princess Toy Shop example shown earlier?

Cash discount Money that may be deducted from the total of an invoice if payment is made within a specified period of time, usually four weeks. The cash discount is calculated after any other discounts have already been deducted.

Trade discount This is money off purchases given by one organisation to another. These discounts are usually given by businesses in the same trade, for example, within the building trade.

Did you know?

Value added tax, or VAT, is a tax that you pay when you buy goods and services. It's normally included in the price. Businesses also have to pay VAT. If a business earns more than £67,000 per year, it has to add VAT to the value of goods that it sells.

Just checking

* What is a cash discount?
* What are trade discounts and why are they offered to some customers?
* Is VAT calculated before or after cash and trade discounts have been deducted?

Small businesses will record all their transactions – receipts and payments – in a cash book. It is a record of all the money that has come into and out of a business's bank account.

What is recorded in the cash book?

All transactions should be recorded in a business's cash book. A cash book is a record that helps businesses organise their finances. It provides a simple means of recording all receipts and payments. A cash book can tell the owners of a business how much money has been paid into the bank, where the money came from, what cheque and cash payments have been paid out, to whom and for what. Businesses should be able to look at receipts and payments on a weekly, monthly, quarterly or yearly basis as a means of monitoring the financial position of the business.

The most frequent entries in a cash book will be receipts from sales of goods or services and other receipts such as any **capital** introduced, money received from sales of assets and possibly any rent received.

Also included in the cash book would be the range of payments made by a business to suppliers for materials, services or other supplies necessary to the business's activities. Other expenses and overheads such as loan repayments, purchase of **fixed assets**, payment of electricity, gas and water bills, and business rates would also be recorded.

It is important that the cash book is started correctly and regularly updated and maintained. This will help the owners of the business to manage their financial position. A well-kept cash book can also help the owners of a business to calculate their cash flow needs for the year, and at the end of each year it will provide the information needed to produce financial statements and calculate business taxes owed.

Setting up and using a cash book

For your assignment, you will be asked to record a number of financial transactions in a cash book similar to the example below. Here are some simple rules for you to follow:

* Traditionally, receipts are recorded on the left side of the cash book and payments on the right.

* Remember to enter the dates of your transactions so it is easy to find transactions in your cash book.

* When entering transactions in the cash book ensure you include enough detail so that it will be clear to you (and your accountant at a later date) what the transaction related to.

* Money taken out of the business for personal use should be noted down as 'drawings'.

* Money introduced into the business (e.g. your own savings) should be noted down as 'capital introduced'.

Capital Money put into the business such as owners' savings or bank loans.

Fixed assets Things owned by the business that cannot be easily converted into cash such as property and equipment.

* It may be useful to indicate whether payments or receipts are in cash or cheque form.

* Start a new page for each new month of trading. At the top of the receipts column insert the words, 'Balance Brought Forward' and enter the closing balance from the previous month.

* At the end of the month, total all the receipts including the balance brought forward and note the amount at the bottom of the receipts column.

* At the end of the month, total all the payments and note the amount at the bottom of the payments column.

* To work out the closing balance, you need to work out the difference between the total payments and total receipts figures. If total receipts is more than total payments, there is a positive closing balance. If total receipts is less than total payments, there is a negative closing balance. This balance is carried forward to the next month's cash book page.

Here is an example of a cash book for a small cake-making firm.

Receipts				Payments			
Date	Details	Cash or cheque	Amount	Date	Details	Cash or cheque	Amount
1/5/08	**Balance brought forward**		**£998.50**				
2/5/08	**A. James - Sales**	Cash	£25.50	8/5/08	Tudor Wholesale – Stock	Chq	£73.99
4/5/08	B. Young - Sales	Chq	£30.00	12/5/08	Cash for stamps	Cash	£6.00
9/5/08	J. Thomas - Sales	Chq	£15.00	26/5/08	Tudor Wholesale – Stock	Chq	£30.00
12/5/08	L. Bircher - Sales	Chq	£45.00	30/5/08	Drawings	Cash	£100.00
14/5/08	C. McKeon - Sales	Cash	£14.50				
20/5/08	D. Mitchelll - Sales	Cash	£24.00				
23/5/08	Tudor Wholesale – Refund	Chq	£18.50				
30/5/08	S. Moss – Sales	Cash	£43.00				£209.99
					Balance to carry down		£1,004.01
			£1,214.00				£1,214.00
	Balance brought down		£1,004.01				

Just checking

* What is a cash book, and what is typically recorded in it?
* What is normally recorded on the left and right sides of the cash book?
* Where does the figure 'balance to carry down' come from?

4.11 Recording transactions manually and electronically

For your assignment, you will be manually producing financial documents. Although some small businesses do manually produce their financial documents and business reports, many now use computerised systems and other ICT software to automate some or all of the accounting process. This topic looks at how computers and software can be used to simplify the accounting process and the advantages and disadvantages of manual approaches.

Financial and accounting software

If a business is very large, it might employ a software design company such as IBM to develop a **bespoke software** package that will help staff carry out their financial and reporting tasks efficiently. However, this sort of one-off software is very expensive.

In small businesses, **generic software** packages are commonly used. For example, 'Microsoft Office Small Business Accounting' allows the owners of a business to use already existing data (such as costs and revenues, receipts and payments) input into Excel (the spreadsheet application) and Outlook (the database application). The package makes it easy for businesses to keep a track of their accounts and even offers the opportunity to buy an add-on that allows the owners of a business to pay its staff quickly, cheaply and securely, through PayPal invoicing.

There is an in-between choice which is more specialised than off-the-shelf software packages. Professional accounting packages such as 'Sage's Business Vision Accounting Software' offers small to medium sized businesses an accounting and management system that will create monthly and annual financial statements (income statements and balance sheets) and management reports to aid the owners of the business in monitoring and controlling the financial performance of their company. Packages such as these reduce the need for skilled accountants, providing facilities such as the ability to input budget figures and perform regular variance analysis.

Bespoke software A one-off specially package developed to meet the needs of a particular company.

Generic software An off-the-shelf package designed to suit a range of companies.

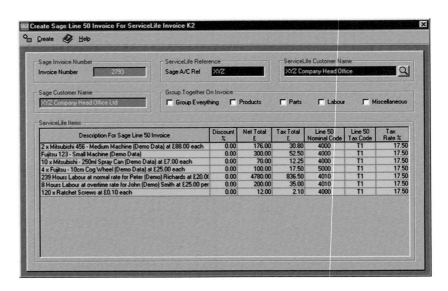

Invoice input screen.

Opposite is a typical example of an invoice input screen in a professional computerised accounting system. As you can see, there are pre-planned data entry boxes for invoice number, customer details and for the customers' order details. This information is stored on the system and used to produce professional invoices which can then be sent in the post to the customer. The staff of the business can view the invoice details on the screen at any time.

Advantages and disadvantages of electronic methods of transactions

Advantages	Disadvantages
Financial information and documents can be processed much quicker freeing up time for other business activities.	Computerised systems may suffer from power failures or attacks from viruses and hackers, all of which can stop the accounting system from operating for a period of time or indefinitely.
Financial documents such as invoices, cheques and statements of account can be automatically created at the touch of a button. They will also look far more professional.	There is no guarantee that the information generated by an accounting system will be accurate and useful if it has been inputted incorrectly. Remember, if you put garbage in, you will get garbage out!
Because of the efficiencies, it can be cheaper to maintain an electronic accounting system than a manual one which is more labour intensive.	Poorly developed accounting systems and software could give business managers inaccurate and misleading information.
Human error (e.g. adding up an invoice, working out VAT) can be reduced by using formulae in an accounting package.	Some computer systems can be open to fraud (changing numbers, creating false accounts, etc.) if the person managing the system does not put proper controls and security procedures in place.
Some accounting packages have been designed to produce a range of useful financial and management reports to help managers in their decision making.	Copies of documents and customer lists could be accessed and stolen by competitors.
Important information can be generated very quickly so effective decision making can take place.	Staff will need to be trained in using specific accounting packages and may probably expect to be paid more than people employed to do accounting manually.
Less need to store paper copies of documentation so more space in offices. A back-up of all files can be safely created every day in a server that is away from the site of the business.	

Activity

1 Which do you think is more appropriate for a small business – electronic or manual methods of accounting? Explain your answer giving examples where necessary.

2 What is meant by the phrase 'manual accounting methods'?

Just checking

* What is the difference between bespoke and generic accounting packages?
* List three advantages of a business computerising its accounting processes?
* List three possible disadvantages of using a computerised accounting system?

4.12 The profit and loss statement and the balance sheet

The profit and loss statement and the balance sheet are the key financial documents that enable an investor or business owner to assess the performance of their investment or business.

Profit and loss statement

Sometimes called the income statement, the profit and loss statement shows the flow of sales and costs over a period of time, usually a year, and the level of profits or losses made as a result of trading. Profit and loss statements are used to measure financial performance over a period of time.

Below is the typical layout of a profit and loss statement for a small business, Kit Kars R Us.

Kit Kars R Us
Profit & Loss Account for Year Ended 31/12/08

	£000s	£000s	£000s
Income			
Sales			125,000
Less Returns			3,250
Net Sales (Turnover)			12,1750
Less Cost of Goods Sold			
Opening Stock		16,000	
Purchases	63,330		
Less Purchase Returns	4,545		
Net Purchases	58,785		
		74,785	
Less Closing Stock		14,350	
Cost of Goods Sold			60,435
GROSS PROFIT			61,315
Less Expenses			
Administration			
Rent & Rates		5,400	
Wages & Salaries		18,000	
Telephone & Postage		375	
Motor Expenses		3,545	
Advertising		3,000	
Sundries		189	
Depreciation			
Buildings		0	
Equipment		7,200	
Motor Vehicles		2,400	40,109
NET PROFIT			21,206

Cost of goods sold is the direct cost of providing the kit car sales (the value of stock used in delivering the sales) and is calculated by taking the value of stocks at the beginning of the year, adding purchases made in the year and taking away the closing stock value.

Gross profit is the profit made on sales after taking away the cost of generating the sales but before accounting for the overheads of the organisation.

Depreciation is the decrease in the value of assets due to their use.

Net profit is the profit made by an organisation once all of its costs have been accounted for such as wages, rent, equipment hire, etc.

A profit and loss statement.

Corporation tax

There is one very important detail missing from the profit and loss statement above if Kit Cars R Us were a limited company and that is corporation tax. As Kit Cars R Us made a net profit of £21,206, the business is liable to pay 21 per cent of its profits in tax if his business has limited status. That would mean a tax payment of £4,453.26. This would leave a profit of £16,752.74.

Balance sheet

The balance sheet shows the value of a business at a given point in time. It details all the **assets** and **liabilities** of the company which should balance with the capital employed within the business (how the business is financed). The total capital employed must be the same as the sum of the net assets – hence the term 'balance' sheet!

> **Liabilities** The debts of a business.
>
> **Assets** The premises, machinery, equipment, stocks and cash owned by a business at a given time.

> **Net book value** is the value of assets after they have been depreciated.

> **Working capital** is the amount the business has to be able to pay its everyday debts (current assets – current liabilities).

Kit Kars R Us
Balance Sheet as at 31/12/08

	£000s Cost	£000s Depreciation	£000s Net Book Value
Fixed Assets			
Buildings	0	0	0
Equipment	48,000	7,200	40,800
Motor Vehicles	12,000	2,400	9,600
	60,000	9,600	50,400
Current Assets			
Stock		14,350	
Debtors		1,650	
Bank		0	
Cash		120	
		16,120	
Less Current Liabilities			
Creditors	2,450		
Overdraft	1,560		
		4,010	
Working Capital			12,110
			62,510
Less Long-Term Liabilities			
Bank Loan			23,000
NET ASSETS			39,510
FINANCED BY			
Capital			
Opening Capital			40,304
Add Net Profits			21,206
			61,510
Less Drawings			22,000
			39510

A balance sheet.

Activity

1 Examine the balance sheet for Kit Cars R Us. Overall, what does the balance sheet show?

2 Does the balance sheet balance? Which figures show this?

3 How much working capital does the business have?

4 What is the most valuable asset on the balance sheet?

5 How healthy do you think this business is? How much money does it owe? Do you think this is a lot compared with the amount the business is worth?

Just checking

✱ What does a profit and loss statement show?

✱ What does a balance sheet show?

Assessment

This unit is assessed internally. This means that you will be set an assignment by your consortium, which should direct your work through a series of tasks connected to the running of a business related activity, so that you cover all of the learning outcomes for this unit. The work you submit for assessment must be original work, produced by yourself under controlled conditions – this will be arranged by your tutor. It will then be marked by your tutor and moderated by the awarding body.

You will be assessed on:

* your knowledge of the nature of business finance and accounting

* your ability to apply budgeting techniques for a product or service

* your ability to record financial information by creating accurate and complete documents and records

* your ability to construct financial reports and interpret financial performance.

To aim for higher grades you should try to:

* offer detailed and accurate examples of finance and accounting jobs and the roles they perform in a business

* produce an accurate and complete financial plan which shows calculated costs and identifies whether relevant sources of finance are internal or external

* provide justified reasons for selecting the method used for processing and storing the financial information, making sure that the cash book, invoice and receipt created are accurate, complete, and containing only relevant information, such as taking account of VAT

* create accurate and complete financial statements making sure they are appropriate for the type of business

* make recommendations on the performance of the business, ensuring your interpretation explores the actual or potential use of the financial information from key business perspectives such as decision-making regarding the need for further investment or reviews its business liquidity.

Introduction

Marketing is one of the most exciting and dynamic business functions that you could take part in. A marketing team will be responsible for the look of a product, how it is presented to customers, its price and the resulting profit. How and where the product is sold, and the way that it is advertised and promoted are other aspects of marketing. By the time you have completed this unit, you should know the principles of marketing, be able to carry out market research, understand how effective customer service is achieved, and be able to handle customers in a sales situation.

How you will be assessed

For this unit, you will be assessed by an assignment based on the marketing and sale of a product or service of your own choice. You will need to produce sample promotional materials based on market research you have carried out, study a business/organisation and show you can deal with customers.

Shop displays are one way of promoting a product.

What you will learn in this unit

You will:

* know the principles of marketing
* be able to carry out market research
* understand how effective customer service is achieved
* be able to handle customers effectively in a sales situation.

THE EXCITING WORLD OF MARKETING

How aware are you of marketing, sales and customer service? In a small group, discuss the things you spend most of your money on – food, clothing, the gym, cinema, computer games, etc. For each area of expenditure, identify what marketing, selling or customer service activities have been part of the buying process.

Personal, Learning and Thinking Skills

Investigating marketing, sales and customer service in business will give you the opportunity to develop a range of skills. When carrying out market research you can demonstrate skills as an independent enquirer; when selling and trying to influence customers you demonstrate skills as an effective participator; when assessing your own contribution to achieving customer satisfaction, and identifying areas for improvement you will be a reflective learner.

Product What a business has to market and to sell. It may be bought or consumed in the form of physical goods or it may be a service.

5.1 Using the marketing mix

Products, or services, that you buy are created, developed, produced and presented in an attractive way to convince you to hand over your money. To get a **product** to the point of purchase requires strategy and planning, based on the manufacturer making a series of decisions about the product. These decisions contribute towards the marketing mix – a strategy for the product based on the features and benefits that define a product to the customer.

Elements of the marketing mix

The basic marketing mix (sometimes known as the four Ps) consists of four main elements: product, price, promotion and place.

Each element is made up of a series of variables that need to be fixed in order to give the product a structure and image. If potential customers like the combination of elements – if it meets their needs – they are more likely to buy this particular product, rather than a similar product from a competitor. Ultimately, it is this mix of elements that a customer buys.

Product

This element of the marketing mix covers variables that make the product what it is: what it does, how it looks and how it is made appealing to customers. They include:

* Product function – what it is, what it is for, what it does, how the consumer experiences it.

* Performance – how well it does, the range, extent or limits to the way it works.

* Product design – its shape, size, colour, what it is made from.

* Packaging form – what the packaging is made from, e.g. paper, card, glass, plastic. Is the item overwrapped or left so that the customer can see and touch it?

* Packaging design – shape, colour, the wording printed on the packaging. Should the lettering be large or small? What colours should be used? Is the packaging graphic or photographic? How do customers expect the product to be packaged? How do competitors package their products?

* Product name – is it a **generic** or **descriptive name**? Does it carry a brand name or logo? These are very important issues when it comes to product recognition and making your product original and distinctive in a competitive market.

Price

This literally covers how much to charge customers for the product, and how much to suggest it sells for to the consumer. Variables here depend on how much the product costs the company to produce and how much profit – the actual return or percentage return that the business wants/needs to achieve.

Competition and market factors also come into play when setting the price for a product. For example, should the price be positioned higher, lower, or the same as the competition? How much will the market be prepared to pay before customers think the price is too high? Alternatively, there may be a lower limit below which customers might perceive the product to be too cheap and consequently of inferior quality.

Promotion

This involves telling people about a product, that is, creating desire, with the aim of generating profitable sales. The most common promotion method is advertising – the use of paid-for space in the media to put across a marketing or sales message. (There's more information on advertising media in the next topic.)

Promotion also includes different forms of publicity that do not take the form of advertising. These include public relations (PR) activities, press briefings and the use of press releases, sponsorship, exhibition space, etc.

You will also come across sales promotions – tactics to stimulate sales. These include discount vouchers, competitions, prize draws, buy one get one free (BOGOF), customer loyalty schemes, etc.

Place

This is where a product is going to be sold and the sales method to be adopted. Place could encompass how a business gets products to its customers – through distributors such as wholesalers, retailers or sales agents, or by choosing a sales and distribution method that is direct to the customer or consumer.

Constraints

The marketing mix also needs to be looked at in the light of constraints, for example internal constraints such as the **budget** available (financial constraints). It would be pointless planning for expensive television advertising when there is only enough money available for local press advertising. You may also find that there are external constraints caused by political or economic factors outside of the business's control, but which affect the market. These may include economic uncertainty (when consumers are less confident in spending money) and tighter regulation on sales activity or concerning the product's function.

Did you know?

When creating a marketing mix for a service, some businesses find it helpful to use an extended marketing mix, incorporating three further Ps for People, Process and Physical evidence. These are not necessarily additional, but a development of the P for Product, emphasising elements that are particularly relevant to a service.

Brand name A name used by a business that gives recognition to a product or group of products which it produces and markets collectively.

Generic name Common or general name for a product, that has to be distinguished by the addition of a brand or company name, e.g. 'television' is generic and needs *Sony*, *Philips* or other name in front to make it distinctive.

Descriptive name This is where a brand name is added to a description of what a product is or does, e.g. 'wallpaper adhesive' would be prefaced by *Solvite*, or other brand.

Budget The amount of money available for spending on a particular project or marketing activity.

Just checking

* What are the main 4Ps of the marketing mix?
* What do we mean by 'constraints on the marketing mix'?
* Think of a famous brand name – how does that company maintain its brand image?
* Can you see the marketing mix at work on products that you buy or use?

5.2 Promotional materials used in business

Scarcely a day will go by without you seeing or hearing an advertisement, being given a leaflet or being subjected to a more subtle form of promotion such as a public relations campaign. Although promotional material comes in many forms, they are all designed to result in more sales of the product.

Types and nature of promotional materials

Promotional materials form perhaps the most exciting and high-profile part of marketing and selling. They are what the customers and consumers notice, often before they realise just what product is being featured.

The most widely recognised types of promotional materials will be broadly classified as 'advertising' materials. Advertising makes use of many types of media, but the main types available to most marketing teams are those shown below.

Print

This includes newspapers, magazines, leaflets, posters, billboards, direct mail, magazine inserts, press releases, and so on. Printed materials can be colour or black-and-white, they may include a mix of photos or illustrations and text, or consist entirely of text, they may have very few words or resemble a newspaper article.

Audio

This **medium** includes radio, recordings, podcasts, public address announcements, and so on. The intended audience may hear a narrator, music and sound effects. It is most commonly used for radio adverts. Audio adverts need to convey their message in a short amount of time because they are fairly expensive to record and broadcast.

Moving image

This medium, which includes television, cinema, video, DVD, can combine images with audio and, if necessary, text. It can be expensive to produce, and having a prime-time advert can carry a high price. As with audio publicity, the messages tend to be short.

Ambient

Ambient is a term used to describe any kind of non-traditional promotional media. It can involve more or less anything, and as such is restricted only by the inventiveness of the marketer. It includes non-traditional, out-of-home media and branding opportunities, such as retail showcards, shelf wobblers; the use of pens, and other desk-top items to carry a **brand** name or message; advertising on street furniture, bus and taxi sides; sky writing.

New media

New media include the use of digital media such as SMS texts, webcasts, email, downloads and web-based media such as pop-ups, screen banners. Promotion through new media may involve any combination of the above, and may direct information targeted at very specific consumer groups.

Activity

In a small group, find examples of promotions in three different media (they don't have to be for the same product or service).

1 How are the promotions similar and different?

2 Why do you think the company chose each medium?

Name of product/service and company

The name of the product/service and the perceived values of the brand are as important as the choice of media for promotional materials. In order for promotional materials to be effective, consumers need to know which product and company is being promoted. This message is essential for converting a company's audience into its customers.

The name chosen for a product – or service – will become part of its brand. The name can be descriptive (e.g. iPod Touch) or abstract (e.g. Vodafone Dolphin), but it needs to be prominent when promoted.

Branding and logos

Promotional materials need to take into account any branding and **logo** guidelines that the company may use. A logo is a visual indicator that clearly identifies products as being produced by a specific company, which may include text or just an image. For example, the Nike 'tick' may be used on its own, or may appear with the word 'Nike'.

There may be different levels of branding that need to work together. For example, a promotion for the Nike Air Pegasus+ 25 SE model of training would include:

* Nike – the parent company logo

* Air – any branding that relates to the Air footwear technology

* Pegasus – any additional branding that relates specifically to the Pegasus model of shoe

* + 25 SE – any edition-specific branding that distinguishes this version of Pegasus from previous models.

A brand may also be shown through a 'house style', such as the distinctive use of red and white in Coca-Cola adverts. A similar approach is to use a sound or 'jingle' that consumers associate with a particular brand whenever they hear it, e.g. Philips 'sense and simplicity' jingle, or the distinctive bleeps made by the telephone in advertisements for Direct Line insurance, etc.

Medium The singular of media. In marketing, it is used to describe a type of communication that carries a message or information to consumers, e.g. print, audio, moving image.

Brand A combination of visual, audio and graphic elements that define a product or service; often designed to present a specific positive experience of that product or service, which may relate to lifestyle, quality, value, etc.

Logo A distinctive graphic or piece of text (or combination of the two) that customers recognise immediately.

Just checking

* Why might a business decide to use posters rather than a television commercial for its promotional material?

* What is the difference between a brand and a logo?

* Identify one example of each type of media.

Door-to-door market research is common practice.

5.3 Introducing market research

Market research is vital for modern businesses. Anyone producing a commercial product or service wants to know the size of their market, the needs of their potential customers and how to reach those customers. They also want to know about their competitors, who will also try to reach the same customers.

Why carry out market research?

Market research generally sets out to answer questions and provide a business with information that is not already known. One of the main objectives is to find out about a market – its size and structure, any trends, and any other facts that can inform a business about the market in which it is interested.

Finding out about customers is another important aspect of market research, which involves identifying who they are, their likes and dislikes, and asking their opinions. Market research is also a valuable way to find out more about competitors, what are they doing, what their plans are and what customers think about them – compared with your business and its products.

Quantitative and qualitative data

Market research data comes in two basic forms: quantitative and qualitative.

Quantitative

This type of data is made up of numbers or statistics that can be manipulated using a range of statistical or analytical techniques. Quantitative data can be used to measure the size and scale of a market, its absolutes (highs and lows), its shares and percentages, and identify any trends.

Quantitative data is collected by different methods that result in numerical data, that is numbers that can be counted. This could include facts and figures such as sales figures or export data. Quantitative data is also produced by counting the number of times an answer is given or the number of times an observed action occurs. It is often collected using questionnaires, survey interviews, and online surveys.

Qualitative

Qualitative data can be used to indicate reasons why, to give explanation and understanding to an issue, and refers to subjective views, opinions, ideas, attitude and motivation.

The data is usually produced from open-ended questions where there is no fixed answer. Focus groups, where a small selected group of respondents give their opinions and discuss a subject, is a common way of collecting qualitative data. The discussions are usually recorded or filmed and the outcome analysed by a psychologist, who can interpret the meaning behind comments and body language, rather than analysed statistically.

The market research process

Market research has to be considered, planned and then put into action, just like any other business plan or activity.

Deciding what questions you want your research to answer

In the early stages of research, the questions considered may be very broad, before getting into the kind of specific questions that are used in questionnaires. Broad questions may include 'How big is the potential market?', 'How many people will buy our product?', 'How much will they want to buy at one time?', 'How much will they be prepared to pay?', 'Who are our competitors?'.

Deciding who to ask and which market research methods to use

Who you ask will depend on what you want to find out. For example, if you want to find out about optimum delivery quantities and transit packaging for your product, it would be no good asking consumers, though business customers will be able to provide answers.

The research method chosen will be the one that is likely to give you the best quality results. You need to decide whether you want quantitative or qualitative information, and whether you want to use primary or secondary research (you'll find out more this in the next topic). In most cases, you will want to use a mix of these.

Planning how long it will take

This will depend on the method you use, how many people you need to survey, and consequently how long it will take you to prepare. Collecting the data will also take time, particularly if you need to make appointments or rely on responses to a postal survey.

Collecting information

The amount of time and effort required for this stage depends on the method of research you use and the size of your sample. Information from surveys, interviews and questionnaires needs to be collected in a meaningful way. For example, the data from a survey may need to be input into a spreadsheet before it is analysed.

Interpreting results and identifying key findings

To start with, your data will need to be recorded and counted. Doing this should show up the main groupings that have given common answers. From this, you will be able to analyse and cross reference your findings to start to give you some answers. If answers are not forthcoming, you will need to review your research method and the questions that you asked, repeating the research exercise with a different method or with modified questions if necessary.

Using results to modify ideas as necessary

Two important measures of the quality of market research are: 'How much can I rely on these findings?' and 'What action can I take or do I need to take as a result?'. Good quality market research findings should always be actionable. For the purposes of the market research that you design, plan and carry out for this unit, your results should be sufficient to produce sample promotional materials based on your own findings.

Personal, Learning and Thinking Skills

When planning and carrying out your own market research and collecting your market research data, you are using the skills of an independent enquirer.

Activity

Take a piece of paper and write down headings for each stage in the market research process. Under each heading, note what you can do unaided, where you may need help or support from a team, and where you might need guidance from your tutor. Try to estimate how long each stage in the market research process will take you, then add these figures together to give an estimate of the total time a research project could take.

Just checking

* How would you explain qualitative data to a colleague?
* What is the main feature of quantitative data?

Target population The defined population from which research results are required.

Profile A general description used to identify a group of people, such as a target market, based on a range of features that would be typical of that group, e.g. a simple profile of your class may be 'aged 14–19, 50:50 male and female, unmarried, live within 5 miles of centre, income spent mostly on entertainment'.

Respondents Individuals that you research, who provide you with results of your research.

Sample The number and profile of the people or organisations – the respondents – that you select to include in a survey.

5.4 Primary research

Primary research is all about collecting data or information for the first time, for a specific project, and analysing it to answer the particular questions or problems (the objectives) that the research sets out to answer. In this topic, you'll look at the main methods of primary research.

Interviews and direct questioning

These are the most well-known form of market research. Interviews may be carried out face to face or over the telephone (a telephone survey). The interviewee may be chosen:

* at random, if the **target population** is large enough

* because of some general characteristic, e.g. the research may only want males, or people aged 65 or over, or shoppers

* because they fit a particular **profile** that has been drawn up as the ideal type of person to interview, e.g. independent business owners in the retail fashion industry who have been trading for less than five years.

By defining the **respondents** precisely to fit the profile that you want to interview, you are more likely to get the type of information that you are looking for, but you may find that there are fewer people that fit your profile.

Interviews and direct questioning will usually be based on a questionnaire that ensures that everyone being surveyed is asked the same questions. As more people are interviewed, this will build up quantitative data that can then be analysed statistically. One advantage of face-to-face interviewing is that if the respondent does not understand the question or is reluctant to answer, the interviewer can help by explaining and encouraging them to answer.

Surveys

This is an alternative to direct questioning that be used to survey large numbers of people. For a postal survey, a self-completion questionnaire is prepared and mailed to respondents with a return-paid and addressed envelope, which will help make sure that you get your completed questionnaires back. Postal surveys can be targeted fairly precisely using post code data. They can be used for a large **sample**.

Many companies now use web-based surveys. These are either hosted on the company's website, or emailed to customers, and consist of the same style of question as a postal survey. This may be a cheaper alternative as it does not incur postage or printing costs, but it reduces your control on the profile of your respondents.

Observations

Observational research may be open, for example traffic surveys or watching and recording how respondents manage a given task such as following instructions for the use of a product. Alternatively, observation may be secret, to see how people behave when not under the researchers' gaze, for example watching how shoppers browse

Case Study: Producing your own questionnaire

There is a lot of skill and judgement used in the development of professional questionnaires to make sure that respondents answer everything that is required. These are the different types of question that you could use when putting together your own questionnaire:

* *Simple dichotomous questions* – these give the respondent the choice of two answers, e.g. agree or disagree, etc. The answers are easy to analyse.

* *Multiple-choice questions* – these allow the respondent to choose their answer from a list that has already been selected and prepared, e.g. Which one of these is your favourite colour: Red/Green/Blue/Yellow? The answers are easy to analyse but do not allow the respondent to voice their own opinion – their favourite colour may actually be purple.

* *Open-ended questions* – these are designed to encourage the respondent to give their own answer or opinion, e.g. Where did you go for your last holiday? These will take longer to analyse as every respondent may give a totally different answer. This will be unusual and you will find that common groupings start to emerge as more respondents give their answers.

* *Scaling questions* – these are designed to provide subjective opinion, that is how strongly the respondent feels about something, e.g. What is your opinion of the service in this restaurant? Would you say that it was very good, good, neither good nor bad, bad, very bad. This is an example of the most common type, the five-point Likert scale.

round a shopping centre. A 'mystery shopper' to see how shoppers or shop staff behave is another common method of conducting observational research.

Focus groups

A focus group is a selected group of eight to ten respondents who are invited to a meeting to give their opinions and discuss a subject. If there are fewer than eight, it is unlikely that there will be sufficient discussion or difference of opinion; if there are more than ten, the group will be difficult to manage and smaller groups may develop.

There will be different group dynamics in mixed sex groups compared with single sex groups. Similarly, different age groups will behave differently when everyone is of a similar age, compared with groups where there is a significant difference in the ages of respondents. Focus groups are a great way of collecting qualitative research data. The discussions are usually recorded or filmed and the outcome analysed by a psychologist who can interpret the meaning behind comments and body language.

Like other primary research methods, it is important to have a plan and structure for the research. Researchers leading a focus group will usually have a series of topics that need to be covered by the group, and they will use their skills at managing people and discussions to make sure that all of the topics are covered. Focus groups are usually planned to last no longer than one or two hours.

Functional Skills

Maths

You will be selecting and applying mathematics to find solutions when you analyse your market research data.

ICT

You will use ICT when entering your research data on to a spreadsheet for analysis and when presenting your research findings.

A focus group is a good way to get opinions and discuss a subject.

Just checking

* Which form(s) of primary research is most likely to provide qualitative data?
* Which form(s) of primary research is most likely to provide quantitative data?

Population The total number of people or organisations that can provide information relevant to a research problem.

Segment To divide up or split a market into smaller parts, then tailoring plans or products for each part of the market (each segment), so that each part is targeted in the most effective way.

5.5 Secondary research

Using secondary research is an effective, relatively low cost way of finding out about a market. In many cases, secondary research may be all that is required to answer questions about a market, to provide basic data that indicates whether a market or product is worth developing.

Secondary research can be done quickly and basic data is usually readily accessible. However, it will have been designed and developed for someone else for a specific purpose. You need to check the source to identify:

* When the research was done – this week, this month, this year, or is it out of date?

* Who conducted the research – a professional market research agency, a business using its own resources, a person unfamiliar with market research processes?

* How the research was carried out, and the sample size and profile – was the method appropriate and was the sample representative?

* Who commissioned the research – a business, a government agency, a political party, a public relations agency?

* Why the research was carried out, that is its purpose – to inform, to make a statement, to change public opinion, to generate a news story?

Internal sources of secondary research

Most organisations will collect and hold a wide range of data which is used by the management team. Once it has been analysed and used for its primary purpose, it becomes a valuable source of data for secondary research.

Sales figures

Sales data will be collected on a regular basis and used to monitor and measure how the business is doing. Depending on the business, this may be purely financial data, the value of sales, or it may be measured in terms of the number of items sold. This data could be for the total business but is likely to be broken down in different ways, for example by individual sales person, by customer, by individual product, or by product type.

As sales data builds up over time, it becomes a very useful source of secondary research. You could use it for further analysis, to identify peaks, troughs, trends, important customers, etc. that be used can help plan marketing activity.

Customer database

Most businesses will keep some form of customer database so that they can record detailed information about their customers. This data can be used to monitor sales, to measure the relative importance of different customers, to identify their likes, dislikes and preferences. A customer database should also include addresses which will indicate their geographic location – very useful for planning sales activity and marketing campaigns.

Activity

The reliability of the source of information for secondary research is of fundamental importance – decisions based on inaccurate or misleading information can result in money being wasted.

Greg has a business idea. He has heard that there is an island off the coast of Florida that is populated by dogs, given a free rein by their owners. His idea is to market Sea Biscuit dog biscuits to the owners who have sent their dogs to the island as food parcels for their beloved canines.

1 Go to www.google.com and look up 'Dog Island' to read the secondary information that Greg is basing his business decision on.

2 Discuss with a partner whether you think that this is a reliable source of information. Why is this?

3 Now use the internet to see if you can find another source of information that confirms or contradicts your decision about this source of information.

4 Should Greg go ahead with his business idea?

External sources of secondary research

External sources of secondary research can be accessed very easily and usually at a relatively low cost.

Published reports

In the main, these are produced on a regular basis by independent market research organisations and made available for sale. You will find that they cover a wide range of information, each report focusing on a particular market, product or industry. For example, a report could focus on the confectionery market, giving background information on its size, history, the main manufacturers and brands, the distribution network, forecasts, etc.

One of the publications from The Consumers' Association.

Organisations that publish these types of report include Euromonitor, the *Financial Times*, Key Note and Mintel. The Consumers' Association and its range of *Which?* magazines are a good source of independent research on products. Trade and industry organisations and journals also publish reports about their own market sector. Some manufacturers produce research-based reports for public relations purposes and to enhance their status in a market.

Government published data

Government departments produce a wide range of data, which is usually available in most public libraries and online. The kind of information that is produced includes **population** and demographic statistics (how many people), social statistics (data on households and living conditions), economic statistics (how the UK economy is doing). You will find that these types of official statistics are useful to build up a picture of a market or customers within a market, particularly if you are looking to **segment** a market demographically or geographically.

Did you know?

Secondary research is sometimes called desk research because the research is usually carried out while sitting and working at a desk, or nowadays at a computer.

Just checking

* Name two places where you should be able to look at official statistics.
* Which Act of Parliament protects the use of personal data held on customer databases?
* Suggest two internal sources of secondary research data.

5.6 Why effective customer service is important

Some businesses clearly spend much more than others on their customer service – some seem to get by, hardly bothering with any obvious customer service support at all. So, what is the point of customer service? First, you need to develop a clear idea of what is meant by 'customer service' – only then will you be able to see why it has become so important for most successful businesses.

Benefits to the customer

The benefits to the customer are relatively clear and straightforward – their immediate requirements will be met quickly and efficiently. Customer service should provide a solution to their needs and their legal rights will be recognised. Much of this will happen as a matter of course during their dealings with a business, and many customers may not even notice that they are on the receiving end of a range of different customer services – so long as they get the product that they want, when they want it, and at a price that they find acceptable.

Benefits to the business

The benefits of good customer service to the business itself are more important from a commercial perspective.

Customer loyalty

This means ensuring that customers are more likely to return to your business when they are next in the market for the products that you supply. This is known as repeat business. The benefit of such customer loyalty is that it costs a business much less to retain its existing customers than it does to attract new customers, so there is a direct financial benefit to the business.

You will see many examples of '**customer loyalty** schemes', ranging from simple cards used by cafés that get stamped each time a purchase is made, to the highly sophisticated loyalty schemes run by major supermarkets that monitor purchases and provide incentives to match your buying pattern. As promotions, these types of customer loyalty schemes may be effective in the short term, but there is evidence to suggest that they have reached saturation point – that most customers are involved in a number of loyalty schemes and just use the one that applies where they happen to be shopping, rather than sticking to just one scheme, thus reducing the benefit to an individual business.

Attracting new customers

Businesses with quality products and an excellent reputation for customer service will attract new business. The company benefits because new customers will enable the business to grow and replace customers who, for whatever reason, no longer buy its products/ services. New customers are also more likely to purchase new products so the business can expand its range.

Another major benefit of new customers is that they have been attracted away from the business's competitors – if they are buying from you, the chances are that they are not buying the same thing elsewhere, so the market share of the business may increase as a result.

Once a business has attracted new customers, the next challenge is to retain them through the continued provision of a high level of customer service on top of maintaining the quality of the product.

Reducing complaints and negative publicity

Dealing with **customer complaints** can take up a lot of time in a business: it can be costly in terms of the human resources required and the direct cost to the business of product replacement or compensation. In addition and of greater concern, a business will get a poor reputation because of the numbers of complaints that it receives – word-of-mouth is a very powerful way of communicating bad publicity as well as good.

A business can reduce the number of complaints it receives by improving product quality and quality assurance. Improving customer service levels will result in immediate benefits. Customer service is a clear demonstration that the business is serious about raising customer satisfaction levels – the cost of replacing products will be reduced, fewer staff will need to be employed to deal with complaints, the reputation of the business will be enhanced and it should start to attract new customers.

Meeting the immediate requirements of customers quickly and efficiently will create a good relationship between the business and its customers and build up their loyalty. Providing a solution to the needs of its customers will mean that they are more likely to return in the future. Recognising the legal rights of customers will protect the business from breaching consumer protection legislation, keep them out of the courts, and avoid negative publicity and associated costs to the business, and so on.

Customer complaints
When a customer is so dissatisfied with an aspect of customer service they receive that they decide to make representations to the business with a view to getting some form of resolution, e.g. an apology, compensation or an improvement in their future dealings with the business.

Customer loyalty
Generating such a positive feeling towards the business that the customer will overlook any shortcomings in customer service and continue to support the business through regular and repeat purchases.

Case study: Getting customer service right at the Terri May Garden centre

When Terri May takes on a new employee at her garden centre, she spends the first day taking them through extensive induction training. In addition to making sure that new employees receive their statutory rights, she explains how to keep the workplace safe and how to work safely with others. They practise the plan for evacuating the premises in the case of an emergency. Before they can start work Terri explains company policy, the reporting structure and how important it is to try to build up a good relationship with customers.

* Which part of the induction training could help build customer loyalty?
* Which part of the induction training is most likely to attract new customers?
* Which part of the induction training is most likely to help reduce complaints?

Just checking

* How would customer services designed to benefit the customer also benefit the business?
* How would attracting new customers benefit a business?
* How would reducing customer complaints benefit a business?

5.7 Who are customers?

'Customer' is the general term used for someone who receives goods or services from a business. Some industries prefer to use the word 'client' as an alternative and some businesses may refer to other organisations as their customers. However, it all relates to being on the receiving end of goods or services. A business needs to find out who its customers are so that it can plan its customer service and market its products and services effectively.

Internal and external customers

Internal customers include team members that you work with, colleagues from other departments who may want you to provide help or information, and managers or people in the business that are senior to you and may want you to perform a task. For example, a person working on a help desk in a shop may be asked to keep a record of the types of enquiries that they receive, and to give their line manager a copy of the list at the end of each working day. In this example, the manager is a customer of the person on the help desk who provides the service.

External customers are more obviously recognised as 'customers', and in most cases they will be paying for goods or services that they want to buy from the business.

There is a direct connection between internal and external customers. If an employee does not provide a satisfactory service for their internal customers, this could have a knock-on effect on external customers as the business's overall standard of customer service expected by the (external) customer may not be achieved.

Typical customers

Is there such a thing as a 'typical' customer? Probably not, as all customers are individuals (and should be treated as such, certainly face to face). However, in order to help plan customer service requirements, and other marketing activities, it is useful if a business can group its customers and try to identify patterns or trends. This is sometimes called 'customer profiling'.

Different organisations will group their customers in different ways, depending on the common features and characteristics that they are interested in.

New and repeat customers

You can probably see that the customer service requirements of new customers may be different from the needs of repeat customers who already know the business. However, you should treat existing and new customers equally well and efficiently since the former are vital to the business and you should make every effort to keep them.

New customers will (most likely) have come from a competitor, and while the business will want to turn them into repeat customers, the fact that they have made one move (away from a competitor) suggests that they could move back again if they have the inclination.

Individual characteristics

Some of the most useful ways of analysing the characteristics of your customers are based on:

* demographic information, such as age, gender, income, employment status, marital status, education, socio-economic group

* psychographic information, such as lifestyle, hobbies, interests, leisure activities, attitude, opinion, values, taste

* geographic information, such as address, postcode, town or region.

By analysing the individual characteristics of customers, a business can build up a picture of its typical customers. From this, it can develop a '**customer profile**', a detailed description of typical customer types.

> ### Case study: Asda.co.uk website
>
> A bold statement in the centre of the home page of the ASDA website reads *"Hello, we're the ASDA Customer Services Team. If there's anything you need, click on 'Contact Us' and we'll be happy to help"*.
>
> * What type of customer is this statement most likely to appeal to?
> * What type of customer does this statement miss totally?

> ### Activity
>
> How would you group or divide up the members of your group? Draw up a profile of each person, which should be a description from the point of view of a business that wants to supply them with products. Analyse these profiles and see what common factors emerge that could be used to group or divide them for sales, marketing and customer service purposes.

> **Customer profile** A detailed description of typical customer types.

Special customer needs

A business may want to know about the special needs of its customers, so that it can make the necessary arrangements to provide appropriate customer services. Special customer needs would include disabilities that might involve physical or access difficulties and customers with visual or hearing impairments or who speak English as a second language. Information about customers is very useful for segmentation and the development of marketing activity targeted at different segments. Once a business knows who its customers are it can start to identify their wants, needs and expectations. From this, it can develop customer services that meet the demands of the customer – as well as the needs of the business.

Finding out about customers

A business can gather much of the information it needs about its customers using primary research techniques (see topic 5.4). In addition, a lot of customer information could be collected from their orders, such as what they buy, how often they buy, how much they spend per order and in total across a year.

> ### Just checking
>
> * What is the difference between a customer and a client?
> * Describe the difference between internal and external customers.
> * Explain why repeat customers are so valuable to a business.

5.8 What is important to customers?

Many a business may think that they know what is best for their customers, and provide the customer with services that they think fit – or that are achievable within their budget. But how can you really know what is important to your customers?

Satisfying customer needs and expectations

Customer service is important to the success of a business. Here are some steps that businesses can take to meet customer expectations.

Customer service policies

A business needs formal **policies** and **procedures** for dealing with customers. Without such policies in place, a business would soon grind to a halt as increasingly frustrated customers confront unprepared staff. The chances are that it will not satisfy customers and they will go elsewhere, to competitors who are more organised and have standard procedures for dealing with customers.

Product knowledge

Customers will expect that everyone with whom they deal in a business will have at least a basic knowledge of the range of products and services being offered. Product knowledge can be acquired in different ways:

* formally – through training
* informally – through taking an interest in the business and learning about its products and services from technical manuals, leaflets or other sources of information.

Another way to increase your product knowledge is to use the product yourself – it will help you to experience it in the same way as a consumer, discovering its weaknesses as well as its strengths.

Two important things to remember about product knowledge are: first, you do not need to know everything about every product in detail, although it helps, but you should recognise the limit of your knowledge and know where to go, what to look up, who to ask, when you reach that limit and cannot provide the answer yourself; secondly, do not lie or make up an answer about a product as it is bound to catch you out at some point when the customers discover it for themselves.

Being proactive

It helps if you are responsive to customer queries, and know where to find information if you do not know the answer to questions. Not being proactive can frustrate the customer, which may mean they take their business elsewhere. Once a customer has been lost in this way, they will think twice before returning.

Sensitivity to customer needs

Customers expect sales staff to be sensitive to their needs – that they will listen and understand what they require. Customer needs are diverse as each customer is different.

Diversity in customer needs may be a function of the business or the products involved, but it may equally stem from the cultural background of the customer. Like product knowledge, if customer service staff feel that they have reached the limit of their knowledge or experience, customers will expect them to seek further advice from senior staff or a specialist who has the particular knowledge required.

Activity

Visit shops, businesses and organisations that deal with members of the public, such as a doctor's surgery or a library, and identify as many different examples of customer services that address the special needs of customers. Think about these particular customer services from the point of view of the businesses or organisations that you visit.

Feed back your findings to your group. See if you can decide why the different places visited felt it necessary to offer these particular services. What would be the main reasons?

Hotlink

The Trading Standards Institute produces a lot of information and training material for businesses as well as for consumers, as it is in their interest to protect consumers by educating businesses. To find out more, visit www.tradingstandards. gov.uk.

Taking responsibility

Most customers will expect that the person with whom they are dealing will see the matter through to its conclusion, and this is an important personal responsibility. Customer service staff should be aware of their individual, as well as corporate responsibilities, to ensure customer satisfaction.

Well-trained customer service staff will remain cool and calm, no matter how outlandish a customer's needs and expectations. In no circumstances should customer service staff engage in arguments or raised voices with customers – it is appropriate firmly to adhere to the policy of the business, but if the situation starts to get out of hand, they should refer the matter to more experienced or senior colleagues.

Recognising customer rights

It is the responsibility of every business, and every employee, to make sure that in all of their dealings with customers they remain legal, decent, honest and truthful – not just in word but also in deed. The Unfair Trading Regulations 2008 are very clear in the way that they outline the responsibilities of a business to deal fairly and honestly with its customers.

Just checking

* State two ways in which you could increase your product knowledge.
* What is good practice when you reach the limit of your product knowledge?
* Where could you find a good source of information on the legal rights of customers?

5.9 Customer service policies and practice

Customer service policies and practices are as diverse as the businesses implementing them. Each will have a different method of managing their policies, and each will have different objectives. The stated objective may be quite different from the internal objective – better customer service may be presented as providing the customer with a more pleasant experience, when really it's about luring them away from a competitor.

Customer service expectations

Businesses provide customer services to meet the needs and expectations of their particular customers. Customers' needs cover practical or physical requirements, for example easy access, staff available when making a purchase, a wide range of payment options, delivery, after-sales service, etc.

Expectations, like wants, are more subjective and personal, and they may vary depending on the attitude of the customer. For example, a customer may need someone to serve them – but they expect that person to be clean, smart, polite and helpful and maybe a lot more. Their expectations do not actually make much difference to the outcome of a transaction in practical terms, but if they are met, they will certainly add value and help create positive feelings towards the business, building customer loyalty and making repeat purchases more likely.

Aims, objectives and ethos of the organisation

The organisation will have set certain aims and objectives for customer service that the management believes will meet the needs and expectations of its customers. To achieve these, all employees must follow the rules, so it may be written into their job description or contract of employment. Customer service policies and procedures may also be dictated by the ethos – the culture – of the organisation, how the organisation is run and how it presents itself to its customers.

Most organisations do not set out to provide poor customer service, but it may occur because management does not realise what customers expect, or there may only be a limited budget available for customer service. Everything has a cost and if the organisation does not have a budget sufficient to provide customer services to the levels expected, then it will show up as a weakness and the business runs the risk of dissatisfied customers.

Industry standards, codes of conduct and legislation

Whether set out in a **customer charter** or **code of practice**, or as a result of historic development, you will find that each industry or sector of business has a general standard of customer service that member companies seek to deliver, and customers have come to expect. For example, businesses in the hotel and catering industry will provide a different set of customer services at a different level from businesses in the energy supply sector. What this means in practice is that customers expect, and are happy to accept, different standards of customer service when they enter a hotel than when they are dealing with energy suppliers.

Industry standards are usually set by trade bodies, that is, organisations that represent the interests of member companies in different industries, such as CORGI for gas installers, or The Chartered Institute of Logistics and Transport, the professional body for everyone in the logistics, passenger transport, transport planning and related industries. Member companies will aim to provide customer services to the standards set by their trade body so that they can benefit from membership of such organisations, such as joint publicity. Most codes of practice will be voluntary or **self-regulating**, but quite often they will be linked closely with legislation that is designed to protect consumers. Thus, by following the requirements of a code of practice members will be sure that their operations remain legal.

> **Customer charter**
> A document that sets out the remit and service standards that a business or organisation aims to work to.
>
> **Code of practice**
> A published set of standards which a business agrees to operate by.
>
> **Self-regulating** The organisation or industry monitors and polices its own standards.

Competitor standards

Closely related to industry standards will be an organisation's aim to match or exceed its competitors' standards. Frequently, the provision of more extensive customer services to a higher standard is used by businesses to demonstrate that they are better than their competitors. This can lead to an escalation of services, with the consequent benefits for customers and consumers, but can become very expensive for the business as it commits more money to the provision of its customer services.

Budget

The customer service provision for a business must fit within the amount of money that it can afford to spend on customer service so that the company remains profitable. This may limit, for example, the number of call-handlers that can be employed at a call centre, which may have an impact on the amount of time it takes to answer calls during busy periods.

> **Just checking**
>
> * Give three reasons why a business might have a customer service policy.
> * What would be the consequence for a business if its customer services did not meet the expectations of its customers?
> * What effect could a limited budget for customer services have on a business?

5.10 Successful selling

The art of selling involves representing and meeting the objectives of the business through satisfying the needs of its customers. Before you can start to become effective at selling, you need to be fully confident about your business and the products that you are selling, and this starts with product knowledge.

SALES TECHNIQUES

Think of the last time you went into a store that sells electronic devices such as mobile phones, MP3 players, etc. What sales techniques (if any) did the sales staff use to convince customers of the benefits of their products? What do you think was most effective? What was least effective? Discuss your experiences in a small group.

What sales techniques do sales staff use in this kind of situation?

Knowing your product/service

To start with, you will need to familiarise yourself with the product. You will need to learn all of its **features** – its specification, how it works, how it performs, how well it compares with other similar products, how it is maintained, how long it will last, how it can be repaired or restored. You will need to be familiar with the features that so that you can convert them to **benefits** for the customer. It will also help if you can identify any unique selling points (USPs) that make your product special and stand out from competition, plus any 'added value' features such as after-sales service, guarantees, etc. Product knowledge will also help you make comparisons with the competition – if you do not know your own product very well, it would be easy to lose out to competition.

It will also help if you know what your customers and consumers use the product for, and how they use or experience the product – in this way, you can advise them, and start to build a positive relationship.

You will need to be familiar with the pricing structure. This is not simply the 'list price' (the selling price) that you are hoping to get, but the bottom-line price below which you should never go as it will cut the profit margin too much.

Features Factual or technical pieces of information about the product, e.g. shape, size, colour, performance.

Benefits The positive gain or advantage that the customer gets as a direct result of each product feature; gives one product an advantage over another, competitor, product.

You will find that discounts are usually negotiable, and quite acceptable so long as you both achieve a satisfactory deal from the transaction.

If you are selling to distributors rather than direct to consumers or end users, you will often be asked for the 'retail price', the price that it will sell for in a shop. Although, as a sales person, you may not have any direct influence over the retail selling price, you should always have a realistic opinion to help you advise the retail customer.

Being familiar with the business's after-sales and support service links directly with customer service. So, in addition to product knowledge, you will need to know the full range of customer services offered by the business. Sales support may also take the form of marketing activity – advertising or promotion that will support your customers as well as your products.

Activity

Choose a product that you are planning to sell. In your group, sit in a circle around a desk or table. Starting with one person, and moving clockwise round the group, each person in turn must state a feature of the product chosen – and then convert the feature into a benefit for your customers. See how many times you can go round the group before you run out of features. For example, consider a 2-pint plastic bottle of milk as the product: feature 1 – it's packaged in a plastic bottle, benefit 1 – this means that if it gets dropped it will not break; feature 2 – there is a tamper evident seal on the closure, benefit 2 – this means that you can see if it has been opened and possibly contaminated; feature 3 – milk is a nutritious drink, benefit 3 – it will help keep you healthy; and so on. You need to note all the features, and attendant benefits, that can be identified. This exercise will build up your product knowledge, which can be used to demonstrate confidence and answer queries that may arise when engaged in selling your product.

Knowing your customers

Good preparation also involves identifying who your customers are – for example, are they trade customers such as distributors, wholesalers or retailers, business-to-business (BTB), consumers or end users? What is the profile – the description – of your target customer? To learn more about customer profiles, see topic 5.7. The target customer is the one (or the group) that is most likely to be in the market and most likely to want to buy your product at a given time.

Just checking

* List the demographic features that could affect your sales plans.
* List the psychographic features that could affect your sales plans.
* List the geographic features that could affect your sales plans.
* How many different prices do you need to know for each product? List them, giving each a brief description.

Customer needs a mode of transport but wants a fashionable model.

5.11 Making a sale

To improve the effectiveness of your sales contacts, you need to become familiar with the basic steps in making a sale. Once you understand these, you can then start to refine them to develop your own successful formula for effective selling. Repeat this and your sales will naturally increase! The more you repeat it, the more sales you will achieve. Thus selling, as the cliché goes, becomes a numbers game.

The basic steps in making a sale

Remember that throughout the selling process, you have an ethical duty to remain legal, decent, honest and truthful in all of your customer interactions.

1. Making initial contact with the customer

Once you have identified who your customer is (see page 136), you must make contact with them to start the selling process. Personal, face-to-face contact can be very effective because you can see the customer, listen to their needs, watch their body language, and immediately decide on the best solution to their needs. Equally, in this situation, the customer can see you, your positive attitude and the enthusiasm with which you present your product.

Cold calling (where you contact the potential customer directly without any warning) can be very hard – you need lots of confidence and you run the risk of receiving a rebuff from the customer. Remember, don't take it personally, if the prospective customer does not know you, then they must have other reasons for an objection. Once you make contact with a customer, you should:

* make it clear who you are and the organisation you represent

* the purpose of your contact.

This should pave the way for your interaction with the customer and avoid any misunderstanding.

2. Finding out what the customer wants

You should be able to find out what a customer **needs** through actively listening to them, and this may be sufficient to satisfy their requirements. Finding out what their **wants** can be more challenging as this is often inferred, implied or left unspoken, but which can be achieved though talking to the customer and having a good, general awareness of them and their circumstances.

3. Presenting them with a solution

When you are selling, the solution to a customer's needs and wants should come from your own range of products. However, if you do not have a product that meets all of their requirements, you still have a number of options for providing a solution:

* Make your product meet the customer's needs and wants by altering it in some way, within the limits of your authority, e.g. changing the price, specification, or other variables.

* Present the customer with a realistic alternative, such as a different colour or a different specification.

4. Overcoming objections

Objections are the barriers that a customer will put up to try to stop you making a sale. They may be rational or irrational, but you should be able to overcome most objections by listening carefully to the customer and then effectively communicating good reasons, based on product and market knowledge, why they should purchase the product or service.

Common types of objections you may face:

* *'The price is too high.'* This can be overcome in a number of ways, by 'adding value' to the sale. This could include emphasising the importance of value over time, rather than absolute price, i.e. the product lasts longer; explaining that you get what you pay for in terms of quality; highlighting that the price includes added value such as after-sales service, a guarantee or warranty, automatic updates, and so on. Try to avoid cutting the price just to make a quick sale, as there will always be someone else who will reduce their price even more and appear to be cheaper, putting the pressure back on you to cut the price further, resulting in a 'price war' where each business tries to undercut the other.

* *'Your delivery takes too long.'* To overcome objections based on timing, you will need to have good knowledge of the real time of manufacture, supply or delivery so you can negotiate a realistic time scale that can actually be met by your business.

* *Features of the product.* To overcome this type of objection, you will need to have good product knowledge so that you can deal with any misunderstanding or assumptions made by the customer. You should also know about your full range of products so that you can present customers with an alternative that meets their needs more closely.

* *'I've always been satisfied with ..., why should I change now?'* No matter how much a customer may favour a competitor, your business and brand will have its own strengths and brand values that you should be able to support through product knowledge and enthusiasm – keep positive, stress your own strengths, reinforced by good reasons why the customer should deal with your business.

> **Cold calling** When you contact the potential customer directly without any prior warning.
>
> **Needs** Objective, functional requirements.
>
> **Wants** Subjective, qualitative desires.
>
> **Objections** Reasons that customers give for not buying something.

> ### Personal, Learning and Thinking Skills
>
> When you are trying to influence customers or presenting a persuasive case for action when demonstrating sales skills, you are using the skills of an effective participator.
>
> When you are showing commitment and perseverance in a sales situation you are using the skills of a self-manager.

5. Closing the sale

This is the final step in effective selling, which we'll look at more closely in the next topic.

> ### Activity
>
> Get in touch with different businesses that have a sales team or a person dedicated to selling. Find out the basic steps that they use when making a sales contact. Do they use a script or a set format for each sales contact?
>
> Identify similarities and differences between the basic steps followed by each of the businesses, and work out which steps help to make the selling successful. Try to build the most successful steps into your own selling activity.

> ### Just checking
>
> * Why is selling sometimes referred to as 'a numbers game'?
> * What are the differences between a 'warm call' and a 'cold call'?
> * How could product knowledge help you to overcome a customer's objections?

5.12 Closing the sale

It's decision time for the customer – you have reached the point where you need to finish the sale and get agreement from the customer to buy. All of your preparation and the sales process should lead them to the point where they say 'yes', and the contract to buy and the contract to supply is made.

Handling customers effectively in a sales situation

You can make the sales process more effective through good preparation and by following a few basic rules.

The right attitude

You need to be enthusiastic and positive – motivated to sell – but without being too overbearing. The customer needs to know that you believe in your business and your product, and this will help give them confidence that you think the product is right for them. Attitude can also be communicated by the way that you present yourself – you should look approachable: be clean, tidy, and dressed appropriately for the selling situation and the customer.

If you have prepared well, have good product knowledge, and can present your answers and arguments effectively, you should be able to overcome most objections. If the customer puts up an objection that you find difficult to overcome, be honest; do not attempt to lie as this will be found out later and the customer will lose trust in you.

Communication skills

Each customer is different, so you will need to adapt your approach to their individual needs and the sales situation.

Use **active listening** to identify what the customer really wants, and use this information to support your product. Your voice and the pace at which you speak when making your sales presentation should help to reassure the customer – stay calm, speak clearly, using language that is appropriate to the situation, at a pace that the customer can take in. Do not shout, gabble, use overlong or technical words (unless, of course, you are selling a technical product to a technical expert when your technical knowledge will be appreciated), pause occasionally and check that the customer understands.

You should also be aware of the importance of non-verbal communication skills – the use of body language to reassure customers rather then dominate them, how using an open posture can make the customer become more relaxed. Eye contact can be important – you can increase your trust and sincerity level by looking the customer in the eye when dealing with them; if you avoid eye contact, you could come across as being nervous, or worse, as shifty and untrustworthy.

Think about how close you position your body in relation to the customer – too far away and you create an invisible barrier, but too close and you would be invading their personal space which could be very off-putting.

IS THERE ANYTHING ELSE?

When you buy something do you notice when the sale is 'closed'? When you are out and about in your daily life, listen carefully to the way the sale is closed. The sales person may say something like 'Is that everything?' or 'Does that complete the order?'. They may be more direct and say something such as 'How would you like to pay?' or 'Will you take it now or shall we deliver?' Discuss with your group which sales closes are most effective.

Active listening Involves not just listening carefully but concentrating on every word or phrase that the customer utters, focusing attention on the customer and engaging with them. Active listening takes in both sounds and body language so that you pick up information about the customer using your senses, as appropriate.

Close The point in a sales interaction when the customer says 'yes' and agrees to buy.

The close

Remember that throughout the selling process, you have an ethical duty to remain legal, decent, honest and truthful in all of your customer interactions.

The **close** is usually recognised by the customer handing over payment – either immediately and directly with cash or card, or indirectly via signing or otherwise confirming the order, and the agreement on a credit arrangement. To close a sale, you must get the customer to agree that are actually going to buy.

There are a number of ways that you can encourage a customer to close a sale, including:

* the use of short-term incentives, such as a discount for an immediate decision

* the threat of an imminent price rise

* the threat of shortage of stock if a commitment is not made

* setting a time limit on a decision, e.g. 'This product/price is only available until the end of this week'.

Although some of the above might sound like 'threats', the threat is implied rather than actual, so as not to intimidate the customer.

A confident salesperson can usually get the customer to close the sale to their mutual agreement, without any loss of face or dignity by either party.

After any sales situation and customer interaction, you should record what happened, what you presented (the product, offer or deal), what the customer bought and how much the customer spent. This can be stored on a customer database for future reference to aid sales planning. In some sales situations this may be done automatically through an ICT process.

It is also worth reviewing your own performance – what went well, what did not go so well, what you may need to do to improve sales interactions in the future and increase the percentage of sales contacts that result in an actual sale.

Agreement is made.

@ Work

During your work experience or a part-time job, seek out the person who has the most experience of sales and selling to customers. Interview them about the use of sales 'closes'. Which ones do they use? Which ones have they found to be most effective? Ask them to explain the reasons why. An experienced salesperson will have a wide range of sales closes 'up their sleeve' that they can draw on and use depending on the circumstances and the customer involved in a sale.

Just checking

* How can you show a customer that you have the right attitude?
* How can the way that you dress affect sales?
* How can you overcome objections raised by a customer?
* Give three ways in which a sales 'close' can be encouraged.

Assessment

This unit is assessed internally. This means that you will be set an assignment by your tutor, which should direct your work through a series of tasks connected to the running of a business related activity, so that you cover all of the learning outcomes for this unit. The work you submit for assessment must be original work, produced by yourself under controlled conditions – this will be arranged by your tutor. It will then be marked by your tutor and moderated by the awarding body.

You will be assessed on:

* your knowledge of how the principles of marketing are applied to the creation of the marketing mix and promotional materials

* your ability to carry out market research

* your understanding of how effective customer service is achieved

* your ability to handle customers effectively in a sales situation.

To aim for higher grades you should try to:

* think carefully about the product or service that you choose for this assignment (your tutor will help).

* produce promotional materials of a high standard that are suitable and appropriate for the product chosen, and consistent with the market research that you carry out

* include in your plan a clear and detailed description of how the four elements of the marketing mix have been used to position the product or service

* make sure that the data collected in your market research is sufficient in terms both of quality and quantity

* give a detailed description of typical customers of the organisation that you have studied, giving clear evidence to support your explanation

* display a positive attitude and demonstrate good communication skills

* assess your performance at different stages of the sales process, identifying specific things you could do differently next time, and give a clear explanation of the benefits.

6 TEAMS AND COMMUNICATION IN BUSINESS

Introduction

It is most likely that when you find a job you will be working in a team. It is recognised that people who work in a team are more productive as they can share work and be more efficient. In this unit you will find out how good working relationships are important to help grow a successful business, and how effective communication skills are an essential part of team working. Every team member has their own particular strengths and skills, and you will investigate different team roles that people can take and learn how these contribute to the achievement of goals. How you will be assessed

How you will be assessed

For this unit, you will be assessed by an assignment connected to a business-related activity. You will be required to plan teamwork together, work towards the team's objectives and finally review your teamworking activity.

What you will learn in this unit

You will:

* Understand the benefits of teamworking

* Know how individuals and team leaders contribute to team working

* Be able to plan and monitor teamwork

* Be able to work and communicate effectively in a team.

WHAT IS A TEAM?

In a business there may be different teams doing different activities which all contribute to the operation of the business. In a small group, discuss the types of teams you think would be in a large office.

Personal, Learning and Thinking Skills

Investigating the different types of teams in a business will give you the opportunity to demonstrate your skills as an independent enquirer.

Activity

Basic skills in English, Maths and ICT – functional skills – are very important in teamworking and communication. Which one of these skills is your strongest? Which one is your weakest? Will you need any extra support in these areas? You will need to think about this and talk about it with your tutor.

Case study: Teamworking

Ishwar has applied for a job in the customer services section of a department store. On the application form, he's been asked to give details of his teamworking and communication skills. Ishwar is a bit unsure of what to include, so he's made a list of all the jobs he's had:

* part-time evening shelf stacker for a supermarket last November/December

* early morning newspaper round for the last three years

* assistant in the ticket kiosk at the local cinema last summer for six weeks

* occasional weekend work as a waiter to help out a family friend who owns a café.

1. Name the jobs where Ishwar has worked as part of a team.

2. What teamworking and communication skills could he include in his job application?

THE DIFFERENCE BETWEEN A GROUP AND A TEAM

In a small group, discuss what you think are the differences between a group and a team. Highlight the key points.

6.1 What is a team?

There is no 'I' in 'Teamwork'. This means that everyone is committed to work together and share problems to complete work activities. In a team, more can be achieved in less time, and employers recognise the value of teamwork. In this topic you will investigate the definition of a team and how it develops.

What is teamwork?

There are lots of sayings about teamwork, such as 'TEAM = Together Everyone Achieves More', 'The whole is greater than the sum of the parts', 'None of us is as smart as all of us', and there are many more. You have probably carried out team activities at school or college, for example in sports teams or in drama productions, and may have some experience in the workplace. So, what makes a team?

A group is a collection of people with different aims and objectives, although there may be a common interest, whereas a **team** can be defined as a group of people with complementary skills, working together to achieve a common goal.

Size is important – groups can be any number of people, but a team seems to have a set size, which allows each player a definite role to play. For example, if a basketball team had 20 players, there would be complete chaos on the court as they wouldn't be able to move freely; likewise, if there were only three players, then they would soon be exhausted with all the running around.

TEAM = Together Everyone Achieves More.

Team development

In order for teams to gel together to achieve their goal, they go through a number of different development stages. These were identified in 1965 by Bruce Tuckman and have been an accepted model ever since. Tuckman's model identified four stages:

1. *Forming* – this is where members find out about each other, learn how they fit in and find out about the task and objectives. They also start to rely on the leader and establish the group culture.

2. *Storming* – during this stage conflict develops as members try to jostle for position. This may cause depression and the group may drift along without a clear sense of purpose.

3. *Norming* – people start to work together having resolved any conflict, trust is developed and they speak and listen to each other.

4. *Performing* – the final stage is reached when all three previous stages have been worked through. People will feel they belong, solutions are found, ideas are implemented and, most importantly, teamwork is achieved as they are working towards a common goal.

Tuckman later added a fifth stage to his model, which he called 'Adjourning'. This stage reflects the fact that teams are often formed for specific tasks and then disbanded.

Team – A group of individuals with a shared vision working together with specific roles and committed to achieving a common goal

Activity

Think about a team in which you are currently involved in or have been in the past such as one at school, college, or through a leisure activity or hobby. Were you aware of Tuckman's different stages? List what happened at each stage.

Case study: Jasmine

Jasmine works part time at a local Italian coffee shop at weekends. There are eight staff altogether, three of whom work full time, and two part timers who started when she did. The part-time staff do not always work on the same shifts and this has meant that, after three months, Jasmine has still not worked a shift with all the staff. She had heard other members of the team discussing that certain individuals had always managed to obtain the best shifts while others were not consulted.

What measures would you suggest should be put in place to create effective team work?

Just checking

✳ What are the differences between a group and a team?

✳ What are the different stages of team development?

✳ Try to relate and describe experiences of stages in team development.

6.2 Benefits of teams

It has been proven that people who work in a team can be more efficient and effective in terms of the quality and quantity of work produced, which is an obvious benefit to an organisation. Organisations establish teams to perform a variety of different functions and this topic will help you explore what makes a team effective, and how teams support the organisation's aims and objectives.

Characteristics of an effective team

Teams make a difference to an organisation's performance, and get better results than a group of individuals who operate within their separate roles. An effective team displays certain characteristics, which are to:

* trust each other

* be loyal

* be open with each other

* be united in a common purpose

* be dependent on each other

* support each other

* be able to work through conflict

* be committed

* have a sense of group identity

* share group efficacy (belief that team members are more effective working together than working alone).

Benefits of teamworking

Team working improves productivity through making best use of people's differing skills and strengths. As we all have different skills, experiences and knowledge, if these are utilised in a team, the results of the work should be greatly improved. For example, if someone was particularly good at finance and the team task involved monitoring a budget, then that person would be the sensible choice to complete those particular tasks. Likewise, some people are good at planning and can see tasks through, whereas another person's strengths might be in coming up with ideas. Each individual team member's skills and capabilities are then reinforced which helps motivate them and feel worthwhile.

Team working also creates more ideas and opportunities for creativity and initiative, especially for solving problems such as improvements to systems and procedures. This is because with the combined knowledge of the team more ideas can be generated and therefore more solutions, which in turn create improved results. Also, team members can test out their ideas and thoughts with each other, and get feedback more easily.

Often one of the main reasons for lack of job satisfaction in the workplace is low motivation of individuals. Employers have found that staff motivation and greater job satisfaction is increased through developing a team spirit of shared vision and sense of commitment. The continual development of the team relationships and enthusiasm of the members in having a sense of belonging, and being part of the work activities, helps to keep the team motivated and able to build on their successes. Also, working as a team helps to improve internal communication within the workforce as a common goal is shared and people feel they can discuss and help each other with the project in hand. Communications are shared much quicker than going through more formal routes, especially matters relating to work performance.

Increased efficiency and productivity is achieved through allocating specific tasks to individual team members. For example, if a project was given to one person to plan, implement and monitor it would take a long time, whereas if the workload is distributed to several team members who were given tasks in parallel, then the overall goal would be achieved much more quickly. In this way team work ensures less duplication of tasks.

Developing performance and stretching people's talents to take on additional responsibilities is better achieved through team working. There are increased opportunities for delegation of tasks to help individuals' develop and acquire new skills, and thereby improve work performance. Employers know that if someone is off sick or on holiday, then other team members can cover the role without too much difficulty. This results in overall less risk to the organisation and a multi-skilled and more flexible workforce. On-the-job training, job shadowing or job rotation is one way to train unskilled members and an improved customer focus benefits the organisation.

Disadvantages of teamworking

So, are there any disadvantages in team working? It could be argued that setting up teams requires a lot of energy and time. Some members may not contribute as much as others, individual strengths may not be so easily recognised and, of course, a clash of personalities and behaviours may affect the **team dynamics** and be a cause of conflict.

Groups also sometimes experience the phenomenon of 'groupthink'. This concept separates teams from groups. Groupthink is 'a mode of thinking that people engage in when they are deeply involved in a cohesive in-group, when the members' strivings for unanimity override their motivation to realistically appraise alternative courses of action' (Irving Janis, 1982). This is where the team is so focused on maintaining group cohesiveness that members lose the ability to think independently – the team tends to drift along towards decisions, which may be inappropriate or unquestioned.

@ Work

See if you can discuss with a few colleagues how they enjoy working in teams. Ask what they like about it, what they don't, what makes the team effective, and how it helps the job. You might need to discuss this in private!

Team dynamics The strength of the team, how people get on together

---

Just checking

* Name four characteristics of effective teams.
* List three benefits of team working.
* List three disadavntages of team working.
* Describe the concept of 'groupthink'.

6.3 Types of team

Teams can be established for many reasons either for the long-term development and operation of the organisation or to meet a short-term requirement or need. Long-term teams include formal support teams and cross-functional teams, whereas short-term teams are often project teams. In this topic you will learn about different types of team and their purpose.

Independent and inter-dependent teams

As well as being either long- or short-term, teams have other features. They can be independent or inter-dependent. An inter-dependent team, such as a football team, relies on other team members to achieve the task (such as defending or scoring goals), so the success of every individual is bound to the success of the team. However, in an independent team, such as an equestrian team where events are won by individuals, the success or failure of one member has no direct effect on the performance of the next member.

Individual success or failure does not affect other members of an independent team.

Formal and informal teams

Teams can also be temporary or permanent to match long- or short-term needs. They can be directed or self managed, real or virtual. Formal teams are part of the organisation's structure, such as the support teams of finance, human resources, administration, IT, whereas informal teams are usually created to work on a specific project or task.

1. Management team

A management team is usually a permanent **hierarchical structure**. It provides direction and coordination of tasks, and allocates resources. Management decides what tasks are to be performed, assigns members to teams, and provides the organisational context within the team functions.

2. Virtual team

A virtual team is a team of people who are physically separated but mainly interact electronically. This means they can work anywhere at any time, and members can be recruited for their competencies, regardless of physical location. A virtual team is often more cost effective as expenses for travelling, accommodation, etc. are reduced.

3. Self-managed team

Self-managed (or self-directed) teams are autonomous where each member of the team shares equal responsibility for the task – the team members develop the goals, assign tasks and monitor performance. Team consensus contributes to improved decision making and ownership.

4. Work team

These teams are stable and permanent, and usually provide services or products. The team leader functions as both a **facilitator** and a team member. A work team may be self managed as the team is largely responsible for determining goals, tasks, assignments and schedules.

5. Quality circles

This is a group of staff empowered to examine quality-related work problems and present solutions – often known as quality improvement teams.

6. Project teams

These teams are dedicated to a specific objective and have limited life spans. They are often cross-functional with members selected for their expertise.

@ Work

Try to find out about as many different types of teams as you can. Which are formal or informal? What is the purpose of each team?

Hierarchical structure
Where there are different levels in a treelike structure, with each level being accountable to another.

Facilitator A person who assists a group of people to plan to achieve their objectives, but without taking sides in the process.

Just checking

* What are the differences between an independent and interdependent team?
* List the features of six different types of team.

6.4 How roles contribute to a team's effectiveness

An effective, cohesive team will achieve an output far higher than the sum of the individuals added together. This topic investigates how different people can contribute to teams in different ways, how teams develop and how an understanding of team roles can aid the development process.

Team roles

When forming or developing a team, the ideal would be to select people whose skills and attributes would fulfil the task requirements while ensuring that all members work together harmoniously. In reality, this may not happen and you may find that the combination of individual strengths and weaknesses causes conflict or disharmony within the team.

This means that your team is a compromise on the ideal. A solution to this problem lies in an understanding of team roles, and how these can be managed to enable teams to develop and maximise their efforts.

There are two requirements when selecting team members – technical and specialist skills, and personal styles. All teams consist of a number of individuals, with each individual having something different and unique to offer. Each member of the team will have been employed to fulfil specific functional roles which are defined in the job specifications or '**roles and responsibilities**' documents. Each member will also contribute to the success of the team by fulfilling a 'team role'.

Belbin team roles

Dr Meredith Belbin carried out pioneering work on team roles and types in the 1970s. He defined a team role as 'a tendency to behave, contribute and interrelate with others in a particular way'. He identified nine different **behaviours**, which he called team roles, each role having its own particular strengths and allowable weaknesses. He concluded that any team member could play one or more of the following roles.

From his research, Belbin found that team roles can help teams gain a better understanding of not only each other but also the task in hand, as well as improving the self-knowledge of the individual team members. He thought that team roles follow a certain behavioural pattern – a snapshot of your behaviour at one time. There are many factors that can influence behaviour, such as a new job, a promotion, or events in your personal life.

Team members will display a number of behaviours directly associated with the team roles they are filling. Effective team members will demonstrate behaviours that are strengths. These effective team members may also have weaknesses that are also directly associated with their team roles. These weaknesses are often the opposite aspects of their strengths. Effective team members understand their weaknesses and therefore take action to avoid demonstrating them – they therefore become 'allowable' weaknesses.

Roles and responsibilities The activities that are to be carried out to perform the job.

Behaviours How people interrelate with others in a particular way.

Role	Strengths	Allowable weaknesses
Plant	Creative, imaginative, unorthodox. Solves difficult problems.	Ignores incidentals. Too preoccupied to communicate effectively.
Resource investigator	Extrovert, enthusiastic, exploratory. Explores opportunities. Develops contacts.	Over optimistic. Loses interest once initial enthusiasm has passed.
Coordinator	Mature, confident, a good chairperson. Clarifies goals, promotes decision making.	Can be seen as manipulative. Often offloads personal work.
Shaper	Dynamic, challenging. Has drive and courage to overcome obstacles.	Prone to provocation. Offends people's feelings.
Monitor evaluator	Sober, strategic, discerning. Sees all options.	Lacks drive and ability to inspire others.
Teamworker	Co-operative, mild, perceptive, diplomatic. Listens, builds, averts friction.	Indecisive in crunch situations.
Implementer	Disciplined, reliable, conservative. Turns ideas into practical action.	Somewhat inflexible. Slow to respond to new possibilities.
Completer	Painstaking, conscientious, anxious. Searches out errors and omissions, delivers on time.	Inclined to worry unduly. Reluctant to delegate.
Specialist	Single-minded, dedicated self-starting, . Provides knowledge and skill in rare supply.	Contributes on only a narrow front. Dwells on technicalities.

Belbin team roles and types.

@ Work

Consider the following in relation to the teams you have experience of:

1 Identify all of the team roles.
2 Are there any roles which are not represented?
3 What are the consequences of an area of weakness?

Personal, Learning and Thinking Skills

Assessing the team's effectiveness requires the skills of reflective learner, which will help you identify what worked well and what didn't work so well.

Just checking

* What is meant by a team role?
* Identify nine team roles and their strengths.
* Name the allowable weaknesses of the nine roles.

WHAT MAKES A GREAT LEADER?

Think of someone whom you consider to be a good leader – they could be historical, political, entrepreneurial, or someone you know. What makes them a good leader? List the qualities they have and the reasons you think they are a good leader. Compare your list with other members of your group.

A great wartime leader - Winston Churchill was the British prime minister during the Second World War.

6.5 The team leader's role

An effective team isn't formed by simply putting people together – it must be led and created by establishing a common purpose, clear roles, sound relationships and open communication structures. In this topic you will investigate the skills and attributes of team leaders.

Types of leader

There are three different types of leader:

* Charismatic – their influence comes mainly from strength of personality, e.g. Churchill, Napoleon, Clinton.

* Traditional – one whose position is as a result of birth, such as kings and queens.

* Appointed – one whose influence arises directly out of their position, such as a manager or supervisor.

Leadership skills

Belbin identified two types of people who might assume leadership of a team – the coordinator and the shaper – depending on the kind of task the team has to undertake. However, there might be instances when the team needs to be led by a specialist, for example if there are technical difficulties, or at other times when someone has had expertise of a particular project or piece of work. This means that leadership is not dependent on seniority or position, in contrast to management.

An effective team leader needs to possess many attributes and qualities, including:

* creating a sense of common purpose

* taking personal responsibility for making things happen

* encouraging and supporting others to take decisions

* making time available to support others

* showing integrity, fairness and consistency

* showing respect

* leading by example.

Action-centred leadership

There are many theories about leaders and leadership. One of the most popular approaches involves relating the leader to the task being carried out, the needs of the team and the needs of the individuals in the team. John Adair represented this as a three-circle model.

The leader's job is to:

* achieve the task through planning and assigning work, managing resources and delegating responsibilities

* help the team with the set task and solve any problems that might arise

* build the group into an effective team by setting objectives and building relationships

* develop and motivate the individuals through monitoring performance, supporting, mentoring, dealing with conflict, giving feedback and recognition.

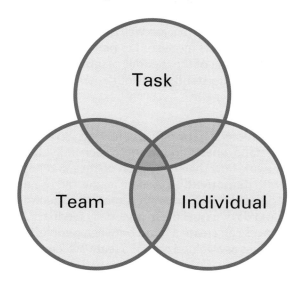

John Adair's three-circle model of action-centred leadership.

Leadership styles

What is a leadership style? This links to the types of leader.

Leadership style	Key features
Autocratic	Make decisions, give instructions and expect them to be carried out without question
Persuasive	Make decisions and expect them to be accepted
Consultative	Seek the views of the team members before making the decisions
Participative	Take problems to the team, exchange views and accept the majority decision

Team leaders can use different styles of leadership. One style will not suit every situation and an effective leader will adjust their style accordingly. For example, during times of emergency or stress, an autocratic style is desirable, but an autocratic style can be very stressful for the team when the pressure is off.

@ Work

Consider three different leaders you work with:

1 What type of leader are they?
2 What is their leadership style?
3 Make notes on the advantages and disadvantages of the style.

Just checking

* Name the characteristics of three different types of leader.
* Which leadership style would you use in an emergency?

6.6 Ways leaders can support teams

Motivation is what makes you behave in a particular way. What you put into something is related to what you expect to get out of it – the reward. Different people are motivated by different rewards, and most of us are motivated by recognition of a job well done. A team leader needs to keep the team members motivated to perform well, and in this topic you will explore some of the theories of motivation and how these can be used to help understand behaviour.

Motivation

Team members may be motivated by different rewards, so a team leader needs to understand what is important to each individual, what they want from their work, how their needs can be met, and how to recognise and deal with **demotivation**. A team leader can use different methods of encouragement to keep members motivated such as social activities, team building days, casual dress days, daily feedback, etc. These shared experiences can create a bond between people, and those who see themselves as a valued part of a team are likely to feel a stronger sense of motivation.

Motivation theories

There are many theories about motivation. Maslow's hierarchy of needs is based on the assumption that individuals try to achieve the goal that will satisfy their needs. These goals may change from time to time.

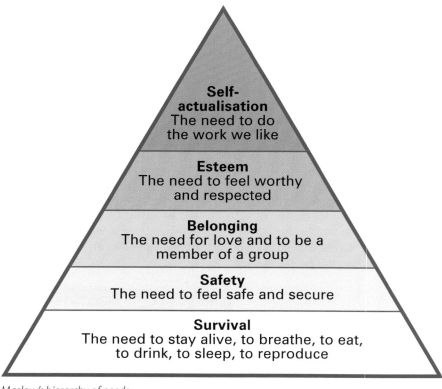

Maslow's hierarchy of needs.

Motivation and job satisfaction

Another theorist, Frederick Herzberg, conducted research into the motivation of accountants and engineers. He concluded that people operate in accordance with two separate and distinct need systems:

* *Motivational needs* are concerned with the job itself and relate to job satisfaction and performance, such as

  * the work itself
  * responsibility
  * opportunities for advancement
  * recognition from others
  * achievement.

* *Environmental needs* are associated with the working situation and are not motivators. However, if these are not met they can become 'dissatisfiers' or demotivators, such as

  * pay and benefits
  * working relationships
  * working conditions.

How people behave at work

Another famous theorist, Douglas McGregor, suggested that companies make assumptions about the way others behave, either:

Theory X – where management assumes employees are naturally lazy and will avoid work where possible, therefore they need controlling under close supervision and threatened with punishment

or

Theory Y – where management assumes that given the right conditions most people enjoy work, will accept responsibility and generally want to do well.

> **Functional Skills**
>
> **English**
> Use speaking, listening and reading skills to find out what motivational rewards are offered by companies. You will need to record your findings in writing, so make sure you write clearly and coherently.

> **Demotivation** Factors which define the job context such as company policy and procedures.

> **Activity**
>
> Split into three groups for different types of business sector – public, private and voluntary. Each group is to research the kinds of motivational rewards offered by at least three different companies. Present your findings on a wall chart and be prepared to discuss this with the other groups.

> **Just checking**
>
> * Name the five stages in Maslow's hierarchy of needs.
> * List three of Herzberg's dissatisfiers.
> * What does a Theory X manager assume about their staff?

6.7 Dealing with problems when planning work

When working in a team and planning work, there will be occasions when the unexpected happens and you will be faced with problems that you will have to deal with. Different types of problems will require different solutions, and this topic will help you investigate different types of problem and ways to resolve them.

Understanding the problem or situation

A problem can be defined as something which stands in the way of achieving a desired goal or objective, or a deviation from the norm. At work, this could be a team member off sick or not pulling their weight in the team. There are different types of problem depending on their levels of complexity and their constraints, such as time, resources and laws:

* **Bounded problems** – these are known and familiar to you and have clear boundaries.

* **Unbounded problems** – these are unknown and unfamiliar with ill-defined boundaries and outside your experience.

Tackling the problem

Problems can sometimes seem to be impossible to resolve. However, thinking laterally will help you to identify the steps you should take to overcome the hurdle.

A good starting point is to try to find the cause of the problem by root analysis, so that all the different ways of dealing with the issue and any possible outcomes can be considered. It can also help to compare it with similar problems that other people have come across, and relate your problem to how they dealt with theirs.

Problem-solving techniques

Idea-storming is a process used to develop highly creative solutions to a problem. It is particularly useful to bring the experience of all team members together during problem solving. Team members meet together to take part in the process, which has a few simple rules:

* appoint one person to note down ideas, often on a flipchart

* rule out judgements, either your own or other team members'

* aim for as many solutions as possible

* be innovative and create as many ideas as you can

* add new ideas immediately.

Another useful method is to draw up cause and effect diagrams, to help visualise the root analysis and any possible outcomes.

Deciding what action to take

Decision making and problem solving are not the same, although people sometimes think they are. Decision making is part of the problem-solving process, and problem solving involves the consideration of a number of possible solutions. A good team leader will involve members in problem solving but still retain the decision. There are eight different steps in the decision-making process.

Once the problem has been solved, it is good practice to see if anything could be done better or differently either to avoid similar problems or to help get through future problems quicker and easier. It is important that you learn from the experience so that you are better prepared for next time.

Functional Skills

English
Use speaking, listening and reading skills when discussing problems in your group and preparing a diagram. You will need to record your findings in writing, so make sure you write clearly and coherently.

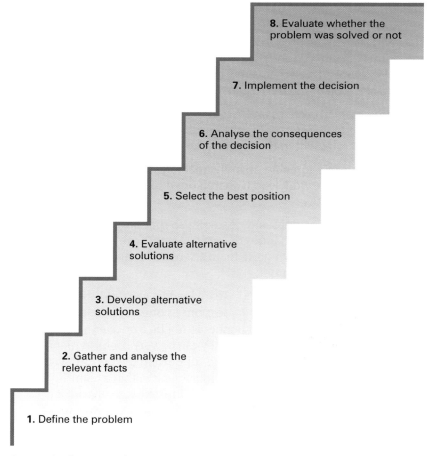

8. Evaluate whether the problem was solved or not

7. Implement the decision

6. Analyse the consequences of the decision

5. Select the best position

4. Evaluate alternative solutions

3. Develop alternative solutions

2. Gather and analyse the relevant facts

1. Define the problem

Steps in the decision-making process.

Bounded problems Those that are easily defined with a clear goal.
Unbounded problems Those that are new and for which information is incomplete.

Activity

Imagine you are planning a visit with a group to an outdoor music concert in another town. What plans and decisions would you need to make? What types of problem do you think could happen? Idea-storm with your group. Prepare a simple cause and effect diagram.

Just checking

* Name the steps in the decision-making process.
* Name two types of problem.
* Identify the benefits of idea-storming.

MONITORING
INDIVIDUAL
PERFORMANCE

What ways do you think a
team leader could monitor
the performance of
individual team members?
Discuss reasons in your
group.

6.8 Monitoring team performance

Teams are made up of individuals who share a common goal. When leading a team, it's important to recognise that different people have different needs. Often the individuals in a team need extra support. Good leaders monitor the performance of their team and the individuals within it. In this topic you will learn the importance of monitoring team performance.

Appraisals

Most organisations have some kind of appraisal system in place because of their value in supporting individuals at work. Appraisals provide a confidential opportunity for setting objectives, evaluating performance, and providing constructive feedback on an individual's performance. Appraisals are one-to-one sessions between a team leader and their staff, and also can be used to listen to issues raised by individuals about things that affect them and their work. During these meetings, there are several key topics that are covered, to ensure that the team is moving forward and working to the required standards. These topics include:

* Setting team objectives and targets as a common goal to work towards, and understanding the specific tasks and requirements of individual roles within the objectives.

* Delegating and agreeing on individual roles for each member of the team so that the work load is shared out equally and contributes to the team objective.

* Establishing milestones and deadlines so that progress can be monitored and any changes or improvements can be made along the way, as well as giving the team a sense of achievement in completion of a set target.

An appraisal helps to support individuals at work.

Team leaders can hold appraisal sessions as often as needed and should not be a once a year activity. They can be very useful in monitoring and supporting the performance of individuals within a team. If an individual needs support, it is important to set objectives for key result areas so that staff are clear about what has to be achieved, when, to what standard, and using which resources.

You should remember that as a team leader you will experience two sides of appraisal – appraising your own staff, and being appraised on your performance by your own line manager.

Prioritising work

It is good practice to make sure that all work is completed in order of priority – that means dealing with the most important first, and so on. You can organise your work into different categories of priority:

You can also organise your work into a list in descending order of high, medium, and low priority. This is particularly helpful when you have lots of deadlines to meet.

Time management

When you have been set tasks and objectives it is vital that you manage your time effectively to complete them within the deadline. Organise and plan your time by making daily and or weekly 'to-do' lists and estimating how long individual tasks will take. Set time limits for each task and negotiate reasonable and achievable deadlines with your team leader. Time must also be allowed for unexpected problems that might arise and cause interruptions to planned work, so that the deadline is not missed. Using electronic or manual diary systems and calendars that you can carry with you at all times help to keep you up to date and aware of important upcoming dates and deadlines, as well as being able to add in new ones on the go.

Objective setting

You looked at SMART objectives in Unit 2 Business Administration, and these apply when team leaders agree work and monitor performance with individual members of their team. Usually, objectives are cascaded through a number of levels.

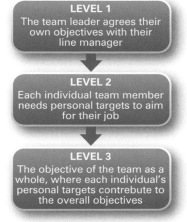

Objectives cascaded through levels of the organisation.

Preparing for appraisal

A good appraisal interview should be a positive experience for both the team leader and the team member. In order for this to happen both need to prepare:

* The appraiser (team leader) needs to remind themselves of what was agreed at the last review and consider how far the team member has achieved those objectives.

* The appraisee (team member) needs to consider how well they think they have achieved their objectives, their strengths and areas where they need extra support.

* Both parties need to collect supporting evidence – negative and positive – as part of the appraisal process is to review past performance and look for ways to build on success and take action on any problem areas.

Appraisal is about evaluating performance, not personality, and it is important for the team leader to take a balanced view, and not focus solely on the strengths of the team, otherwise performance will not be improved.

6.9 Participating in a team

Everyone is different and as a team member you will need to work effectively with other people. There may be times where you can help others complete a task when you have time to spare, or do a favour for someone and so build a positive working relationship. Other times you may have to cope with a difficult person, which could lead to conflict. This topic will help you understand the skills and attributes needed when working in a team.

The ideal team member

Working in a team can be demanding and difficult when people do not cooperate and are unwilling to work. For a project to move forward and a team to develop, its members need to have the following qualities:

* A positive attitude. Positive staff results in positive work output, which is what the employer is looking for. Showing that you are committed to the team's success and that you are willing to take collective responsibility is a positive attribute to the team's progress.

* Willing to participate. Taking on a fair share of the workload improves team culture and respect for one another, as well as moving the project closer to completion.

* Supporting the team. A strong team has respect for individual team members, allowing each person to speak without interruption. Each member should be polite to the rest of the team and cooperate well with them. They should be willing to listen to other points of view.

* Effective communication. Communication is vital within a team, so strong listening and speaking skills are required. Non-verbal communication such as body language, eye contact and gestures makes the team more personal, but should be kept positive and professional.

* Recognising and dealing with conflict. Recognising conflict is usually a lot easier than dealing with it. It can be hard to rise above the conflict and take action among fellow employees. However, there are some strategies that can be used to make it easier, including:

  * active listening

  * trying to understand the situation from both sides of the argument

  * focusing on the issues, not the people involved

  * negotiating compromise to result in **win-win solutions**.

When resolving conflict it is important to ensure that any allegations are supported with evidence. If the conflict cannot be resolved using unofficial means, further action involving third parties may need to be taken.

Types of conflict

Constructive conflict

This can be beneficial to teams. For example, creative teams may argue before an idea is developed and agreed, but as long as the discussion focuses on the issue rather than the person, then the outcome is purposeful as it can release emotion, anxiety and stress.

Destructive conflict

On the other hand, destructive conflict is harmful to everyone who is involved. It is a situation out of control where people become upset and productive work stops. Early indicators can include body language and open disagreement.

> **Win-win solutions** When both sides benefit from a compromise.

Teams make a difference to an organisation's performance.

> ### Functional Skills
>
> **English**
> Use your speaking and listening skills in group discussions.
> **ICT**
> Use your ICT skills to select and use software to prepare a table.

> ### Personal, Learning and Thinking Skills
>
> When working in a team towards a common goal you will demonstrate your team working skills. It is important to collaborate with others and resolve any conflicts that may occur.

> ### Activity
>
> There is a conflict between two people regarding shifts at a café. Natalie is being accused of taking all the busy shifts where there are statistically more tips. Soreya wants Natalie to swap some shifts with her to make it more even and fair, but Natalie is refusing. Soreya takes the issue to her manager, who negotiates a compromise between the two to resolve the conflict.
>
> In a small group, decide who will play the role of Natalie, Soreya, and the manager and see if you can resolve the conflict effectively with a win-win outcome.

> ### Just checking
>
> * List the key qualities of an effective team member.
> * Name the stages when dealing with conflict.

6.10 Giving and receiving feedback

Feedback is important as a tool for maintaining and improving performance. It lets us know about ourselves and the effect our behaviour has on others. Part of the aim of the appraisal interview is to let the team member concerned know how well they are doing. As a team leader, you will go through the objectives and give feedback on performance for each objective. In this topic you will learn about different types of feedback and why this is important when working in a team.

Types of feedback

Positive feedback

This involves giving praise for achievements. It is important when working in a team to acknowledge good performance as it lets people know they are doing things well and encourages high motivation. Everybody likes to receive positive feedback and, as a team leader, it is best not to wait until the official appraisal session to give positive feedback but to give it regularly to inspire the team to keep working hard.

Negative feedback

This involves identifying problems and areas for improvement. It is important to give and receive negative feedback, but it must be given in such a way that will lead to improvement and increase motivation.

Effective feedback

This is usually a balance between giving and receiving both positive and negative feedback.

* Constructive feedback stresses the positive achievements but also deals with the negative by providing support and guidance on how improvements could be made. This is important to make the other person feel valued.

* Destructive feedback is mainly critical and focuses on the negative aspects, and does not offer any guidance on how performance could be improved.

Activity

Reflect on two occasions when you have received feedback, one of which was constructive, the other less so. Make notes on the positive and negative feelings you had when receiving both types of feedback, and what impact it had on your performance.

Giving feedback

Preparation for giving effective feedback is essential. This includes gathering facts and information to support specific comments and focusing on what is important. When giving feedback to another team member you should use the 'sandwich' approach – start with the positive, move to the negative, then end by focusing on positive action. It is important to refer only to behaviour that can be changed, not personality, and give the other person the opportunity to respond.

Feedback helps to improve performance.

Receiving feedback

When receiving feedback it is important you listen carefully to what is being said so that you do not react defensively or justify what you have done. You should regard the session as a way to help you improve and develop your skills, and to think about what you do well, and what you do not so well. If you are unsure about something, then ask for clarification or specific examples of the performance in question. Be willing to accept advice and agree an action plan to move forward. Often people think a performance appraisal is always going to be negative, so it is important to accept praise when it is given.

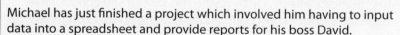

Case study: Giving and receiving feedback

Michael has just finished a project which involved him having to input data into a spreadsheet and provide reports for his boss David.

David: 'I see you've just finished the project. Why is it so late?"

Michael: 'I haven't used that particular spreadsheet program before, and I had to ask Layla to show me how to do it.'

David: 'Well, there are lots of mistakes. I suppose I will have to spend time correcting these now.'

Michael: 'I'm sorry, but I just couldn't make head or tail of it ...'

David: 'I should have known better and done it myself.'

1 Which type of feedback is David giving to Michael?

2 How would you give constructive feedback to David on his feedback technique?

Functional Skills

English
Use your speaking and listening skills in group discussions.

Personal, Learning and Thinking Skills

When giving constructive feedback to others you are demonstrating your team worker skills. Make sure that you offer support to help others improve their performance. Also, when receiving feedback you need to deal positively with praise and criticism and not become defensive. In order to make changes to further your learning and development, you should use your reflective learner skills to consider ways forward.

Just checking

* What is involved in giving effective feedback?
* Why should you avoid a negative approach to feedback?

169

Assessment

This unit is assessed internally. This means that you will be set an assignment by your consortium, which should direct your work through a series of tasks connected to the running of a business-related activity, so that you cover all of the learning outcomes for this unit. The work you submit for assessment must be original work, produced by yourself under controlled conditions – this will be arranged by your tutor. It will then be marked by your tutor and moderated by the awarding body.

You will be assessed on:

* your understanding of the benefits of teamworking

* your knowledge of how individuals and team leaders contribute to teamworking

* your ability to plan and monitor team work

* your ability to work and communicate effectively in a team.

To aim for higher grades you should try to:

* use a diary or calendar for the plan with individual goals and activities entered and showing how tasks have been categorised into high/medium or low priorities

* demonstrate good time management skills showing how you have set time limits for the various activities as well as how progress of own tasks has been monitored such as adapting the plan

* demonstrate good team working skills such as making a clear contribution to the task, being able to maintain a consistently positive attitude, and supporting team members

* communicate effectively by giving thoughtful and constructive feedback to other team members and being able to accept feedback from others well

* demonstrate good conflict management skills when faced with a situation during the team activity; if this does not happen during the activity then you need to offer convincing suggestions of how you would deal with conflict situations

* offer explanations of how effective you and the team were in the activity, including whether a team leader would have been of benefit

* think carefully about how organisations can benefit from team work and support your answer with examples from your own experiences of the team activity.

Introduction

In 1859, the great naturalist and evolutionary philosopher Charles Darwin wrote, 'It is not the strongest of the species that survive, nor the most intelligent, but the one most responsive to change' (www. wikiquote.org). Darwin was discussing the development and survival of animal species. The same applies to businesses – if they do not evolve and change with the times they will, at some point in the future, no longer exist. Just like dinosaurs! This unit looks at how organisations and employees respond to change in today's dynamic business environment.

Case study: 'The 50 Cent Machine'

The American rapstar 50 Cent is responding to change in a way that his fans might find a little unusual. He has decided that there is profit to be made in the precious metals market. As a result, 50 Cent has invested a lot of money in an ore mine in South Africa that digs for platinum, palladium and iridium ore. The long-term plan is to use 50 Cent's brand name and attach it to the precious metals. In business terms, 50 Cent is increasing his portfolio of business interests, that is, investing in businesses outside of music. (To read the full story, see 'The 50 Cent Machine' by Zack O'Malley Greenburg at www.forbes.com.)

1 Why do you thing 50 Cent might want to invest in an ore mine?

2 What does 50 Cent mean when he says 'I've got a diverse portfolio'?

3 Which current major economic factors do you think influenced the decision to make this investment?

4 What is your personal opinion on the likely success of this venture. Support with reasons.

How you will be assessed

This unit will be assessed by a short written examination lasting one hour. It will contain a range of questions based on changes in different organisations.

What you will learn in this unit

You will:

* know why and how change occurs in businesses
* understand the impact of change on employees.

Personal, Learning and Thinking Skills

An important part of improving your own work is to evaluate what you have done. In doing this, you need to question all aspects of the work you have completed – this will range from group to individual work, and maybe presentations. It is also very important to question the quality of the research you have used to ensure accuracy and validity. By reviewing your work, you will be demonstrating the skills of a reflective learner.

7.1 The changing business environment

'Production moved to China – 300 jobs axed!' We often take such newspaper headlines for granted but, in making such decisions, businesses take months – sometimes years – to plan their future strategies. Very often though, for people who are part of the change process, it is the manner in which change takes place that has a major effect. In this topic you will investigate why and how change takes place in business, which will help you to better understand the implications of the newspaper headlines you may read.

Activity

Look at the illustration showing business change. Now, create a timeline that shows how industry in your local area has changed over the last 100 years. By using the internet or visiting your local library, it will be possible to research and find out the types of industries that were popular in your local area in the twentieth century.

Demography Studying the population by analysing age, gender, socio-economic groupings, earnings and area in which people live.

Economic growth An increase in the amount of goods manufactured and sold by a country.

External factor A factor that affects the business but which is beyond its control.

Changes to business over the past 100 years

1900s
1950s
1970s
2000s
The future: nanotechnology?

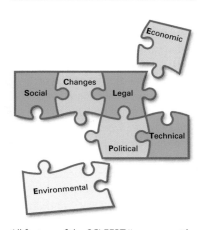

All factors of the SCLEEPT jigsaw must be analysed before change can take place.

'Social, Changes, Legal, Economic, Environmental, Political, Technical' factors

It is often said that 'no business is an island' and that a business cannot operate without **external factors** impacting upon it. External factors are factors about which the business can do (in some cases) very little. These factors are referred to by the acronym SCLEEPT, which stands for **S**ocial, **C**hanges, **L**egal, **E**conomic, **E**nvironmental, **P**olitical and **T**echnical.

The SCLEEPT factors

Below the SCLEEPT factors are detailed, and indicate the types of things in business that must be thought about when considering making change.

1. Social	2. Changes specific to the organisation or sector
Social factors are those that are concerned with population changes (known as demography) and issues associated with norms and values, e.g. the value placed on education in a particular area. Social factors also concern cultural issues such as people's attitudes to work, health and religion. In addition, population movement has increased with the expansion of the European union. This means that companies now have to consider the needs of a much wider audience than they did ten years ago.	A business might decide to change: ✱ its suppliers ✱ the country where something is manufactured ✱ how and/or by whom an item is distributed. Other factors relating to changes include an increase in competition or even a change in customer numbers, for example as a result of the construction of a new housing estate, or the introduction of online shopping.
3. Legal	4. Economic
Legal factors are those that require a business to act in a certain way by law, e.g. not using false or misleading advertising. They include laws that protect consumers and employees. In addition, legal factors ensure that products are manufactured to a certain standard to avoid injury or death.	These factors include **economic growth**, changes in interest rates and increases or decreases in the rate of inflation. Economic factors are also concerned with the level of unemployment, taxation changes and the supply of resources. They affect the price or supply and demand of goods.
5. Environmental	6. Political
This factor has become one of major significance in recent years and refers to the way in which organisations reduce their impact on the environment. Businesses want to be seen as environmentally friendly and it is generally agreed that business has a responsibility to lead the way on the issue of global warming. Some analysts also argue that tackling environmental issues provides organisations with an opportunity to promote positive public relations. Businesses can be heavily fined if they are found to be heavy polluters.	This factor relates to the way in which political changes might impact on an organisation's future strategic plans. Political factors abroad, which may affect UK business, must also be considered. An example of political change would be if a company was receiving tax incentives for locating in a deprived area and if those tax 'breaks' were later withdrawn by the government. Such a change might have a dramatic effect on a business, possibly forcing redundancy or closure.

7. Technological

Technological factors relate to those issues involving the use of new technologies, such as nanotechnology used in MP4 players and mobile phones. Technology is a major factor when considering change. If a business does not keep pace with technology, its processes will become outdated and its rivals will gain competitive advantage.

Advancements in technology also allow businesses to produce and market products in new ways, such as using SMS messages to advertise to a target audience. It also means that products can go from design to full production to obsolescence much quicker. Therefore, it increases the need for a business to keep its eye firmly fixed on its market.

Mechanisation has also changed the way businesses manufacture products. For example, most cars are now produced by robots; 50 years ago they were mainly built by hand. Other technological changes include developments in consumer technologies such as mobile phones, which have changed the way business is conducted.

No longer do people have to be in the same building to take part in a meeting – video conferencing, for example, allows staff in different locations to take part in a meeting. This type of technology has led to an increase in the size of world economies. Modern mass production methods have also made many consumer technologies, e.g. MP3 players, affordable for most people.

Just checking

✱ Why is it important for businesses to research demography when planning for the future?

✱ How will an economic slowdown impact on a business's ability and willingness to invest?

✱ How has technology changed the face of modern business

The Sinclair C5.

7.2 Changes in the external environment

A business is said to be only as successful as its last big contract – if a company loses business and also fails to win new business, then it will soon cease to exist. It is therefore essential that companies pay close attention to the SCLEEPT factors that we looked at in the last topic. If they fail to do so, their products or services may not continue to appeal to their target markets.

It is likely that when one of the external (SCLEEPT) factors changes, it will have a 'knock on' effect on a number of the other factors, and as result they will also change. When we discuss factors in this collective way they are referred to as the 'external environment'. When the external environment changes it can lead to businesses also having to change in order to stay competitive. For example, when the economy is growing, new business opportunities occur, but when the opposite is true it can lead to job losses or closures. There are a number of ways in which business can respond to change.

Beginning of new businesses

Positive change in the business economy is usually the catalyst to encourage entrepreneurs to follow their dreams and start up new businesses. In 2000, 178,900 new businesses were registered; by 2006, this figure had increased to 182,200. These figures clearly show that during the post-millennium growth period, business people across the UK were taking the opportunity to start their own businesses.

This was due in part to very good economic trading conditions – reasonably low interest rates and inflation, with the additional benefit of low levels of unemployment, which was creating demand for products and services. Growth during this period mainly focused on the tertiary or service sector. Businesses such as estate agencies and recruitment firms grew at a fast pace to meet the demands of a growing and prosperous economy.

Closure of businesses

While change can bring opportunities for business, it can also have negative consequences. Very often on the news, you will see that XYZ company is 'shedding 300 jobs'; this is usually as a direct result of change. The reasons for change can be many and varied. However, change normally takes place for two reasons: first, to improve **efficiency** and, secondly, to improve profit, although there are a number of other reasons that can lead to business closure.

New technology

Over the past 30 years, the use of technology in the workplace has significantly increased. In effect, machines have replaced the routine tasks that humans used to carry out. Using machinery is an efficient use of a business's capital; once the initial investment has been

Efficiency A measure of how well a business uses its resources.

made (apart from servicing and running costs), machines can run 24 hours a day, seven days a week without a break. Humans require breaks, sometimes have time off through illness, can go on strike and, of course, take holidays. Therefore, businesses have embraced technology, in some cases, at the cost of jobs, which, in turn, has led to the closure of offices and factories.

Relocating all or part of the business

The main reason for a private limited or public limited company to exist is to make a profit for its **shareholders**. In order to do this, businesses seek to find opportunities to reduce costs. One increasingly popular way involves relocating all or part of the business abroad to take advantages of cheaper labour and materials costs. The relocation of call centres to India has been a feature of recent years. Bangalore, for example, has been transformed by the influx of western businesses relocating there, which has proved beneficial for both the business and the area:

* The business benefits from lower labour costs, as the average call centre worker in India gets paid around £3,500 per year in contrast to £16,000 in the UK.

* The area benefits as business relocation brings much needed new jobs and an increase in wealth.

Restructuring

Restructuring is the process of changing an organisation and the way it is managed. To do this, businesses usually introduce new departments or remove job roles and departments from the company's organisational structure. Again, restructuring can present both opportunities and threats to employees. For some workers, it may involve a change in their job role to increase their **span of control**; for others, it may mean that their job role disappears altogether, leaving them with the prospect of moving into another job role or possibly facing **redundancy**. Restructuring is another activity that a business undertakes to improve its efficiency and hence profits.

Changes to job roles, processes and procedures

The drive for increased efficiency is a never-ending task for businesses; they are constantly seeking to improve the way tasks are carried out. This is not a new idea. In 1911, the famous US engineer and work study guru, F. W. Taylor in his book, *The Principles of Scientific Management,* wrote about the need for businesses to examine their job roles, processes and **procedures** to increase efficiency.

Changes to job roles might involve taking on more responsibility, for example a bank manager may be asked to oversee two branches, rather than just one. When an organisation changes processes and procedures, the focus will be on how tasks are

Shareholders Individuals or corporate investors who buy shares in a business in the hope that these will increase in value.

Span of control The number of workers that a supervisor is responsible for.

Redundancy Where a company identifies that a person is no longer required for a particular job. The person is relieved of their duties and leaves the business. If the employee is eligible, they will receive a sum of money called a 'redundancy settlement'.

Procedures Either written or accepted methods of how to complete a job or task.

Car manufacturing involves heavy use of machinery and technology.

completed and ways in which tasks can be completed more efficiently. As mentioned above, this can involve greater use of technology, or maybe changing the workflow of a procedure to make it more streamlined.

It is important to remember the well-known phrase 'time costs money' – the quicker a task can be completed, the cheaper it will be for a business, and this will impact on profit.

Case study: South Bradford Vocational Centre

A specialist educational centre has been set up on the outskirts of Bradford in order to cope with the increased demands of the employment market.

The South Bradford Vocational Centre (SBVC) offers an innovative approach to educating 14–19-year-olds by providing them with a range of training from school/college staff, training providers and industry. The benefit of the SBVC approach is that students get to learn in different ways, in small groups and in fully equipped learning suites, including a production kitchen, beauty salon and a fully functioning office.

The approach used by SBVC is designed to provide learners with the skills that a fast-moving employment world requires, so the only courses taught there are vocational enabling students to gain industry standard recognisable qualifications.

1 Why is it important that learners develop vocational skills alongside their traditional school learning?

2 Employers are becoming more involved in helping to design courses. Why do you think this is the case?

3 Why do you think employers are increasingly looking to employ people with both academic and vocational skills?

Just checking

* How might a downturn in the economy affect some businesses negatively but benefit others?
* Think of three different industries that have taken on board the principles of F. W. Taylor.
* Do you think that restructuring is the best way to make a business more efficient?

7.3 Types of change

In business, change can occur in different ways. Some changes will be radical, others less so. It is therefore important both to understand the speed at which change takes place and how it happens. The two main types of change that you will look at in this topic are step change and incremental change. You will also need to understand how change takes place – either through directive or organic change

Step change

At first glance, it might appear that when a business makes a **step change** it is only making minor changes, but this could not be further from what step change means. A step change is very significant and will affect the value or size of an organisation.

Take, for example, Lehman Brothers (Holdings), the fourth largest investment bank in the world, which filed for bankruptcy on 15 September 2008. It was a victim of the **credit crunch** – the business simply had no money to carry on trading on the investment markets. When Lehman Brothers went bankrupt it reportedly owed investors about £335 billion. The demise of Lehman Brothers sent shockwaves through the banking sector, and many financial institutions have had to make step changes in the way their businesses operate.

Incremental change

This differs from step change in that the changes made are a lot smaller and usually take place in a pre-planned manner. **Incremental changes** tend to be more focused on changing the way a task is carried out, with the intention being that lots of small incremental changes will lead to large-scale change in the organisation. An example of an incremental change would be the upgrading of a piece of software to make the processing of a task easier. That, combined with the correct training to use the software should, in theory, lead to a much larger change within the organisation, the aim being to improve efficiency.

Change usually happens in two main ways, either through **directive change** or by happening **organic change**. It is important to understand the difference between the two methods as they affect employees in different ways.

Directive change

Directive change is a management tool that is used to change the way something is done in the workplace. A directive is an instruction that needs to be carried out. Directive change uses the notion that within a business a **hierarchy** of power exists, and as a result employees are accountable to other employees, typically a line manager. Directive change can be implemented by the use of **formal authority**, whereby managers can use their authority to make changes if they face resistance from the workforce.

Directive changes tend to take place when an immediate effect is required. For example, in 2008, the UK government made directive

---

DEALING WITH CHANGE

Think about a time in your life when you have had to deal with change. It could be changing schools, maybe starting a part-time job or some other type of change that has affected you. In a small group, make a list of the changes and then discuss how you dealt with the change.

Step change Large-scale change that has significant effect on the size and value of a business.

Credit crunch When banks do not have enough cash to lend businesses and consumers.

Incremental change Smaller scale change, e.g. looking at improving the way a task is completed.

Directive change A change that takes place via one person issuing an instruction to another person.

Organic change Change that naturally occurs within a business through the efforts of an efficient workforce.

Formal authority A concept whereby a hierarchy of power exists in a business and the power is used by managers to make directive change.

Hierarchy Employees ranked by order of level of responsibility.

A year before Lehman Brothers (Holdings) went bankrupt, it would have been inconceivable to imagine that a business with such a strong reputation and a history spanning 158 years could collapse. After all, Lehman Brothers was a bank – an institution that should be able to manage its own finances. The reasons for the bankruptcy are very complex. One of the main ones was simply that Lehman Brothers ran out of cash – in other words, the bank's cash-flow dried up.

The root of the problem was this: Lehman Brothers had lent money to other banks in the form of huge loans, and, in turn, the borrowing banks had loaned the money to the general public in the form of mortgages. However, as inflation and bank interest rates began to rise, borrowers found it increasingly difficult to repay their mortgages. Eventually, millions of bank customers defaulted on their mortgages – they had no money to repay their loans – which meant that the borrowing banks did not have the money to repay Lehman Brothers. Finally, this led to Lehman Brothers having no capital to re-invest to try to get them out of the problem.

1 Do you think that Lehman Brothers could have avoided this disaster if they had taken a step change earlier?

2 Make suggestions as to what changes Lehman Brothers could have taken.

3 Could Lehman Brothers have saved the business by making a series of incremental changes? Provide suggestions.

---

changes to the ways banks could merge with each other to help stabilise the economy. When we consider directive change in business it can occur in many situations. A common example is a change to the way work procedures and processes are carried out. Another popular example of directive change is the use of performance management techniques. This system involves a meeting between an employee and their line manager during which targets are set which should be achieved before the next performance management review (typically within 6 or 12 months). This is a directive change because the employee is agreeing with their line manager to change the way they do certain things.

> **Laissez-faire** A concept whereby employees let the business operate without intervening.

Organic change

Organic change is change from 'within' the business, which means that employees of all levels do their jobs to the best of their ability and positive change should occur naturally. This **laissez-faire** approach is generally well received by employees as they feel empowered to make decisions without having directive change forced upon them.

Critics of this system argue that this type of change is random and unplanned; you cannot accurately measure the success of change that takes place. Additionally, others argue that you need people in charge to take responsibility for managing the change process; otherwise the process is not carried out efficiently.

Activity

For this activity, you are to assume the role of expert (management consultant) who has been brought into a business to turn it around as it is losing profit and market share to competitors.

Background: Exquisite is a manufacturer of high quality chocolate products. The company has been in business for 150 years and, for most of that time, has been a market leader. Recently, it has been losing out to more dynamic, younger manufacturers.

The business has a vast range of goods but no longer effectively targets its products at customers; also the products are still made by hand whereas its competitors use machinery. Additionally, the business is overstaffed by 15 per cent of its workforce, mainly shop floor workers and middle managers. As a result, staff fear that the business is in difficulty and that it may close resulting in the loss of everyone's jobs. Staff morale and motivation are rock bottom.

Task: You are required to put together a proposal to improve competitiveness at Exquisite. Remember, there are many issues that are contributing to Exquisite's problems, and you will be required to address each problem in sufficient detail.

Did you know?

Much of the success experienced in the Japanese manufacturing economy has been attributed to an American, Professor W. Edwards Deming. Deming's philosophy of production and management invited workers from all levels within a business to make suggestions on how to improve productivity and efficiency. Prior to Deming's involvement, workers had no say in how businesses should be run and simply accepted orders from their superiors.

Just checking

* Which type of change (directive or organic) do you think is most effective?
* Which type of change do you think is best received by employees?
* Which form of change is most likely to occur if a business needs to respond quickly, and why?

7.4 Businesses keeping pace with change

If a business does not keep pace with the competition, it will eventually cease to exist. Businesses, like human beings, are followers of trends and fashions. The commercial market is continually changing, with ideas and concepts going in and out of fashion. The trick for a business is to identify which trends will help them to increase their profits. As Darwin observed, '...the one most responsive to change' will survive.

Business survival

In the first year of trading, the main objective of all businesses is to survive. However, once the first year has passed, and assuming the company is breaking even, it must not lose sight of this initial objective. A successful organisation will spend a large percentage of its budget on research and development to enable it to track and keep ahead of market trends. Due to the commercial market being extremely competitive, any lapses in concentration will allow competitors to steal market share and customers, which, if not remedied, could be very costly to a business.

Better fit with business environment

As mentioned in Unit 7.2, a company must be fully aware of and keep up to date with any changes to SCLEEPT factors. To some extent, these external factors control the direction in which a business must go. Each individual factor could harm a business if not considered when strategic plans are being made. If a business understands these factors, then there is a good chance that they will be dynamic enough to respond to consumer and market demand.

Advantages over competitors

By understanding business change, an organisation has a better chance of predicting what is likely to happen in the future. A business which can do this also has the capacity to spot new openings in the market and exploit them. In the past, many businesses saw greater use of ICT as being a way of gaining **competitive advantage**. While ICT is still a major contributor to the success of a business, the advantages once gained by using ICT are not as great. There are two reasons for this:

* Mass production techniques mean that the price of equipment has fallen and so is more readily available to smaller businesses.

* Businesses are much more aware of what is available in the market and it is rarely possible for a business to have a piece of software that is unique (unless it can afford to have tailor-made software tailor).

Increased chances of success

By following market trends and keeping pace with business changes, a company increases its chance of success. As mentioned earlier, an 'intelligent' business – one that keeps it eye on what consumers want – is more likely to attract and keep customers.

Better able to change as need arises

When the time comes that business has to make a change, the most successful organisations are those that are able to make small changes rather than large directive changes since the latter can take a long time to have an effect. Imagine if the change requires all staff in a large business to be retrained. This cannot happen instantly and there will be a time lag during the training period. Therefore, if a business remains focused on market changes, it should only have to make minor adjustments to its procedures rather than step changes.

Competitive advantage
Gaining an advantage over competitors by means of superior manufacturing and design processes or by providing goods and services with unique features.

Case study: How Microsoft responds to change

In order to remain on top of the business and home user software market, Microsoft has made a massive investment in research and development over the last few years. This is essential as many software companies are competing for Microsoft's market share. However, as you would expect from a pioneering business, Microsoft is determined to maintain its position as number one in its market sector, and in 1991 set up Microsoft Research to help it to do this. Today, Microsoft Research employs over 800 researchers who focus on 55 different areas of software research. To ensure that Microsoft attracts the best people in terms of abilities, its research operations span the world from Europe to Asia and the USA. Microsoft researchers are expected not only to work on developing new ideas but must also present their work at conferences in the form of presentations and academic papers. All work is peer-reviewed, meaning that a co-worker checks it for accuracy and validity, thus ensuring the quality of research.

Microsoft Research views software not just from an IT perspective but from the viewpoint of the end user. To promote success, it utilises the skills of a wide range of experts ranging from mathematicians and psychologists through to anthropologists and medical doctors. These skilled people enable the organisation to judge the effect that its products will have on the buying public and, as a result, maximise the sales potential of its goods. In managing change Microsoft use what they refer to as 'incubation teams.' The role of an incubation team is to develop and nurture new product ideas from the beginning; such teams keep Microsoft at the forefront as they allow the business to diversify and develop into new markets. (Based on information available at Microsoft Research, www.research.microsoft.com)

1 Microsoft is one of most successful companies of the last 50 years. Explain how you think it has achieved this.

2 Why do you think Microsoft Research requires the support of so many diverse scientists?

3 What do you think is meant by the term 'incubation team' and how can these help Microsoft deal with change?

Just checking

* Why do businesses need to respond to change?
* How do external influences impact on a business?
* Give three examples of step changes that businesses might make.

7.5 The effect of change on employees

So far, you've looked at change and how it may affect the business. It's also important to look at change from the employees' perspective. Change can be viewed in two ways: one person might see it as an opportunity to take on a new challenge and develop themselves professionally, while another might react to change with anxiety and dread. Much of this is to do with how change is managed and how well informed staff are before, during and after the change process. One thing is certain, however, as the business world changes pace at an ever increasing rate, you, as an employee are likely to be an agent of change.

Different roles at work

When a business is restructured this will usually impact on employees. As mentioned earlier, businesses are constantly trying to become more efficient, as a result of which employees may be required to change their jobs roles in order to fit in with new business requirements. For example, a major bank feeling the full effect of a downturn in the economy decides to make a number of employees redundant. It also changes some of the job roles of its existing staff, including the way in which the IT support department is run. The bank has decided that all IT support staff must repair problems remotely rather than visit branches to make repairs. This type of decision can either motivate or demotivate workers depending on the type of personality of a person.

New location of workplace

Very often businesses decide to relocate. This can be for a number of reasons. The business may decide that it requires more office or factory

Case study: Vickers Defence Systems

In 1915, in an attempt to help the British war effort, a large Royal Ordinance manufacturing facility called Barnbow Works was opened on the outskirts of Leeds. The factory remained open until 1999 when production of the Challenger 2 tank was stopped. At its peak between 1915 and 1950, the factory employed about 17,000 people. To give you some idea of scale of the factory, it is approximately 600 m length and at its widest point is 100 m wide – that's equivalent to eight football pitches! When it was built Barnbow was one of the largest in Europe. By 1999, when the factory closed, many of its employees had spent their whole working lives there, as well as their families before them, and that was all they had known.

1 How do you think employees felt when they discovered that Barnbow Works was going to close?

2 Using the case study, make a list of words to describe the feelings of the employees when they were told the factory was going to close?

3 What do you think are the worst aspects of losing your job as a result of factory closure?

4 Do you think that some employees may have felt that the closure presented new career opportunities for them?

space to run its operations, or it could be that a new facility has been built which is more appropriate than the buildings being used at present. Businesses often view moving as way to cut costs; for example, they may decide to move from a town centre to the outskirts of town where rents will be cheaper. This simple change can have an effect on employees. Imagine, for example, that you have worked in the same town centre office for a long time and that you do not drive. The thought of a more complicated route to work using public transport may not motivate you. On the other hand, you may see the benefits of working in a brand new facility which has been designed for your purposes and should make your working life easier a motivating factor

New colleagues and managers

If a company decides to change its structure or move location, this could also mean that employees have to work with new colleagues or a new manager. Some people may find this daunting as they have over many years built up a good working relationship with the people around them and they know what to expect of each other in working terms. However, some employees enjoy working with new people as it provides them with new ideas on how tasks should be carried out.

Loss of familiar colleagues and managers

As you saw in the case study, when a business decides to reduce staff numbers or close down completely many employees initially find it difficult to continue in their normal way. Sometimes this might be because a trusted employee has left who could be relied upon to get work completed. The loss of staff in a department can also put the remaining employees under pressure. Individuals may experience apprehension and sadness if they fear their own jobs might be under threat.

Different work processes and equipment

Some people do not like the thought of changing the way they do their jobs. For many people who have been doing a particular job for a long time, they may feel that their way is the best. However, this type of attitude can lead to inefficiencies in business. A prime example was the growth of ICT in business throughout the 1980s and 1990s. Many employees felt that ICT posed a threat to the security of their jobs, while others believed that ICT would hinder rather than help them, and a minority of workers decided that they would reject ICT completely in favour of doing their work in the way they always had. A good example of this is in education, where many older teachers feel that their traditional paper systems are as efficient as ICT based methods. Many of these problems were associated with a lack of training and mis-information about how ICT can help. Today, many employees openly embrace changes in technology and see it as a way of developing their knowledge and skill levels; they also see the advantages for the business they work in.

Job losses

For many employees the thought of change automatically raises fears about losing their jobs. Very often the impact of change is only reported in the media when it involves a business closing or redundancies being made. However, when the economy experiences a downturn there are certain business sectors that are generally more affected than others. Construction is one example. When the economy is slowing down people tend not to move house, so the demand for new houses diminishes as a result.

Activity

Think of a time in your life when you have had to deal with a major change, for example when you moved from primary to secondary school, or, if you have a part-time job, changes that may have taken place there.

Make a list of the changes, then think about how you felt when the change was taking place and how dealt with the situation. What emotions did you feel at the time? How did the change impact on you and the people around you.

Just checking

✱ Why might an employee be required to change their job role?

✱ How might a change of business location impact on employees?

✱ How might the introduction of new ICT equipment be of concern to some workers?

7.6 Case study: How employees deal with change

Sonal Chaudhry and Charlie Smith both have degrees in Business. When they left university recently, they decided to set up their own management consultancy, ChangeCo. They have been asked by the directors of MakeIt Ltd, a manufacturing company, to help their employees cope with a period of major change in the business.

In a small group, think about the area where you live. Which businesses existed in your locality three or four years ago? Compare these with the businesses that there today. How would a recession impact on your local area? In a small group, make a list of businesses and business sectors which might be positively affected during a slowdown or recession and those that might be badly affected.

From their business course, Sonal and Charlie know that there are six golden rules when trying to implement change on people who work in business. They have decided that they must make a presentation to the workforce to educate them about the changes.

Activity

MakeIt Ltd is a car parts manufacturer. Set up 35 years ago, it employs 650 employees. Due to the current economic crisis, the sales of new cars are down, and therefore the products that MakeIt supplies to car manufacturers are no longer needed in such great numbers. MakeIt's Board of Directors has put together a rescue plan. However, for this to be successful, they need to halve the size of the workforce. MakeIt is the major employer in the area and reducing its size will affect other local businesses.

Task: You are to make a presentation to the whole workforce about the planned changes. In the presentation you will need to cover the following:

✱ Explain to workers what is going to happen, the reasons for the changes, and that there could be opportunities from retraining.

✱ Try to think how people might feel about the changes. How could they deal with this?

✱ Advise workers why they need to stay positive and introduce workers to the concept of career planning.

✱ Advise workers the ways in which they can seek support from others.

As you can see, this is a tough task and is the main reason why ChangeCo has been brought in. The board of directors feels that an outside company may be able to present the case in a better light than they could themselves.

Demotivated The lack of desire to do a task; in extreme cases requires pressure applying from elsewhere to complete a task.

Trade union An organised group of workers set up to protect their interests in the workplace. Unions offer advice and support to their members, and may negotiate pay and working conditions with employers.

1 Finding out information

A good way to reduce the anxiety that surrounds change is to find out exactly what is happening and how it is going to affect you. Very often, rumour and speculation upset people and make them anxious. By establishing the true picture, informed decisions and reasoning can take place.

2 Assessing the benefits and risks

As mentioned earlier, people can view change at work either as beneficial or potentially risky. By finding out about the changes, an employee may be able to assess their future course of action. For example, if they see that the changes might provide career opportunities, they may decide to continue to work for their employer in the hope that they might have a chance of gaining promotion. On the other hand, an employee may decide that their only course of action is to look for another job in another company.

3 What do people feel about the changes?

When businesses make changes they need to consider the feelings and emotions of the people who work for them. You may have heard about the company that informed its staff by SMS text message that they were being made redundant. How would you feel about this? For an employee to make a rational decision about how the changes might affect them, they will need to spend some time working out how they truly feel.

4 Trying to stay positive

Imagine you have been informed that your company is relocating to another site 200 miles away. You have the option to move with the company, or take redundancy. In this situation it is very difficult to see how you might stay positive. Some people would see it as an opportunity, while others would find the prospect of moving rather daunting. Nevertheless, maintaining a positive attitude in this situation is vital. Once negative feelings start to creep in, people become **demotivated** and the quality of their work may deteriorate.

5 Planning your career

Over the past 50 years, attitudes towards work have changed greatly. As recently as the 1970s, it was considered normal for a person to be with the same organisation all of their working lives. Nowadays, research has shown that an average working person is likely to have at least three job changes in their career. This poses an interesting question: when you start a job do you view it as a long-term career option or a shorter-term measure that will enable you to move on to your next career? With this in mind, employees need to have clear career goals and, more importantly, set objectives which will enable them to achieve those goals. Actively planning your career is essential.

6 Seeking support from others

If an employee knows that a change is likely to occur, they should discuss the situation with colleagues, and also seek the advice and support of professionals such as the human resources department or their **trade union** representative. Talking to other employees can be supportive for everyone concerned. Professional advice can help the employee to understand the details of the change, for example the terms of a redundancy package.

Activity

The workforce has requested that you provide them with information on the trade unions that are relevant to them. MakeIt's workforce is made up of workers from both administrative and manufacturing sectors.

Trade unions are set up to protect the interests of their members. There are many trade unions which cover all aspects of industry ranging from administration jobs to medical vocations. However, many trade unions are not referred to as such. For example, a lot of unions are known as societies or associations.

For this task you need to find out the names of as many trade unions as you can. Then choose five from your list and write down which industries they support. Next, research your five trade unions further and find out exactly what services they offer their members.

Tough decisions have to be taken by the Board of Directors of MakeIt Ltd.

Just checking

* Why is it important that employees find out as much as possible about future change before it happens?
* Why does staying positive through difficult change help the process?
* How can seeking help from others enable change to be less difficult?

7.7 Employees keeping pace with change

Businesses are constantly seeking to stay one step ahead of their competitors, either by gaining market share from them or becoming the best in the sector in which they operate. For this to happen, employees must be aware of the changes occurring. Workers who keep pace with change will be viewed as a more valuable asset to an organisation, particularly if a business is planning to reduce its workforce.

Improving your chances of keeping a job

Organisations want to employ people who are adept at keeping up with changes in business practice. There is an important reason for this: if a company is to remain competitive, employees must be able to adapt to change and embrace new procedures and systems. Since these are often introduced to save the business money, an employee who can demonstrate the ability to adopt new ideas easily is an important asset. At the same time, such employees show that they have an interest in their job and a willingness to go the extra mile. In the face of redundancy, a person who has kept pace with changes is likely to be in a safer position than one who has not.

Developing new skills

The skills that businesses require are continually changing; for example, 20 years ago email was not a common form of communication, today it is used very frequently. As a result, you will need to keep developing new skills throughout your career. This is the reason why respected employers put great emphasis on developing the skills of their workers, known as **Continuing Professional Development**. Organisations see great value in this because it not only improves the skill and knowledge level of employees but also **motivates** them as employees feel the business is taking an interest in them.

Opportunities inside and outside the organisation

Employees who are pro-active in developing their careers can find that other opportunities present themselves either inside or outside of the organisation they work for. For example, a highly motivated and skilled worker is likely to be recognised for their abilities in the form of promotion; they may be called upon to use their knowledge within a team that is solving a specific problem or helping plan strategy for the business. Very high ranking managers in organisations are often asked to give lectures and talks to groups of people about their strategies and ways of working to move a business forward. Nowadays, employees of all levels may have the opportunity to help others outside of their organisation, for example when a company allows an employee to visit a school to talk to pupils about an issue.

THE WONDERFUL WORLD OF BUSINESS

The course you are studying has been developed to keep pace with the business world – people from business actually contributed to its design by explaining what should be included.

In a small group, discuss why you think the course has been developed. Why do you think the business community has been involved in designing the diploma?

Continuing Professional Development The process of continually improving knowledge and skills by receiving training and guidance

Motivates Encourages a person to do a task without pressure being applied from elsewhere.

Advantages of staying positive about change

When change occurs in a business it is important to see it as something positive. This will help to make the process a lot easier, even though the benefits may not be immediately obvious. If employees see change as a bad thing, they will soon become demotivated, which will affect the quality and efficiency of the business. While sometimes it may be difficult to accept change, employees need to be able to adapt to whatever they are presented with.

Positive attitudes when employing staff

Businesses need employees who have positive attitudes; they want people who say 'I can do that' not 'I can't do that'. A positive attitude can go a long way to help solve problems in difficult situations. A negative attitude indicates a lack of interest in what the business is doing. Positive attitudes are infectious – who do you prefer to be around, a happy motivated person or someone who is not interested in what they are doing? Businesses want to employ people who do not see problems only 'challenges'.

'I can do that'.

Activity

Spend a few minutes thinking about yourself and your personality. Then ask yourself the following questions:

1 At which times in your life have you been really motivated to do something?
2 When have you felt totally de-motivated?
3 Compare your answers to questions 1 and 2. Which was the most productive time, and why?
4 What 'barriers' in life stop you from being motivated?
5 What can you do to avoid these 'barriers'?

Personal, Learning and Thinking Skills

The main way in which we improve our performance is to reflect and evaluate a piece of work we have done and the process by which the work was completed. As a reflective learner, you are required to reflect and evaluate your work and look at ways in which you could do the work better.

Just checking

* Summarise the benefits of keeping abreast of change.
* Why is it important to take advantage of opportunities both inside and outside of the workplace?
* Why do businesses use direct and indirect observation methods?

7.8 Evaluating the impact of change on employees

When change takes place in an organisation it is important to evaluate its impact so that the company can assess if the change has been beneficial or not to the business. A number of methods are used to evaluate the impact of change. One of the most important involves consulting employees to find out what impact change has had on them.

As an employee, how do you feel about the news? Would you think that the changes might pose a threat to your job security?

Direct methods of evaluation

Observation

This method involves an expert observer watching an employee or team carrying out their routine tasks. This is a very useful technique, but it has to be done over a long period of time to ensure that employees get used to having the observer around, otherwise they may act differently and the results of the observation will not be valid. Sometimes the observer will sit in a booth behind one-way glass allowing them to watch but not be seen.

Interviews

This method is particularly useful as the feedback is direct and the interviewer can also examine the facial expressions and tone of voice of the interviewee.

Staff surveys

This type of evaluation may not always be helpful. If the general feeling in the workforce is that the change has had a negative effect, then the chances of receiving quality feedback that will be useful and useable is minimal. If change is seen as positive, then employees may be happy to complete questionnaires accurately. Once again, the survey reviewer must be mindful of overly positive responses as this might distort the actual picture. Another benefit of staff surveys is that a lot of people can be questioned in a short space of time.

Indirect methods of evaluation

Measuring productivity

This method of evaluation is useful because it provides an accurate picture of how beneficial change has been. If productivity is increased, then it could be argued that the change has been positive, but if it has remained the same or reduced, then the changes may have had a negative effect on the business.

Customer satisfaction

This is usually carried out by using a questionnaire which customers are asked to indicate how happy they have been with the service they have received. They key to this method is to compare current data with data from previous surveys, which will show if customers are more satisfied now than they were before the changes.

Staff turnover

This involves measuring the number of employees who leave the business and comparing this with the number who left before the change took place. A company can assess if the change has positively or negatively impacted on staff motivation and morale.

Case study: The Hawthorne Studies

Between 1927 and 1932, the social scientist Elton May carried out a series of experiments at the Hawthorne Plant of the Western Electric company in Chicago. They formed what was to become known as 'Human Relations School' of management. Mayo's ideas focused on changing the way people worked in order to improve productivity. Mayo discovered that no matter how he changed working patterns productivity increased – this became known as the 'Hawthorne Effect.'

1 What was the focus of Mayo's work?

2 Why do you think Western Electrical, owners of the Hawthorne Plant were interested in these findings?

3 What was the Hawthorne effect?

Activity

Copy and complete the mind map below. It will provide you with a summary of Unit 7.

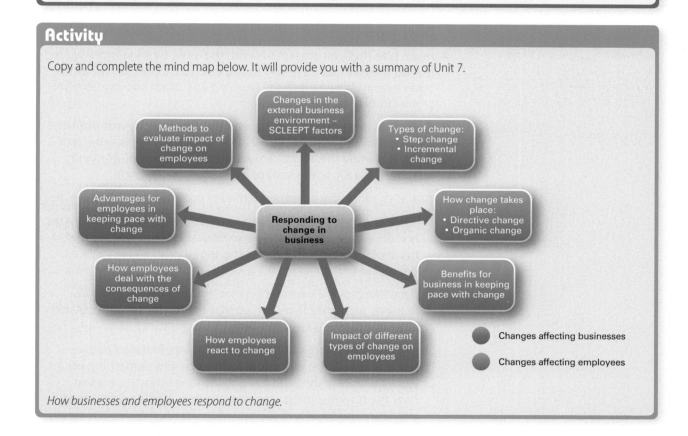

How businesses and employees respond to change.

Just checking

✱ Have you understood how change affects employees in a business?

✱ Do you understand how people react to change differently?

✱ Do you know why it is important that employees keep pace with change?

✱ Do you understand why it is important to measure the impact of change?

Assessment

This unit is assessed externally. This means that you will be set an external assessment, a 60-minute examination under controlled conditions, based on a series of questions that will test your knowledge and understanding of the learning outcomes for this unit. This will be marked by the awarding body and the mark you receive will be based on how well you answer the questions, based on a mark scheme that will have been developed specifically for the paper set in each examination series.

You will be assessed on:

* your knowledge of why and how change occurs in businesses

* your understanding of the impact of change on employees.

To aim for higher grades you should try to:

* use past papers to study the structure of the question paper and the types of question that are used; this should mean that there are no shocks when you sit down to take the examination

* review the content and approach of the mark schemes produced for past papers

* make sure that you are familiar with the basic terminology used in real businesses that have had to respond to change, as well as the basic terminology used in the learning outcomes and assessment criteria in the unit specification

* make sure that you are familiar with the command words used in the questions so that you know what kind of answer is expected; this will identify the kind of answer that is required. Command words are usually at the start of a question, for example:

  * assess: judge the extent or degree of something

  * compare: to show the similarities and differences, or advantages and disadvantages between two or more things; additionally, this may be extended by bringing together the findings in a description

  * describe: provide information that includes relevant actions, features, elements, facts, etc. so that the reader can understand what it is that you are describing

  * explain: give a summary of the main points/features; to give reasons and/or the procedure for/how or why something occurs, e.g. explain why the business chose that method or, explain how the business overcame that problem. You would normally introduce the topic and then provide details showing the depth and also a breadth of your knowledge about the topic

  * identify: name, mention, select or list key elements, facts, features, etc. as appropriate from information given

  * outline: provide reasons for a decision, a procedure, a feature, etc.

8 CORPORATE SOCIAL RESPONSIBILITY

Introduction

In the 21st century, it is not acceptable for businesses to exist solely to make a profit. Indeed, companies must be able to demonstrate that they can operate successfully without damaging society and the environment. This relatively recent concept is known as 'corporate social responsibility' (CSR). There are many ways in which large and small companies can demonstrate CSR. For this unit, you must understand why organisations need to act responsibly, the ways in which they can demonstrate their commitment to CSR and how they review, evaluate and recommend improvements to business practices In this unit, you will research how a company's actions impact on its stakeholders and society around it.

What is corporate social responsibility?

Corporate social responsibility is a wide ranging concept which covers many aspects of a business's operational activities. Traditionally, we have come to think of CSR in relation to protection of the environment. However, CSR goes much further. If we break corporate social responsibility down into its basic form, the corporate (business) aspect of CSR is concerned with looking after the well-being of a business. This includes financial control, investment, how the business is managed and governed and all other issues that impact on the way the business is viewed by the general public. The social aspect of CSR relates to how well the business interacts and impacts on the people who work for it and its surroundings, for example providing its employees with a safe place to work and the actions it takes to protect the environment.

How you will be assessed

This unit will be assessed by an individual assignment based on a single organisation. You will be required to look at what the organisation is doing at the moment, assess its impact and make recommendations. This will involve describing ways in which the organisation is already acting responsibly; assessing the positive and negative effects of the organisation on a local community; identifying an issue that is relevant to the organisation and recommending steps it could take to show it is acting responsibly; and explaining the benefits of doing this.

What you will learn in this unit

You will:

* understand why organisations need to act responsibly

* know ways in which organisations can demonstrate corporate social responsibility

* be able to review and recommend improvements to business practices.

8.1 Non-governmental organisations and pressure groups

Non-governmental organisations (NGOs) and pressure groups play a major role in placing pressure on businesses to act in a socially responsible way. Many of today's business practices have developed through pressure placed on businesses via interest groups. If companies choose to ignore the demands of NGOs and pressure groups, it can cost them dearly in terms of image and profits. This topic looks at the role of NGOs and pressure groups in raising awareness of corporate social responsibility.

Non-governmental organisations

Non-governmental organisations have been around for many hundreds of years. One of the most famous activists was William Wilberforce, campaigner against the slave trade and founder of the Society for the Prevention of Cruelty of Animals (now the RSPCA). More recently, organisations such as Friends of the Earth have campaigned against business practices that damage the environment, such as building business parks on greenfield sites that reduce the amount of natural habitat for animals.

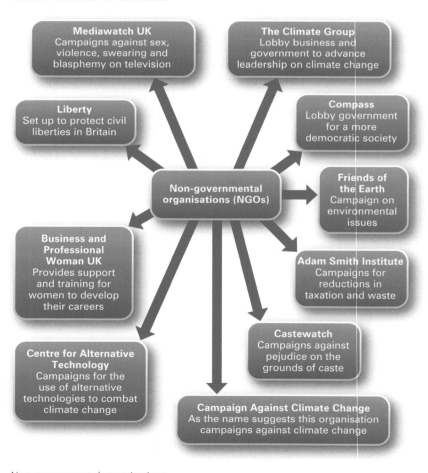

Non-governmental organisations.

NO PRESSURE!

In pairs, write down the name of as many **non-governmental organisations (NGOs)** and **pressure groups** as you can think of and explain what they are campaigning for or against. After you have made your list, discuss with your partner how successful the organisation has been in forcing changes on businesses and the way they conduct their business. Try to think of three examples where pressure group/NGO campaigns have been successful.

Non-governmental organisation (NGO) An organisation set up to influence government and businesses. It has no connection to government.

Pressure group A group of like-minded individuals who work together to campaign for a common cause.

Ethical consumers A consumer who chooses to buy goods and services that will not harm the environment.

Did you know?

There are hundreds of non-governmental organisations in the UK. The mindmap below contains information on a few interesting NGOs that could help with your research. A full database of NGOs can be found at www.dango.ac.uk

Pressure groups

Pressure groups are made up of people who hold the same values, political beliefs, ethnicity, religion or simply a common goal. They voice the opinion of people who otherwise may not be heard in society. By forming a pressure group, individuals seek to put pressure on institutions such as local and national government in an effort to change policy. However, pressure groups also seek to put pressure on businesses as well. One of the most famous campaigns in recent years has been the medical profession's fight to tighten up the advertising and selling of tobacco products. (In this case, the medical profession has been the pressure group.) In your life time, you will have noticed how tobacco sponsorship has reduced, especially of sporting events, and you will also have seen how the advertising on cigarette packets has changed. These now include graphic images depicting the harm that tobacco can cause. This example demonstrates that a determined pressure group can force great change.

Consumers

Consumers are also important in placing pressure on business. Quite simply, if the business is causing a consumer concern, they can affect the business by shopping elsewhere. If enough consumers do the same, then this will impact on the business's profits.

The effects of negative publicity

Large businesses rely on shareholders investing money in them, which in turn enables them to do things like expand or develop new products. Investors can use the image of a business as one measure of an organisation's potential success, for example they can look to see if the business is socially responsible. Therefore, it is important that businesses try to avoid negative publicity as this will ultimately affect how attractive a firm is to an investor.

Case Study: People and Planet

People and Planet is a student-based pressure group that runs campaigns on a wide range of issues. These include campaigns to raise awareness about economic justice, corporate power and the environment. People and Power aims to target young people between the ages of 16 and 24 to join their campaigns. Visiting www.peopleandplanet.org will provide help to answer the following questions:

1 How much impact do you think young people can have on changing major issues around the world?

2 Why do you think People and Planet target young people to join their group?

3 What are the main intentions of People and Planet?

Type of negative publicity	Effect on business
Financial problems	Consumers may lose trust in a business that appears to be in financial trouble, and may decide to move to a competitor.
Safety issues	This may affect a business's ability to recruit and retain staff if they are seen as an employer who is not safety conscious.
Ethical issues	If a company operates in a sector which is ethically sensitive (e.g. the production of genetically modified crops), the business may suffer as **ethical consumers** may choose to purchase alternative goods elsewhere.

The effects of negative publicity on a business.

Just checking

* What is a non-governmental organisation?
* What is a pressure group?
* How can ignoring corporate social responsibility attract negative publicity to a business?

8.2 Ethical consumerism

Ethical **consumerism** has become big business over the past decade. The principle of ethical consumerism means that products or services should be manufactured in a way that isn't harmful to the natural environment or exploits the people who make or provide goods or services. It pays businesses to be ethical – as the world becomes more selective in the goods and services it buys, businesses must meet these changing demands or face being ignored by consumers who demand a higher level of social responsibility from what they buy.

Increasing popularity of ethical consumerism

Due to pressure from consumers and pressure groups over the last decade, manufacturers and service providers have become more ethical in many ways. As a result, consumers have developed a better understanding of **ethical consumerism** and now demand much more in terms of assurances that products or services are provided in an ethical manner.

Ethical consumerism has given the consumer the opportunity to protest against issues that they feel are unfair. Consumers can protest against a business in several different ways, although the intended outcome is always to either gain publicity and highlight unethical practices or deter other consumers from dealing with a particular business and as a result damage the company's profits. The following are examples of how consumers can protest:

∗ Only deal with companies that have a commitment to **Fairtrade**.

∗ Boycott a business or product if it is believed to be unethical.

WHO'S ETHICAL AND WHO ISN'T?

Think of all the ways in which businesses have become more ethical over the last few years. Use the internet to research and find out which businesses use **ethics** to promote their company. Make a note of any fair trade organisations that the firm may be associated with and find out what these groups stand for ethically.

To help you with this research, visit Ethical Consumer magazine's site at www.ethiscore.org.

Case Study: The Fairtrade Foundation

The Fairtrade Foundation is an independent non-profit organisation.

Our mission is to work with businesses, community groups and individuals to improve the trading position of producer organisations in the South and to deliver sustainable livelihoods for farmers, workers and their communities by:

being a passionate and ambitious development organisation committed to tackling poverty and injustice through trade

∗ using certification and product labelling, through the Fairtrade® Mark, as a tool for our development goals

∗ bringing together producers and consumers in a citizens' movement for change

∗ being recognised as the UK's leading authority on Fairtrade.

∗ Our four key areas of activity are:

1 Providing an independent certification of the trade chain, licensing use of the Fairtrade® Mark as a consumer guarantee on products.

2 Facilitating the market to grow demand for Fairtrade and enable producers to sell to traders and retailers.

3 Working with our partners to support producer organisations and their networks.

4 Raising public awareness of the need for Fairtrade and the importance of the Fairtrade® Mark.

Source: www.fairtrade.org.uk

The Fairtrade® Mark

* Only deal with businesses that demonstrate socially responsible investment, meaning only investing in projects that will not disadvantage people, the environment or society in general.

Case study: Oxfam raises consumers' awareness of ethical consumption

Oxfam's campaign to fight poverty and climate change is world famous. In 2007–08, Oxfam GB teamed up with the design consultancy IDEO to try to increase consumers' awareness of ethical consumption as a way to tackle social and environmental problems. Oxfam had identified that if it was to have a real impact on understanding what motivates shoppers to buy ethical goods, it needed to seek guidance from a specialist company. The reason for choosing IDEO was simple – its philosophy is to focus on consumers' buying behaviours when designing products rather than relying on market trends.

Market research indicated that consumers trust the brands they buy regularly and that the look of a product is often more important than its function. Although consumers were in favour of ethical consumerism, they didn't believe they had the power to **influence** businesses to act in an ethical way. With this in mind, a number of concept ideas came into being. These focused on making promotional campaigns 'sexy' – so that ethical consumption would become an informed choice rather than a 'guilt' purchase.

The full case study can be found at www.ideo.com/work/featured/oxfam and this will help you to answer the questions below.

1 What do you think is meant by the term ethical consumption?

2 Oxfam wanted to 'connect with people'. What do you think this means?

3 Evaluate the case study and decide if you think Oxfam is conducting itself in the correct way.

Just checking

* What is ethical consumerism?
* Explain the term fair trade.
* What is socially responsible investment?

Consumerism Creating happiness through buying material possessions.

Ethical consumerism The process of buying goods or services that are made or provided with minimal negative impact on humans, animals or land.

Fairtrade A world standard which ensures that producers are operating in acceptable working conditions and being paid a reasonable amount in return for their product and labour.

Ethics Moral codes which guide an individual or organisation to act in the correct manner.

Influence Power to affect other people.

Personal, Learning and Thinking Skills

It is important to understand why an increasing number of consumers are buying goods and services that are produced in an ethical way. Some major retailers are using ethical trading as a tool for advertising. However, you must be able to show your understanding when your work as an independent enquirer is being assessed. Therefore, when you make conclusions in your work they must be supported by the evidence that you have gathered and researched. Arguments must be clear, logical and most of all sensible.

In pairs, discuss ethical consumerism and then individually create a one-page report on the topic. Preparing a formal report requires the skills of self management, independent enquiry and creative thinker. How can you use these skills to ensure that your report is a success?

8.3 Benefits of corporate social responsibility

The benefits of being socially responsible are many and varied for business. Not only does it make a business look like a 'good citizen', it also has more practical benefits. For example, a good reputation makes it easier to recruit and keep staff, which in turn has a positive impact on a business' profits. A good reputation can also encourage people to invest in a business, and this is important when a company is trying to raise finance. In many industries it is vital to have a good reputation as without it other companies will not deal with you.

What are the benefits for business?

Consumers' interest in the activities of business has never been greater and, as a result, organisations have had to respond to this by ensuring that their business operations are undertaken responsibly. For example, many companies that produce goods in China and the Far East have set guidelines and standards regarding the working conditions and pay of their workers in these countries. Over the years, these guidelines have improved the working conditions and living standards of workers.

Positive publicity

Many businesses use corporate social responsibility to their advantage, for example it is often used in advertising to make a business look like a 'good citizen'. For many organisations, it has become a major factor when choosing which other businesses to trade with – the need to maintain a positive image is now a leading factor in many organisation's strategic planning.

Customer loyalty

Consumers have a vast range of places to go to buy their goods. Many businesses seek to develop customer loyalty by telling them of their corporate social responsibility credentials. This could be through the abolition of plastic carrier bags or providing recycling bins.

Businesses use corporate social responsibility to be good citizens.

Recruiting and retaining staff

Corporate social responsibility can be a useful tool to attract employees in a competitive market place. As society becomes more aware of social issues, many people may choose to apply for a job at a company with a strong social responsibility record. In addition, employees may be more likely to stay with such a business as they will feel well respected and valued by the company. Many businesses have discovered that if they treat their staff well, their workforce will be motivated and more productive. Generally, businesses that treat their employees badly have high staff turnover and recruitment costs. Add to this the cost of training new staff and it makes sense to treat people as the business' most valuable resource.

Case study: BP

The oil and gas producer BP has invested in a programme to ensure the security and human rights of its workers and the communities in which it operates. This involves training employees and contractors to make them aware of potential security hazards and human rights violations. BP also has a code of conduct called 'Voluntary Principles on Security and Human Rights' which highlights the dangers of security hazards and human rights infringements.

To find out more, visit www.bp.com

1 Why do you think that BP is concerned with the human rights of its employees?

2 What do you think BP means by 'security'?

3 Does BP seem a good employer to work for? Explain your answer?

Activity

As you saw in the case study, BP takes its social responsibilities very seriously. Visit BP's website and make a list of points that could you write about in your project work.

A diverse workforce

Corporate social responsibility promotes diversity in the workplace. It helps companies to attract a variety of talented workers because people often prefer to work for businesses that care about society and the environment. This, in turn, benefits the business in many ways, including improved working relationships among workers of different backgrounds, which will improve the productivity of a business. Other benefits include employees having a greater commitment to their work though a shared vision of what needs to be done, and enhanced flexibility, creativity and participation in decision making.

Diversity Difference or variety.

Just checking

* Why is it beneficial for a business to be corporate and socially responsible?

* To what extent, do you think employees are attracted to a business based on its CSR reputation?

* Why is diversity important in a workplace?

IDENTIFYING SOCIAL RESPONSIBILITIES

Think about how businesses interact with their consumers. In a small group, choose a large, well-known business and make a list of all of its responsibilities towards consumers. Why do companies take these responsibilities seriously?

8.4 How can businesses be socially responsible?

When you think about how a business can be socially responsible, your first thought might well be how it impacts on the environment and climate change. However, corporate social responsibility goes much further than that. A business that fully adopts a socially responsible attitude will seek to minimise negative impacts on all of its stakeholders, including employees, suppliers, consumers and the general public, and the local community.

The environment

Businesses, like human beings, have to adopt a socially responsible attitude to the environment. Over the years, companies have often been seen as some of the main offenders in causing damage to the environment. However, through the work of pressure groups and successive changes in the law relating to the production and disposal of damaging waste, companies are now leading the way in the fight to save the planet. This issue has become of such importance to many companies that they devote millions of pounds to improving manufacturing processes and safeguarding the environment.

Managing waste

At a local level, businesses will often look at a range of ways to minimise their impact on the environment. Many businesses have discovered that by changing the way they do things, they can save money and develop a higher profile in terms of public relations. This is a list of steps that a business can take to be more environmentally friendly:

∗ Have well-designed procedures for managing waste.

∗ Recycle as much as possible.

∗ Use **sustainable resources**.

∗ Reduce the amount of energy used, which will, in turn, reduce their carbon footprint.

∗ Encourage good environmental practice by customers.

Case study: Simple Shoes

Simple Shoes' philosophy is simple – the company acknowledges that its workers have to earn a wage to pay the bills, but importantly it believes that it is possible to make a profit and pay workers without damaging the environment. That is why all of Simple Shoes' products are made from 100 per cent **sustainable materials**, which includes the rubber for the soles of the shoes – recycled car tyres. The primary reason for using recycled materials is simple – why produce new materials (rubber, etc.) which damage the environment when there is an endless supply of rubber and other materials available that could be used which will have not additional environmental impact?

To find out more, visit www.simpleshoes.com.

1 Do you think it is possible to have a profitable business which has little impact on the environment?

2 Why do Simple Shoes use car tyres for the rubber parts of their shoes?

3 Why have Simple Shoes adopted the philosophy they have on using recycled materials?

Employees

It is often said that an organisation's most valuable resource is its workers. Over the last century, employers have realised that if they treat their employees fairly, then the workforce is likely to be happier in its work and productivity will remain high. So how can a business be socially responsible for its workers? Below is a list of ways that firms can demonstrate their social responsibilities:

* Promoting good health in the workplace.

* Providing staff with good pay and benefits.

* Providing staff with appropriate training and development opportunities.

* Ensuring a safe and secure working environment.

* Ensuring that diversity and equal opportunities prosper through staff training, recruitment and pay policies and the use of monitoring.

* Recruiting staff ethically and having clear pay structures.

Suppliers

When thinking about a business's social responsibilities, suppliers do not immediately spring to mind. The reason is that they are seen as being a separate business. However, if suppliers are not socially responsible, it could be argued that the company they are supplying isn't responsible either. These are some considerations that organisations need to be aware of when choosing suppliers:

* Does the supplier promote a socially responsible attitude?

* Does the supplier provide its employees with fair working conditions?

* Does the supplier demonstrate concern for the environment in the way it runs its own business?

* If the supplier buys components from another person or company, does it treat this business ethically?

It is important also that socially responsible companies treat their suppliers fairly, for example by paying them on time.

Consumers and the general public

Some people may argue that consumers are the most important factor when considering an organisation's corporate social responsibilities. This is because it is often said in business that 'if you do not have any customers, you do not have a business'. The question is: what can a business do to demonstrate it is socially responsible towards its customers? Below are several ideas that promote a business's social obligation towards its customers:

* Advertising products and services in an honest and fair way.

* Treating customers fairly so that their buying experience is a pleasant one.

* Ensuring that all customers are catered for and providing for those who are vulnerable.

* Promoting responsible consumer behaviour.

* Consideration of the health and wellbeing of customers so as not to act in a way that is damaging to customers.

* Supporting other local businesses by choosing them as suppliers.

> **Sustainable resources**
> Materials that can be produced with little impact on the environment, e.g. fast growing wood – providing a tree can be planted straight after another has been felled, the impact on the environment should be minimised.

@ Work

You will need to carry out research to find a global business that has recently had to respond to an environmental or ethical problem. Your work needs to investigate the effect that your chosen business has had on other businesses and the local community. You will need to show that you have researched the following areas: what the problem was; how it came to light; the effects of the publicity on the organisation; how the organisation responded to the problem; and why the issue is important to the organisation and others.

Your project should be in the form of an interactive presentation, and must be accompanied by slides or handouts.

The local community

Over the past 20 years, businesses have become more aware of the communities that they serve. A business needs to consider its impact not only on the environment in which it operates but also the social implications of locating in a certain area. In many cases, the location or relocation of an organisation to a new area is seen as a positive thing, because this will create jobs and wealth locally and eventually lead to a more prosperous future for the area. For example, during the 1980s and 1990s many large foreign companies made massive investments in establishing business facilities in the UK. Such businesses included the Japanese car maker, Nissan, which opened a massive production facility in Sunderland.

Organisations now understand the need to work with local communities, because if they are seen to be 'good citizens', positive public relations can be beneficial in attracting employees and new business. Companies can demonstrate their responsibilities to a local area by:

* finding out the needs of the local community and providing support, if possible

* providing financial support for local projects through grants, sponsorship and charitable donations

Case study: Nissan in the North East

For many years, Nissan's plant was the most efficient and productive car manufacturing plant in the UK. However, the company was hit by the recession of 2009 and had to lay off staff. Nissan is an interesting case study because since the Sunderland factory was opened in 1986, it has provided many employees with a good income in return for their hard work. The North East had suffered a similar fate in the 1960s and 1970s. At that time, the north east of England was famed for ship building. However, during the 1980s ship building slowly ground to halt, as it was cheaper to produce ships abroad. When the Nissan factory opened, many people believed it would be a new start for Sunderland in terms of job creation. While for over 20 years that may have been true, time will only tell with regard to the most recent job losses. These are the responsibilities that Nissan has to its local community.

* To provide jobs that are available to local people.

* To operate in a manner that does not impact negatively on Nissan's environmental surroundings.

* To provide employees with the skills and training so that they can remain competitive in the car production industry.

* To utilise locally sourced materials where possible.

* To focus on the needs of the local community – can Nissan support any projects to raise awareness and interest in local issues?

* To promote a health and safety ethic in its workplace to avoid accidents and injury.

* To encourage employees to be enterprising, thus empowering workers to develop creative solutions to problems. This working ethos is key to how Japanese companies achieve success. It benefits the community as a whole, as employees are trained in a solution focused manner and, as such, should problems in the community occur there will be people available who can solve these problems.

1 Why do you think Nissan wanted to employ local people?

2 Why do you think Nissan wanted to source materials locally?

3 Evaluate the costs and benefits of Nissan both recruiting and sourcing materials locally.

* providing non-financial support, e.g. encouraging employees to act as mentors or volunteers for others

* offering work experience places for schoolchildren, or educational visits and visiting speakers to schools

* promoting local interest groups

* having a policy of social inclusion whereby each person in the local area has the same opportunity to apply for jobs regardless of abilities.

Did you know?

There is an organisation that is devoted to promoting business in the community. Visit its website – www.bitc.org.uk – to see the many creative ways in which business is trying to meet the needs of its communities.

Activity

1 Research two companies that place great emphasis on corporate social responsibility. Compare and contrast their policies with particular focus on: environmental concerns, employees, suppliers, consumers and the general public; the local community.

2 After you have analysed both businesses, draw a table and write in similarities and differences.

3 Using your research, do a simple evaluation saying which policy is best and why you think this is so.

Personal, Learning and Thinking Skills

In deciding what responsible business practice is, you will have to question your own assumptions and the assumptions of others. By doing this, you are demonstrating the skills of a creative thinker.

Functional Skills

ICT

When carrying out research for your written work you can use ICT to find and select information. This could include:

* using a search engine to find relevant information
* being selective and finding useful information
* keeping a record of websites visited.

You could also use a spreadsheet to create any charts that you wish to include, a word processor for typing up your work or even desktop publishing software for creating any illustrations.

English

When completing written pieces of work ensure that you pay close attention to your use of language. It is important that you use the correct vocabulary and tone for the piece that is being written. For example, when you are completing the report, it is important that you use formal language which is clear and concise.

Just checking

* Why is it important for businesses to show a socially responsible attitude?
* How can a business show its commitment to the area in which it is situated?
* List the responsibilities that businesses have to their employees.
* Explain why businesses need to consider the corporate social responsibility of their suppliers.
* To what extent do you think that customers and the general public are the most important stakeholder group in a business?

8.5 Gathering information

Businesses are constantly seeking to review and improve the way they work, otherwise in the long run they may cease to exist. In the fifteenth century, the Italian philosopher Niccola Machiavelli was quoted as saying, 'The one who adapts his policy to the times prospers, and likewise the one whose policy clashes with the demands of the times does not'. The process of reviewing business practices in order to recommend improvements involves three steps: gathering information, analysing information and gathering information.

Collecting information

When thinking about change, businesses need to 'capture' or collect information from different sources to assess the impact or potential impact of their decisions. It is only after this information has been gathered that any analysis can take place and decisions made.

Choosing how to collect information

It is important to carry out research using a number of sources. One of the main problems with data collection is eliminating 'bias'. Bias is when a person or group of people are 'persuaded' to give a certain response; this causes the researcher problems as the information received is not necessarily accurate. It is for this reason that companies will carry out research using a range of methods to give an accurate picture of the data they require. It is also important to remember that corporate social responsibility affects the general public as a whole and not just the internal stakeholders of a business.

The process of collecting data

The diagram below shows the process that has to be gone through when collecting information for research purposes.

Primary research methods

Primary research is also known as 'original' research. It is called primary research because the information collected is 'new' and has not come via another source. This type of research is undertaken by the business (or a research agency employed by it) to collect information. A business can obtain primary information in a number of ways, as described below.

Face-to-face survey

A face-to-face **survey** is where a **market researcher** asks a person if they would be willing to spend a small amount of time answering a number of questions. The benefits of this method are that it is quick and easy to carry out. The main problem with this type of survey is getting people to stop in the first place to answer the questions. Some market

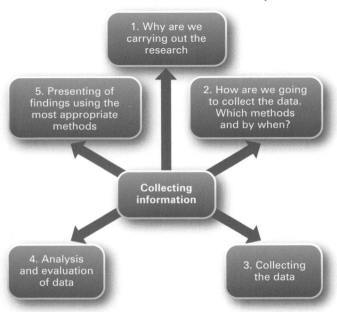

The process of collecting information.

research companies try to overcome this problem by offering small incentives to attract **participants** to answer the survey. This method of research was very popular until quite recently but has now been superseded by technology based methods.

Postal survey

This involves sending consumers a questionnaire through the post. The consumer then completes the questionnaire and sends it back to the market research company or business. The main problem with this method is that it has a very low return rate, in some instances as low as 20 per cent. To improve this, businesses offer incentives to attract people to return the surveys.

Telephone survey

This involves asking consumers questions over the telephone. The benefits of this technique are that it is cheap and a lot of consumers can be contacted very quickly. However, this method has a number of drawbacks – it is time consuming and sometimes consumers can be offended if unsolicited phone calls are received at home. Additionally, some consumers will not give honest responses as they just want to end the call.

Observation

This type of research method is commonly used when a new product is being designed. It involves observing how participants respond to a new product or idea. The researcher monitors all aspects of the people involved including what is said, facial expressions, how they touch, hold and use a new product. In some circumstances, the researcher may become involved with the research activity so they can get a better understanding of what the participants feel about the product or service in question. This is known as participant observation. This is a very good method of research but is time consuming and expensive.

Internet-based survey

This is where you either visit a website and are asked if you would like to complete an online survey or you receive a survey via email. This is becoming an increasingly popular method of surveying as many people can be targeted at a very low cost. Even if only a small percentage of people respond, the business is still likely to receive a lot of useful feedback. In addition, the data can be analysed by computers, saving further time and money.

Secondary research methods

Secondary research is information that is collected from sources that already exist, unlike primary research which is carried out specifically for a business purpose. Secondary sources include newspapers, magazines, trade journals, company accounts, information from the internet and the news. Businesses can buy information from specialist market research companies that specifically focus on the area that they are researching.

Primary research The process of gathering data first hand in a way that is specific to a business' needs.

Survey The process of carrying out research which involves a large number of people.

Market researcher The person who carries out the research on behalf of a business.

Participant A person who is being surveyed as part of the research.

Personal, Learning and Thinking Skills

To be successful in this piece of portfolio work you must organise your research and resources in order to produce a successful article and report. In successfully completing this task you will have to demonstrate that you are a self manager.

Activity

For this task you are required to work with a partner and investigate the different types of research methods available. As part of your discussion, you must identify which methods are most appropriate for different situations, for example if a business is launching a new product, which type of research would be the most appropriate?

Just checking

* Why is it important that businesses carry out primary research?
* Give three advantages of primary research over other methods
* What problems might market researchers carrying out primary research face?

8.6 Analysing information and drawing conclusions

When a business implements change, it has to consider the impact that the change has had on the business. It does this by gathering data and then analysing the information that it has collected, after which the company is able to draw conclusions.

Analysing information

When a business implements any type of change, it has to consider the impact that the change has had on the business. To do this, a company assesses its position before change and then after change has taken place. The way in which a business collects information can vary. If a business has implemented change that impacts on consumers, it will carry out research with that group of people in mind. If a business has made changes which affect its workers, it will survey them. The results will then be analysed, sometimes using a spreadsheet or specialist software, and the results will be put into a report and passed to those staff members that requested it.

WAYS TO GATHER INFORMATION

In a small group, list as many methods as possible that businesses can use to gather information and monitor the effectiveness of change on the business. Try to identify the specific type of information that each research type can offer a business.

@ Work

In carrying out your research you will need to identify a relevant issue that the company you researched earlier could address. This issue can be best investigated by taking a 'before' and 'after' approach – looking at the business before and after change has taken place. Examples of potentially controversial issues are included below.

Personal, Learning and Thinking Skills

While you are carrying out your research and assessing how well businesses use responsible business practices, you will be using the skill of a reflective learner.

Assessing positive and negative impacts		
Change	**Negative impact**	**Positive impact**
A major local employer decides to expand its factory.	Local community worried that the new factory will be built on greenfield and damage animal habitats.	Local community thinks that there may be more jobs made available at the business after expansion.
A major mobile phone company wishes to site a large phone mast in a village community.	Local community fears there could be health implications and that the value of their houses will be affected.	Local community thinks it would be good for the area as mobile reception is poor.
A local farmer decides to expand his business and grow more crops but does not currently have the manpower to work his fields.	Local community fears that any new jobs may be taken by foreign workers.	If the jobs are taken by either local or foreign workers, greater wealth through extra spending power and taxation for the area will be created.
A local hospital decides that patients can choose where they have their operations.	Local community may feel that the treatment they receive from another hospital may be inferior to their local hospital.	Local community think that the changes are of benefit because hospital waiting times are shorter and so patients should get better more quickly.
A local engineering business decides to change its hours from a two shift to a three shift system.	Workers are unhappy that they will have to work through the night.	Local community think this is a good idea as it shows the company has plenty of business and workers jobs are safe.

Assessing the impacts of change on a community.

Local communities can be very sensitive to change. An issue that one person or a group of people may consider trivial or unimportant, another group might find to be of great significance. Above is a list of ideas that may impact either positively or negatively on a community.

Identifying issues and assessing ideas

It is likely that in the course of your research you will identify many areas that you feel are need of investigation and where you could make both practical and timely recommendations. To gain good marks you should investigate all of the areas. However, while it would be advisable to mention them in your final report, you must remember that your report must not exceed 1,000 words. Therefore, you must decide which issue you are going to focus on in-depth. In your report you must clearly state which corporate social responsibility issue you are discussing and how this impacts on your chosen business. It is always worthwhile using other company examples to explain a point if it is something that should be happening in your company but is not. All ideas have to be well thought out, clear and practical.

Activity

Referring to your research, create a mindmap that summarises the tasks and requirements that you need to carry out in order to review and recommend improvements to business practices. By doing this task, you will be recapping what you have learned and also have a better idea of what needs to be contained in your report. This task will improve your reflective learner skills.

Drawing conclusions

After data has been analysed and reported on, it can then be used by a company to draw conclusions. A business will be looking specifically at how the changes have affected it. Obviously, companies are looking for positive results from the changes they make. However, sometimes organisations make changes which adversely affect the business, as Coca-Cola found to its cost in 2004. The company launched a bottled water product in the UK called 'Dasani'. The product was supposed to be the purest bottled water money could buy. In fact, it was later revealed that the water was actually from a tap. Coca-Cola immediately withdrew 'Dasani' from the UK. For a short time, this issue affected the image of Coca-Cola, but the brand recovered quickly due to its strong name.

Just checking

* Have you considered the different methods you could use for researching that will allow you to make recommendations and judgements in your report?
* Have you considered how you are going to present your supporting research in your report?
* Have you discussed both positive and negative impacts of any changes made by your chosen business?
* Are your recommendations practical, convincing and written in way that shows balanced judgement?

@ Work

To achieve good marks for the portfolio work for this unit, you must make it clear in your work that you have carried out research. In order for this to be achieved you must support all your work with research and findings.

When you are presenting your recommendations and conclusions make sure that you include charts and written analysis of what is being written about – this clearly indicates you have undertaken the required research and know what you are talking about.

For your project

For AO3 you are required to investigate the impact of an organisation on your local community, and consider the impact of the business's positive and negative aspects. To do this there are very specific areas in which you need to conduct research on. These are:

* the impact of the organisation on the local community, both positive and negative
* the financial and non-financial investment of the organisation in the community
* the needs of the community in the area served by the organisation, and whether the organisation responds to these
* provide your own recommendations for improvement.

This evidence will need to be compiled into a report of between 500 – 1000 words long.

Assessment

This unit is assessed internally. This means that you will be set an assignment by your consortium, which should direct your work through a series of tasks connected to the running of a business related activity, so that you cover all of the learning outcomes for this unit. The work you submit for assessment must be original work, produced by yourself under controlled conditions – this will be arranged by your tutor. It will then be marked by your tutor and moderated by the awarding body.

You will be assessed on:

* your understanding of why organisations need to act responsibly

* your knowledge of ways in which organisations can demonstrate corporate social responsibility

* your ability to review and recommend improvements to business practices.

To aim for higher grades you should try to:

* think carefully about the organisation that you choose for this assignment; it could be any type of organisation, public, private or voluntary, but it must be a real organisation; larger organisations will provide greater scope when completing the first and second parts of the assignment, but smaller organisations may also be suitable – your tutor will help you to choose

* make sure that examples of corporate social responsibility that you give are clear and well justified, and considered broadly from different perspectives

* make sure that when giving examples of ways in which organisations can demonstrate corporate social responsibility that they are relevant

* be specific and detailed when reviewing business practices and recommending improvements, giving a broad range of examples to support your judgement.

* use appropriate and realistic examples that relate clearly to the organisation that you have selected to study

* make clear and realistic recommendations about specific steps the organisation can take to improve its corporate and social responsibilities.

Introduction

This unit will help you to think about finding a career that will suit you in business. The Higher Diploma in Business, Administration and Finance will give you the opportunity to look at many different aspects of business, including the administrative side of business and finance.

You have a wide variety of choices and lots of options to think about. The unit will guide you through those choices and help you to think about the type of career that you might like and how you might get there. You will also learn about some of the most important aspects of being employed and your rights in the workplace. You will discover how organisations get the best performance out of their staff and the processes that are used help employees to work as well as they can.

How you will be assessed

For this unit, you will be assessed by a single assignment connected to careers and your future employment. You will be required to use careers information to produce a simple career plan (which includes information you have found out about a chosen career), a short-term plan to help you achieve this, and goals for your work experience. In addition, you will create job application documents, and then prepare for, and take part in, a job interview. You will also be expected to use your work experience to identify statutory and contractual rights and responsibilities of people in the organisation in which you are working, and describe which performance management methods are used and what they are used for. Finally, you will review what you have learned and assess whether you have achieved the goals you set in your career plan.

What you will learn in this unit

You will:

* be able to use sources of job information

* be able to plan for and set goals for your career

* be able to prepare for and participate as an interviewee in an interview for a job

* know how employment legislation, procedures and processes operate in the workplace.

Case study: What famous business people say

'For me, the drive to succeed is not about proving something to others; I just want to make sure I don't lose out on the opportunities I've been given. I come from a humble background but given the opportunity, anyone can succeed.'
Tim Campbell

Tim Campbell

9.1 Sources of careers information and recruitment methods

Before you start finding out about a career in business, you'll need to know where to go for information and help. On your course, there are many people who can help you, including your tutors and other students in the class. You can ask your family and friends for advice too, but there are also many specialists such as careers advisers who can assist you. First, you will need to think carefully about the information that you require. This topic will help you to access suitable sources of information and advice to help you plan your career.

Sources and types of information

Careers advisers

You will find it useful to book an appointment to talk about your career with an adviser.

Company websites and career packs

You can find out about different companies and the jobs they offer through their websites (see the grid opposite for some ideas). Some employers will send out careers packs of information so that you can consider the types of employment available.

Employment agencies and Jobcentres

Employment agencies and Jobcentres can offer you a range of advice. The JobCentre website (www.jobcentreplus.gov.uk) provides information on jobs. You can also use the internet to help you find employment agencies in your area: www.agencycentral.co.uk, for example, is a recruitment agencies and job sites directory; or to see a range of different types of jobs, look at the recruitment site www.reed.co.uk.

Newspaper articles, job advertisements and specialist journals

There are many newspapers and journals that include information on different types of careers; for example, the *Guardian* advertises many marketing jobs every week and also makes them available online. Specialist journals such as *The Grocer* advertise retail vacancies every week, both in the magazine and online.

Careers guidance software

In your school or college library, you will find a variety of different software packages and online services that can help you make decisions about careers.

College prospectuses, open days and careers fairs

You may find it helpful to look at the opportunities for education that might be available to you after you leave school or college. You can find out about the different options, including specialist courses, by visiting colleges and universities at their open days or evenings and talking to the staff who work there. Careers fairs may also be run in your local area.

9.2 Planning and setting career goals

Case study: 'This is not just *any* career ...'

Some large companies, such as Marks and Spencer (M&S), offer a range of interactive activities and information on what it is like to work for them. These are designed to help you think about whether the organisation would be a good employer for you. The M&S website – http://corporate. marksandspencer.com/mscareers – provides information about qualifications needed, experience required, training and development offered and even quizzes to help you think about whether or not you might want to work for the company.

Visit M&S's website and try some of the activities for yourself.

Information provider	Type of information
Connexions www.connexions-direct.com	Advisers may visit your school/college or be available online – find out which is the best option for you.
Careers advisers www.direct.gov.uk/careersadvice	Advisers may visit your school/college or be available all the time. You will need to book an appointment. You can also get advice over the internet by accessing the website, which includes email/phone contacts and even useful podcasts.
Careers fairs	Fairs usually happen at least once a year in your town or city. Look in the local paper, or search the internet to find out about the next one.
Visiting speakers	You may have the opportunity to listen to visiting speakers about how they have been successful in their careers or what they have been studying at college or university.
Newspapers/specialist journals	Most newspapers include a section on job vacancies and feature articles giving advice on job options. The job vacancies can be looked at online as well as offline. For some careers, there might be specialist websites or journals, e.g. Retail Week or Marketing, where you will find additional information about working in a particular industry.
www.careersa-z.co.uk www.alec.co.uk www.careers-gateway.co.uk	These websites provide more general information about job finding.
www.acca.co.uk www.cim.co.uk www.cipd.co.uk www.lawsociety.org.uk	These are specialist websites which will give you information on: Accountancy Marketing Personnel and Development Law

Where to get careers information.

Just checking

* Name three different sources of offline careers advice.
* Name three difference sources of online careers advice.
* What is the purpose of a careers pack produced by a company?

Now it's time to start thinking ahead to your future career. The first stage is to see where you are now and then prepare a career plan. There are five steps to producing a plan: 1 Self analysis of your current situation; 2 Researching your career; 3 Planning short-term activities; 4 Setting goals for work experience; and 5 Reviewing your goals. You will go through each of these steps in this unit to help you plan your future career!

Self-analysis

Thinking about where you are now is the first step. Use the mini self-assessment activity below to get yourself thinking.

Activity

For each of the statements in the self-assessment chart, give yourself a rating from 1 (extremely important) to 6 (extremely unimportant). Discuss your results in pairs. What do they show about you?

Statement	Rating	
I want to earn lots of money	1 2 3 4 5 6	
I want lots of time off for holidays	1 2 3 4 5 6	
I want to be in a safe and secure job	1 2 3 4 5 6	
I want to receive good sick pay, pensions or other benefits	1 2 3 4 5 6	
I want to manage others	1 2 3 4 5 6	
I enjoy doing paperwork	1 2 3 4 5 6	
I like meeting people	1 2 3 4 5 6	
I would like to be my own boss	1 2 3 4 5 6	
I enjoy working with numbers or finances	1 2 3 4 5 6	
I enjoy creative work	1 2 3 4 5 6	
I want to work for someone else	1 2 3 4 5 6	

What I want and need from a job

Now that you have carried out a self-analysis of your current situation, it is also important to think about what you want and need from a job. This means you can match the type of activities that you enjoy to the type of job that you think you might be interested in. For example, if you really want a career in business that allows you to be creative, you might think about a career in marketing so that you could use your skills in advertising. If you enjoy working with numbers, you might want to think about accountancy or banking.

Activity

Look at the aspects of work that you thought were important to you and consider different business areas that you might be interested in. Use the mind map below to help you.

Which business areas are you interested in?

Choose one area that you find interesting, or maybe there are others not listed here that you think are for you!

Case Study: 'Shift Happens'

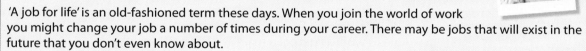

'A job for life' is an old-fashioned term these days. When you join the world of work you might change your job a number of times during your career. There may be jobs that will exist in the future that you don't even know about.

Watch the 'Shift Happens' videos, authored by Karl Fisch, on YouTube to give you some thought-provoking ideas about what is likely to happen to the world of work in the future.

1 What does the video suggest might happen to jobs in the future?
2 How might careers need to be planned differently in the future?
3 Why is it going to be important to be flexible in terms of what you might want to do?
4 How important are skills and training?

Did you know?

The world of work is changing and there is now a move towards everyone becoming a 'career entrepreneur'. This means that you take responsibility for all aspects of your own career and see it as your responsibility to sell yourself to employers by telling them about your unique skills!

Just checking

* What skills, qualifications and experience do I have now?
* Why will I have to be more adaptable in terms of the experience and choices that I need to make for careers and employment in the future?

9.3 Researching your career

Now you have chosen a possible career, the second step in your career plan is to consider what you need to do to get into that job or career and the rewards that you will receive when you get there. For your Business, Administration and Finance assessment, you will need to find out about a particular career and the qualifications and experience that you will need to get to that career.

Planning your career

Work

Choose examples of three jobs from your career choice. Then find out about the qualifications and experience that each will need. Copy and complete the table below with the information you find. An example is given to help you. If you need more information about where to source careers information and jobs, see the careers information chart on page 209.

Job title

Marketing Assistant in Hampshire

Qualifications needed (education)

BAF Higher or Advanced Diploma

Experience needed (knowledge and training)

Work experience in a marketing environment, especially advertising

IT training, especially website maintenance and design

Skills

IT skills

Able to work as part of a team

Potential earnings/Other benefits

Creative £17k–£18k pa

Choose examples of three jobs from your career choice. Then find out about them. Compare the three jobs. Are there any similarities in the experience and knowledge that you might need?

Now that you have looked at three possible jobs of interest to you, the next step is to find out more general information about the type of career you are considering. For example, if you are thinking of becoming an accountant, you should consider the general qualifications that you might need by visiting websites of accountancy firms and checking which types of qualification you might need.

Did you know?

… that many employers do not want specific work-related skills. Instead, they want skills that you can develop through your personal, learning and thinking skills (PLTS) and functional skills work. The most important skills that many employers look for are:

* confidence and the ability to communicate
* the ability to work in a team
* the ability to use IT
* the ability to plan/organise
* honesty
* flexibility and adaptability.

Think about which of these skills you already have (many probably!), which ones you need to work on and how these relate to your career choice.

Bibliography A list of sources of information that you have used in your work. Make sure you quote other people's work that you have found on websites or in books.

The last stage of this process is to match your qualifications and experience so far to those that are needed for the career that you would like to work in.

A short-term career plan

You will need to put together a short-term career plan, which will be assessed as part of your BAF Diploma. The first part of the plan will include all of the activities that you have completed so far and the final part will show what you now need to do to get you to your chosen career. Remember, your plan could include personal, learning and thinking skills and functional skills as well as those directly related to your Business, Administration and Finance Higher Diploma.

Functional Skills

English

In pairs, discuss the experience and qualifications that you have so far on the BAF Higher Diploma course. Explain to your partner the skills and knowledge that you already have and the gaps that you have noticed. Why do you want this career? What are the particular features that make you want to do this job? Are there any difficulties that may come with this job?

Activity and time scale	Why this activity will help me with my career	Additional information
Getting involved with the Student Council – nominations are due by April	It will show that I can work with other people and this will be important for my career in marketing	I am going to think about whether to stand as a candidate for the President of the Council to show extra responsibility

Short-term career plan (usually for the next two years).

Just checking

* Which different types of information do you need when choosing between different types of jobs?
* Which skills are employers looking for now?
* How can your skills and personal qualities help you choose the ideal job for you?

9.4 Setting and reviewing goals for work experience

While you are doing your Business, Administration and Finance Higher Diploma it's important to use your experiences of work as well as you possibly can. By setting yourself some goals for work experience and then assessing them, you will be able to measure how you are doing.

Setting goals for work experience

Below are some key areas that you will need to consider when setting your goals for work experience.

Which skills and attributes (qualities) are relevant for the job?

Each job will have a different set of skills and attributes that are needed to perform it. You will need to think about what those skills are before you go on work experience and then decide which skills you need to develop.

Your strengths and weaknesses.

You will also need to think about your own personal strengths and weaknesses. Are you punctual, well organised, a hard worker, a good communicator?

Which areas do you need to improve on? Is there anything you are less good at, for example remembering your books or papers for class, doing your work outside of classes?

Skills and attributes you want to improve or show you can do.

You should think about the personal skills and attributes which you will need to develop or demonstrate on work experience; for example, how you work with others, IT skills, ability to carry out work such as filing, dealing with customers or helping colleagues.

How you can set goals to help you do this.

Finally, you need to set yourself some goals or targets. You should try and make sure that they are SMART. This means that they are specific, can be measured, can be achieved, that they are realistic and have a time constraint on them. It may not be possible to make all of your goals SMART but it may help you to review them if they are! (To find out more about SMART objectives, see Unit 2.9, page 46.)

You might have some more specific goals that you wish to achieve when you are on work experience. There might be certain types of experience or people you would like to talk to in order to find out more about your future career.

Employers expect all employees to get to work on time.

Activity

Write a set of instructions to show how you would research more information about a company. Where would you look for information, how and why? Type up your instructions and place them on the wall of your classroom. Ask others to read them – how clear are they to follow?

Reviewing your goals

When you return from work experience you will need to revisit your goals and assess what you have achieved and what else you might have learned.

Achievement of goals

You can measure the goals that you set yourself, see how many you achieved and whether there were any that you did not achieve, and why. You need to make judgements about how useful the experience was in helping you to achieve your goals. You should also consider how useful your goals were to begin with – were there other goals you should have set? You will need to provide good evidence of how far you achieved your goals as part of your assessment.

What else you learned

There will be other experiences and learning that will have taken place during work experience. You will need to decide what else you have learned. You might consider problems you have solved, how you feel about your future, including your hopes and dreams, what you think of yourself and how you performed, what you have learned about how you work with other adults in the workplace. All of this learning is very important for your future!

Personal, Learning and Thinking Skills

Remember at regular points during your work experience, it is important that you reflect on your goals. Don't just leave them to the end. If you have not completed something, ask your employer or supervisor to help you find a way to achieve it!

You will need to keep a note of what happens every day on work experience. You might wish to do this as a diary, in a notebook, on a blog, in your e-portfolio or through a social networking site. If you decide to go for an online version that may be viewed by others, make sure you are professional with your comments and don't write anything that is not true! This will help you to become a reflective learner.

Just checking

* What does SMART mean and why is it useful?
* Why is important to think about your skills before when setting goals for your work experience?
* How can you develop your own personal strengths and weaknesses for work experience?

9.5 Case study: preparing your job application

You've seen an advert for a job that seems just right for you. You've contacted the organisation and they've sent you a job information pack. The next step is to prepare your application. You'll need to produce an up-to-date CV, write a covering letter and fill in the application form using key employment documents. Getting your job application right is a really important first step to secure employment. This topic will guide you through what you will need to do.

Key documents

There are several key documents that you need to know about, including:

* **job description**
* **person specification**
* **curriculum vitae (CV)**
* **covering letter**
* **application form.**

Job description

A job description gives all the most important information about a job. It describes the role.

Job title	This is really important as it will give the job applicant an idea of what the job involves and the level of responsibility, e.g. Office Assistant.
Department and location	A job description will often be written for a particular department within a large organisation.
Job purpose	This gives the applicant guidance on the role and extent of their responsibilities, e.g. whether they supervise others or can make management changes.
Responsibilities and terms	This gives a very rough idea of what is involved in the post. Many job vacancies have open-ended terms, which means that they can change slightly to take into account the needs of the business or employee. This section tells the employee about any people or resources they are responsible for.
Responsible to whom	This tells the employee who they will be expected to report to with any problems or queries, for example a line manager or supervisor.
Name of compiler and approver	The people who designed and agreed the job.
Date of issue	This is when the job description was issued. In a fast changing business world, it is important to know when changes were last made to the job.

What's in a job description?

Person specification

The person specification gives all the details about the type of person that the business is looking for, including special skills, qualifications and experience required for the job.

PERSON SPECIFICATION

Post Title: Administrative Assistant
Directorate/Division: Corporate Services
Legal & Democratic Services
Scale / Grade: 2/3

QUALIFICATIONS/TRAINING:
It is **essential** that the postholder is:
- Educated to GCSE level or equivalent Including English at Grade 'C' or above

It is **desirable** that the postholder has:
- Evidence of continuing professional development and education, e.g. HNC, 'A' levels

EXPERIENCE/KNOWLEDGE:
It is **essential** that the postholder:
- Is computer literate, and has a good knowledge of MS Office
- Working within an office environment

It is **desirable** that the postholder has:
- Previous experience of working in a local government or public service environment

SKILLS AND ABILITIES:
It is **essential** that the postholder has:
- Good communication skills, both oral and written
- Good organisational skills
- Good interpersonal and customer service skills
- An ability to work using own initiative within boundaries
- An ability to work effectively with people across a wide range of levels and responsibilities
- Good attention to detail
- Good teamworking skills
- Good keyboard skills
- Good numeracy skills
- Legible handwriting
- An ability to write messages, semi-routine letters and simple reports which are clear and structured
- Has tact and diplomacy
- The ability to maintain confidentiality

ADDITIONAL FACTORS:
It is **essential** that the postholder has:
- A willingness to undertake appropriate training
- A commitment to maintain high customer care standards

It is **desirable** that the postholder has:
- An ability to travel in and out of the county and at times when public transport may be limited

---

A person specification.

Job description Gives information about the job.

Person specification Describes the type of person the business is looking for.

Curriculum vitae (CV) Gives employers information about the job seeker, such as their qualifications, education, and so on.

Activity

Find a vacancy for a full-time job that you could apply for when you have completed your BAF Higher Diploma, e.g. admin assistant, marketing assistant, accounting assistant or retail assistant.

Print (if online) or look at the job description and highlight the key elements of the post that interest you.

In a small group, discuss the reasons why you think that the job is the right one for you. How does the more detailed information in the job description help you to be sure that this job is one that you really want to apply for.

Now print (if online) or look at the person specification.

Highlight and write down for each point on the job description which skills and experience you have that match what the job requires. Do you have all the skills and knowledge necessary? Is there any additional experience that you should plan to work towards?

Covering letter

When sending an application for a job it is usual to enclose a covering letter. This should give details of the post that you have applied for and highlight the skills and knowledge that you believe make you particularly suitable for the job. You can also include any additional contact information that you want employers to know.

Activity

Look at the example of a covering letter shown below. Now draft a covering letter for the full-time vacancy you researched above. Ask a classmate to have a look at it and tell you what improvements you could make.

Curriculum vitae (CV)

A CV gives employers details about you – your qualifications, education, experience and leisure interests. It is good practice to update and improve your CV for every job that you apply for.

Curriculum Vitae

Personal Details

Name	Jacob Smith
Address	18 Hill Lane Southampton SO15 5RL
Telephone	023 80511822

Education

2006 – 2011	Besthampton College

Academic Qualifications

BAF Higher Diploma	Predicted Grade A
GCSE Maths	A* Grade achieved 2009
GCSE English	Predicted Grade B
AS Maths	Predicted Grade B

Work Experience

2009	Work experience at HMV using the till, pricing stock and stock management as well as dealing with customers

Personal Statement

I am a really outgoing person who likes to play sport. I am a member of the Rugby Team and also play at the weekend for my local team. I enjoy computing and am able to use a number of different software packages. I am hard working and am always on time.

Referees

Mrs Sharp
Head Teacher
Besthampton College
76 Laxford Avenue
Southampton
SO26 8PU
02380 876233

A curriculum vitae.

Dear Sir

I would like to apply for the job as Office Assistant. I am studying at City Technology College at the moment and am due to finish my BAF Diploma soon. I am taking my Maths GCSE this year and I am predicted to get a B this time.

In my summer holidays I have worked in an Estate Agent's office helping customers, filing and answering the telephone. I have enclosed my CV for your attention.

Please call me on 078666234 if you would like to discuss my CV with me.

Yours sincerely

S E Bough (Miss)

A covering letter to accompany a job application.

Activity

1 Using the example of a CV to help you and with the help of the websites you learned about on page 209, update your own CV.

2 Now adapt your CV to suit the full-time vacancy you researched earlier.

Application forms

Application forms differ depending on the organisation advertising the job. Generally, application forms ask job applicants to complete a standard set of questions and boxes. This makes it easy for the organisation to compare potential candidates. Some businesses use online application forms instead of paper ones. You should take care with online application forms to ensure that you use appropriate English and not 'text speak' as this 'myt nt giv da ryt impreshun'!

Activity

Now find the application form for the full-time job vacancy that you have researched, and complete the application. If you can't find an application form for that employer, use a search engine to find a 'standard application form', print it out and complete it. Alternatively, your tutor may give you a suitable form.

Just checking

✳ Explain the difference between a person specification and a job description.

✳ When would you send a covering letter, and why?

✳ What is a CV and what does it contain?

HOW MANY TIMES?

Think about how many different interviews you have had in your life so far. You may have been interviewed by a teacher, by other professionals helping you with your education, by other younger students wanting to know more about your school or college, by governors or by community groups, by inspectors such as Ofsted, as part of the school or college council? What was the experience like? How did you feel?

9.6 Case study: preparing for interview

Your carefully prepared job application has won you an interview! The next stage is to think about the interview itself. In this topic, you will learn about interview **protocols**, how to prepare questions to ask at interview and be prepared to answer questions that you may be asked.

Interview protocols

At interview, employers will expect you to have a smart appearance, so you should:

* dress in a business-like style – wear a suit or other smart clothing and clean shoes

* look clean and tidy – avoid wearing too much make-up, perfume or aftershave

* avoid chewing gum.

You should arrive in plenty of time for the interview.

During the interview, remember to:

* shake hands with the interviewer as you enter the room

* say only positive things about your employer or school/college.

At the end of the interview, thank the employer for their time.

Activity

Using the list of protocols above, produce a poster that can be put on to your classroom wall explaining how you should arrive at an interview.

Remember to shake hands with the interviewer when you enter the room.

Preparing questions to ask at interview

When you are in an interview situation it is often hard to think of questions that you might want to ask about the job. Although it is possible to ask about the rate of pay in an interview, it can be thought of as impolite, so it is better to avoid doing this. Be careful not to ask questions about things that you should know already – use the website or company information to find out the answers before interview! Below are some areas that you may find useful to consider when thinking about questions to ask:

> **Protocols** A set of rules or expectations setting out how you should behave in a given situation.

* What training or development opportunities are available?

* What are the organisation's strengths and weaknesses?

* Who will review my performance and how often?

* What do you like best about working in the organisation?

* What further career opportunities are there likely to be for someone in this post?

* How does the organisation reward talent?

Activity

Using the questions above or ones that you can think of yourself, practise asking a partner the questions and trying to answer them for the job that they have chosen. How easy or difficult were they to answer? Make sure you ask and answer the questions as an interviewer and interviewee.

Preparing for questions you may be asked

It is not possible to predict in advance all of the questions you might be asked in an interview, but you can prepare for some of the most likely ones, such as:

* What made you apply for this job?

* What do you know about our organisation?

* What skills do you think you could bring to the post?

* What experience have you got?

* What training or development do you think you might need to be able to do the job effectively?

* What do you think will be the main challenges of this job?

* Give me an example of when you have worked effectively in a team.

* Tell me about something you have done recently that you are really proud of.

* Where do you see yourself in five years' time?

Just checking

* Name two ways that you can prepare for interview.
* Why is it important to practise questions that you might be asked before you go?
* What two things should you remember to do during an interview?

9.7 Case study: the interview

It's the day of the interview! There's just one more thing you'll need to have in order to turn the interview into the offer of a job – good interviewing techniques and skills. You'll learn about these in this topic.

Techniques used by interviewees

There are many ways that you can do well in an interview, and you will need to be aware of different ones that you can use, including selling yourself, showing enthusiasm and demonstrating your knowledge of the job/organisation.

Selling yourself

Selling yourself at interview means promoting yourself. You need to tell the interview why they should employ you rather than someone else. It is about letting them know why you are special and the best candidate for the job.

Showing enthusiasm

Being enthusiastic is very important. You need to sound willing to take on tasks, even if the tasks sound a little boring, and be flexible and adaptable to new challenges you will be given.

Remember to smile and be friendly in an interview and don't forget to show you care about work that you have done before or projects that you have been involved with.

Demonstrating your knowledge of the job and organisation

It is very important to show that you know relevant information about the job and organisation that you are applying to. You will need to know some information about the products or services they sell, the size of the organisation and any other relevant information from their website or other published resources.

> **Activity**
>
> Choose a book, magazine or website to find a piece of text of about 500 words. In pairs, read the text to your partner and then ask them to repeat back what they have heard. Now change over and do the same exercise again – how much could you remember? How well were you listening?

Techniques used by interviewers

The job of the **interviewer** is to make the interview process as easy as possible for the **interviewee**. It is impossible for you to be completely relaxed, but you should be put at ease. The interviewer will also be using different types of questioning techniques to try to find out more about you.

Communication skills

At the interview you will be assessed on your oral communication skills, the way you respond to questions and non-verbal communication.

BACK TO BACK

Sit back to back with a partner and interview each other about a favourite hobby or pastime that you do at the weekends. Take it in turns to talk for three minutes each and then ask each other questions. How does it feel to interview each other in this way? What is missing and why is it important to see someone face to face for interviewing?

Did you know?

Open-ended questions allow the interviewer to find out how you think and what you are interested in, e.g. why you would like to work for the organisation.

Competency-based questions consider specific requirements of the job and may ask you to use examples to show your skill/competencies, e.g. 'Tell me about a situation when you dealt with a difficult customer'.

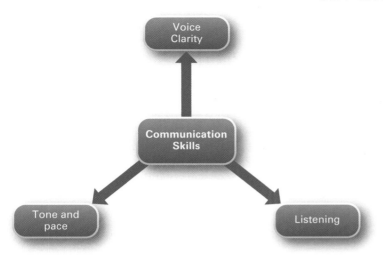

You'll need to have these key oral communication skills.

Interviewer The person who asks the questions.

Interviewee The job applicant who is being asked the questions

Pace The speed at which you talk, e.g. fast or slow.

Tone The way you talk, e.g. a deep or high voice, do you sound serious or fun?

Activity

1 Using a voice recorder, camcorder, a mobile phone with video or other software, carry out a role play in pairs. One of you should be the interviewer and the other one the interviewee. Use the questions you prepared in Unit 9.5.

2 Record your voice and think about what you sound like – exiting, enthusiastic, boring or dull. Experiment with changing your voice. Are you clear to understand, do you speak clearly or slowly. Assess yourself using the checklist below to help you:

　✳ How clear was your voice – could you easily understand yourself?

　✳ How did your voice sound?

　✳ How quickly or slowly did you speak?

　✳ Did you sound or professional?

Hotlink

Access the website www.bbc.co.uk/bbcfour/audiointerviews/professions and listen to some of the famous voice clips available. What do you notice about how clearly they speak, how their voices sound, what was the **pace** and **tone** like? Now think about your own voice and compare!

Some of the key oral communication skills are shown below:

Asking and responding to questions

You have already learned about the different types of questions that you may be asked, but it is also important to think about how you ask and respond to questions. You have learned some skills already such as being enthusiastic and selling yourself. Here are some other tips to help you.

✳ When you ask a question think carefully about what you are trying to find out and make sure your question asks for the right information.

✳ When you are asked a question leave enough time for you to think about the answer but not so long that the interviewer will think you don't know the answer or find the silence too long and then interrupt you.

✳ Make sure you don't interrupt the interviewer – let them finish speaking and then speak.

* If you don't understand a question, ask the interviewer to **rephrase** the question.

* Watch out for 'leading questions', either asking them or being asked, e.g. 'You do like doing lots of self study, don't you?'. This type of question leads you to an answer.

* Make sure that you always respond in a positive way about yourself and experiences that you have had. Sometimes interviewees will say negative things about places where they have previously worked – this is very bad practice and should be avoided. Even if you did not enjoy an experience, focus on elements of it that you found useful, e.g. 'My experience helped me to realise that I would prefer working in marketing rather than human resources because …'.

* Remember to listen! It is much more difficult than you think.

Activity

With a partner, using a timer, practise the interview questions, Start by answering the question after 10 seconds, then extend this to 20, 30, 40 and so on up to a minute. How does it feel to wait this length of time as an interviewer and as an interviewee? What impact does it have on the interview?

Non-verbal communication

Body language

Gestures such as shaking hands are important. A firm handshake is a way of showing that you are confident and a suitable person for the job, but watch out that you are not over-confident as the interviewer may perceive you as big-headed.

Shyness and nervousness can come out in your body language too. Try to calm your nerves during the interview because you will often give away clues to the interviewer about how you are feeling without saying anything; for example, swinging your legs, tapping your foot or not looking someone in the eyes tells the interviewer that you are not comfortable!

Posture

The way you sit at the interview can also give signals to the interviewer. If you slouch backwards, you may appear uninterested. You need to sit up straight (but not too rigidly) and lean forward slightly to show you are interested.

Rephrase Reword a question in a different way to make it easier to understand.

Your posture can tell the interviewer whether you are enthusiastic or uninterested.

Activity

Find a newspaper and read an article about any aspect of business. In groups of three, ask one person to interview another about the article – the third person should make notes. The note taker should give feedback to the interviewer on body language, posture, eye contact and facial expressions.

Eye contact

It's important to look the interviewer in the eye when you are talking to them as this will encourage them to believe that you are honest and trustworthy. Looking at the interviewer shows that you are interested in what they have to say.

Facial expressions

Your facial expression will tell the interviewer a great deal about your personality. Remember to smile – this shows that you are happy, friendly and approachable. (To learn more about facial expressions, see topic 2.7, page 42.)

Just checking

* What is meant by eye contact?
* Why is communication so important in interviews?
* What is a leading question and why should it be avoided?
* How can you show your enthusiasm in an interview?

9.8 Rights and responsibilities of employers and employees

All employers and employees have rights at work. This topic will help you to understand those rights and enable you to know your right and responsibilities at work.

Contractual employment rights

When you start a job, you and your employer form an agreement known as a contract. You can agree any terms in the **employment contract** with your employer. There are two types of terms in any contract: **express terms** and **implied terms**.

Express terms

These terms have to be agreed between the employer and the employee and must include:

* amount of wages
* hours of work
* holiday entitlement and pay
* sick pay
* redundancy terms
* how much warning (notice) the employer must give you if you are dismissed.

Activity

Find out what is meant by redundancy and what happens when someone is made redundant.

Implied terms

The following terms are not specifically agreed between the employer and employee but are customary to include in a contract:

* the employee and employer have a **duty of trust**
* the employer should provide a safe working environment
* the employee has a duty to obey any reasonable instructions given by the employer
* the employer has a duty to pay the employee's wages and provide work as long as the employee is willing to work.

Employment contract
An agreement between an employer and employee setting out the terms of work, such as hours of work and wages.

Express terms Terms in a contract that must be included by law.

Implied terms Terms that are customary to include in a contract.

Duty of trust The 'term of mutual trust and confidence' between employer and employee not to act in a way that could destroy, or damage, the relationship of trust and confidence.

Employment protection rights

Most employees have rights given by law. Some of these are shown below and include a right to:

* a written statement of the terms of employment

* an itemised statement of pay

* security of employment after maternity leave

* maternity, paternity or adoption leave

* statutory sick pay

* meal breaks

* compensation for being made redundant

* not to be unfairly dismissed

* belong to a trade union

* not to be victimised, harassed or discriminated against.

Generally, you and your employer can agree any terms in the employment contract. However, you cannot agree to a contractual term which gives you fewer rights than your statutory rights.

Employees have a statutory right to a pay slip.

> **Did you know?**
>
> The main rights of an employee in an employment contract can be found in the Employment Rights Act 1996, Employment Act 2002 and Employment Act 2008.

Activity

1 Why is it necessary to include statutory rights in an employment contract? What might happen to workers if these rights did not exist?

2 In a group, create an imaginary new job. Then visit a website like www.simply-docs.co.uk and create a contract of employment for that job using both statutory and contractual terms.

Health and safety at work

Employers have a statutory duty to take care of the health and safety of all their employees, for example they should ensure all machinery is safe. Employees also have a duty to make sure that they do not do anything that would harm or endanger the lives of themselves or their colleagues. There are also specific laws and regulations which cover the following:

* fire safety

* cleanliness

* noise

* lifting and carrying heavy weights

* hazardous substances

* first aid facilities

* temperatures

* hours and rest periods

* computers

* smoking at work.

Activity

In a group, create a health and safety checklist using some of the headings opposite and then check your own classroom for any obvious hazards (there shouldn't be any!).

Case study: The paper factory

Lauren has just left school and has started her first job as a general assistant in a paper factory. Her duties include sweeping floors, moving small boxes from place to place and making tea.

One day the factory is very short staffed and Lauren is told by her boss to work on the paper-cutting machine. Without any training, Lauren begins to work. When the paper gets jammed, she puts her hands inside the machine to pull it out; the machine starts up and severely damages her hands.

1 What have Lauren's employers failed to do?

2 What could Lauren have done to prevent this accident?

Functional Skills

IT

Produce a checklist, using a software package of your choice, listing the list of welfare provisions that should be present in every workplace. Now go through the checklist to see if every part of it is met – it should be! What should you do if anything is missing?

Welfare rights at work

As well as health and safety responsibilities, employers have a duty to consider their workers welfare. This means that they must provide:

* toilet and washing facilities

* fresh drinking water

* a place for workers to put their own things and change clothing if necessary

* a place where employees can rest and eat meals.

Activity

In a small group, discuss what employers can do to reduce risks for young workers?

Working hours and paid holidays

Working hours

All workers are entitled to be paid at least the minimum wage for the work they have done. They have the right to be paid if they are unable to work because they are off sick or away from work on maternity leave, paternity leave or parental leave.

Employees may be entitled to unpaid time off work in other circumstances, for example in a family emergency or on jury service.

Workers' hours are governed by the EU Working Time Directive, known in the UK as the Working Time Regulations. These cover:

Activity

1 Find out the National Minimum Wage for the following workers (be careful they usually change each year):

  ✳ Workers aged 22 years and over
  ✳ Workers aged 18–21
  ✳ Workers aged 16–17

2 How much do you think workers under 16 should be paid?

3 How do you think differences in rate per hour for different age groups might affect the way that employers recruit new staff?

Did you know?

South Korean workers have the longest working hours in the world. They work on average 2,317 hours per year, which is around 600 hours (or 50 working days) a year longer than workers in the UK!

✳ holiday entitlement (see below)

✳ the maximum average working week

✳ the right to rest breaks during the working day and the right to rest periods between working days

✳ hours when working at night.

In general, workers aged 18 years and over are entitled to work no more than six days out of every seven, or 12 out of every 14, take a 20-minute break if they work more than six hours and work a maximum 48-hour average week. Workers aged 16 and 17 should take at least 30 minutes' break if they work more than four-and-a-half hours, no more than eight hours a day and 40 hours a week and have 12 hours' rest between working days and two days off every week.

Holiday rights

Case study: Paperboy claims holiday pay

In 2002, 14-year-old paperboy Edward Des Clayes launched a groundbreaking legal challenge in an attempt to make his employers, Herts & Essex Newspapers Ltd, give him paid holiday. He believed that paperboys/girls should be entitled to claim paid holiday under the Working Time Regulations, but lost his case at an employment tribunal hearing. The tribunal ruled that he was too young to be entitled to a paid holiday (visit www.bbc.co.uk. to read more about this case).

1 Do you think it is fair that under 16s cannot claim holiday pay?

2 How could this law be changed?

3 Write a list of all the reasons why under 16s should or should not receive holiday pay.

Paperboys and girls are not entitled to holiday pay

Activity

Why do you think the police, the armed forces and emergency services are excluded from the right to holiday pay even though they usually receive it?

Nearly all workers have the statutory right to a paid holiday. The self-employed, the police, armed forces and other protection services are exempt from this right. Employees have the right to holiday based on the formula of 5.6 weeks' holiday a year times the number of days per week worked.

For example:

* if you work a five-day week, you are entitled to 28 days' paid holiday a year (5.6 x 5).

* if you work 2.5 days a week, you are entitled to 14 days' paid holiday a year (5.6 x 2.5).

From 1 April 2009, the minimum amount of statutory paid holiday you are entitled to is 5.6 weeks, which is 28 days. Any other holiday is a contractual point agreed at the time of starting work. Employers may ask employees to take bank holidays as part of this paid holiday.

Anti-discrimination legislation

Employees are protected at work from discrimination because it is unlawful to discriminate against a person at work because of their:

* sex
* colour
* religion or belief
* race
* nationality
* sexuality
* disability
* ethnic or national origin
* age.

Discrimination can be either direct or indirect. Direct discrimination occurs when a person is treated less favourably at work because of their sex, race, religion, age, sexuality or disability. For example, if a worker with disabilities is not selected for promotion because of their disability, this is direct disability discrimination. Indirect discrimination occurs where a particular employee cannot meet a requirement which is not justifiable in terms of the work and they are at a disadvantage as a result; for example, if an employer only gives training to full-time workers, this may indirectly discriminate against women, as most part-time workers tend to be women.

Did you know?

According to the employment relations organisation, ACAS, the UK's working population is getting older. There are currently 20 million workers aged 50 and over in the UK. By 2030, this figure is expected to reach 27 million – an increase of 37 per cent!

Activity

1 What type of employment should be exempt from age discrimination?
2 What special procedures should be in place to deal with employing older workers?
3 Research the following anti-discrimination legislation and describe how it affects employers and employees.

Activity

In a supervised group, look around your school or college and make a list of the special provisions in place to allow access to the college for disabled students and staff.

Legislation	Effect on employer	Effect on Employee
Disability Discrimination Act		
Race Relations Act		
Equal Pay Act		
Sex Discrimination Act		
Employment Equality (Age) Regulations		

Case Study: British Airways and the necklace

In 2006, British Airways asked a member of staff to hide a necklace with a cross because it contravened the company's uniform policy.

Heathrow check-in worker Nadia Eweida was placed on unpaid leave after refusing to cover up the necklace that she wore to signify her Christian faith. She stayed at home from September 2006 to February 2007 without pay until the airline changed its policy and made it acceptable to display a faith or charity symbol.

Nadia took her case to an employment tribunal to make a number of claims against BA, including claims under the Employment Equality (Religion or Belief) Regulations 2003 of direct and indirect discrimination and harassment. She lost her case and then tried to appeal against it but again lost in December 2008 when it was found that she had not been discriminated against.

1 What grounds did BA give for banning the necklace?
2 Why was this different to other religious items such as turbans and hijabs?
3 What did BA do as a result of the case and why do you think they did this?

Just checking

✱ Which types of discrimination are employees protected from at work?
✱ Name two employment protection rights that employees have.
✱ What is the minimum statutory holiday pay in weeks from 1 April 2009?
✱ Name two pieces of legislation that cover employees at work.

The final topic of this unit looks at how employees are helped to perform to the best of their ability. High performing employees help businesses to be more effective and make best use of resources.

Goal setting

Goal setting is when you set specific goals that you want to achieve. You have already learned about how to set goals earlier in this unit. If employees have goals to work towards, their performance can be measured against them. This means employers and employees can see how much progress has been made.

Learning and developmental activities

These are key activities for all employees because they help to improve performance. The more activities that employees take part in, the more competent they are likely to be become at their jobs. Below are examples of different activities:

* going on a training course
* studying for a qualification
* team building
* learning a new skill
* **work shadowing** a colleague
* doing work experience at another location
* doing charity or voluntary work.

Monitoring and appraisals

Monitoring employees at work is the way that employers check to see how well their staff are performing. It might be informal monitoring where the line manager checks how employees are doing on a daily or weekly basis. It could also be monitoring of the activities that employees are doing at work, for example using email or internet (if it is permitted). **Appraisals**, on the other hand, are formal systems that organisations use to encourage employees to give their best performance. The targets or goals that are agreed between the employer and employee should be a mix of what is needed for the business and employee. There are both advantages and disadvantages of using appraisals at work and these are shown in the table below.

MEASURING PERFORMANCE

How can the performance of the following people or groups of people be measured: doctor, football team, charity organisation, pop concert and restaurant. Discuss the different types of measurements in groups – think of different ways people can be measured.

Did you know?

All teachers now have to undertake a minimum of 30 hours of Continuing Professional Development (CPD) every year.

Work shadowing Learning how someone does their job by watching them.

Appraisal A formal system used by organisations to monitor how well staff are performing.

Advantages	Disadvantages
The employer and employee can work together on improving performance which helps to use resources in the best way.	May seem unfair if different managers in a business do them differently.
May be linked to payments so rewards are given for good performance, e.g. pay rises, bonuses or time off in lieu.	The goals need to be achievable but not so easy that this is likely to take away their worth; costs may go up if performance is exceeded.
May allow the employee and the employer the chance to get to know each other better and therefore improve their working relationship.	May not be given enough time and therefore doing an appraisal interview badly is worse than not doing one at all.
Allows the business to plan training that is needed.	May be a limited amount of money available for training so it may not be possible to give everyone all the training that they would like.

The advantages and disadvantages of appraisals.

Activity

Think about times in your life when you have had your performance measured, e.g. when you did SATs, a part-time job, work experience. For each of the performance reviews (similar to an appraisal), think about how you felt:

1 Who was in control of your performance?
2 Did you agree performance targets?
3 How did you feel after each review?

Personal, Learning and Thinking Skills

This activity will provide evidence for your creative thinking skills.

In a small group, discuss how you would like to be rewarded for hard work and good performance. Would you prefer to receive an award or be sent on a course that you would really like to take part in, or would you prefer to have time off or extra pay instead? If you chose extra pay, what type of pay – in one lump sum or added every year to your pay.

Consider the different options that people prefer and why this is the case. Now, how would you reward your employees if you were the boss?

Performance-related pay

Performance related pay (PRP) can take many different forms. Some organisations, such as banks, monitor and reward performance by using individual employee appraisals to see how well employees are doing. If they do well they get a monetary bonus or an increase in their pay. Some companies such as Tesco award free shares to virtually all of their employees if the company does well. Many teachers in further education receive performance-related pay based on how well pupils achieve at the end of their courses. Companies may also use PRP to decide on annual pay increases – a different percentage increase will be given to employees depending on how well they have performed over the past year. It is very important to make sure that if PRP is being used by a business that it is fair and does not discriminate against anyone (see anti-discrimination legislation on page 230).

Just checking

* What does PRP stand for?
* What is the difference between employee monitoring and appraisals?
* Name three developmental activities that an employee in an office might do.

Assessment

This unit is assessed internally. This means that you will be set an assignment by your consortium, which should direct your work through a series of tasks connected to the running of a business related activity, so that you cover all of the learning outcomes for this unit. The work you submit for assessment must be original work, produced by yourself under controlled conditions – this will be arranged by your tutor. It will then be marked by your tutor and moderated by the awarding body.

You will be assessed on:

* your ability to use sources of job information

* your ability to plan for and set goals for their career

* your ability to prepare for and participate as an interviewee in an interview for a job

* your knowledge of how employment legislation, procedures and processes operate in the workplace.

To aim for higher grades you should try to:

* include detailed and relevant information in the career plan that you produce

* set specific and realistic goals for your workplace experience

* provide good supporting evidence in the review of your progress and lessons learned

* address the specific requirements of the job you applied for

* prepare well for the interview, identifying a range of relevant questions you think they may ask you, and identify a range of relevant questions that you could ask

* show a good understanding of the difference between statutory and contractual rights, in the employment rights and responsibilities that you identify

* show a good understanding of methods of performance management, how and why they are used

* show a good level of interview techniques in terms of selling yourself and showing enthusiasm, demonstrating a good level of oral communication skills, showing the ability to answer simple questions well and giving good answers to more unexpected or open-ended questions

* show non-verbal communication skills that are good and sustained throughout the interview.

Account balance	The amount of money that a customer owes for goods or services supplied by another business.
Active listening	Involves not just listening carefully but concentrating on every word or phrase that the customer utters, focusing attention on the customer and engaging with them. Active listening takes in both sounds and body language so that you pick up information about the customer using your senses, as appropriate.
Appraisal	A formal system used by organisations to monitor how well staff are performing.
Assets	The premises, machinery, equipment, stocks and cash owned by a business at a given time.
Bank reconciliations	Checking transactions shown on a bank statement match with the records held by a business.
Bankruptcy	When a person or a business is unable to pay its debts.
Barter	Swapping goods to pay for things, not using money at all.
Behaviours	How people interrelate with others in a particular way.
Benefits	The positive gain or advantage that the customer gets as a direct result of each product feature; gives one product an advantage over another, competitor, product.
Bespoke software	A one-off package specially developed to meet the needs of a particular company.
Bibliography	A list of sources of information that you have used in your work. Make sure you quote other people's work that you have found on websites or in books.
Bounded problems	Those that are easily defined with a clear goal.
Brand	A combination of visual, audio and graphic elements that define a product or service; often designed to present a specific positive experience of that product or service, which may relate to lifestyle, quality, value, etc.
Brand name	A name used by a business that gives recognition to a product or group of products which it produces and markets collectively.
Budget	The amount of money available for spending on a particular project or marketing activity.
Budgets	The amount of money each department is given to run the business.
Bureau de Change	French for 'currency exchange'.
Cambio	A currency exchange bureau, from the Spanish word for 'change'.
Capital	Money put into the business such as owners' savings or bank loans.
Cash discount	Money that may be deducted from the total of an invoice if payment is made within a specified period of time, usually four weeks. The cash discount is calculated after any other discounts have already been deducted.

Close	The point in a sales interaction when the customer says 'yes' and agrees to buy.	**Customer complaints**	When a customer is so dissatisfied with an aspect of customer service they receive that they decide to make representations to the business with a view to getting some form of resolution, e.g. an apology, compensation or an improvement in their future dealings with the business.
Code of practice	A published set of standards which a business agrees to operate by.		
Cold calling	When you contact the potential customer directly without any prior warning.		
Collateral	A security pledged for the repayment of a loan.		
Commission	A charge for changing money from one currency to another.	**Customer loyalty**	Generating such a positive feeling towards the business that the customer will overlook any shortcomings in customer service and continue to support the business through regular and repeat purchases.
Companies House	The government department responsible for the registration of privately and publicly owned companies in the UK.		
Competitive advantage	Gaining an advantage over competitors by means of superior manufacturing and design processes or by providing goods and services with unique features.	**Customer profile**	A detailed description of typical customer types.
		Debit card	A card which can be used to take money from a person's bank account.
		Debits	Money that you owe.
		Debts	Money owed to a business.
Competitors	The other businesses which a company trades against.	**Dedication**	When you totally devote yourself to do something.
Consumerism	Creating happiness through buying material possessions.	**Demography**	Studying the population by analysing age, gender, socio-economic groupings, earnings and area in which people live.
Contingency	An emergency or unexpected expense that must be prepared for.		
Continuing Professional Development	The process of continually improving knowledge and skills by receiving training and guidance.	**Demotivated**	The lack of desire to do a task; in extreme cases requires pressure applying from elsewhere to complete a task.
		Demotivation	Factors which define the job context such as company policy and procedures.
Credit crunch	When banks do not have enough cash to lend businesses and consumers.	**Denomination**	A unit of measure, especially in monetary value. The different amounts coins and notes come in are known as denominations.
Credits	Money that is owed to you.		
Curriculum vitae (CV)	Gives employers information about the job seeker, such as their qualifications, education, and so on.	**Descriptive name**	This is where a brand name is added to a description of what a product is or does, e.g. 'wallpaper adhesive' would be prefaced by *Solvite*, or other brand.
Customer charter	A document that sets out the remit and service standards that a business or organisation aims to work to.		
		Directive change	A change that takes place via one person issuing an instruction to another person.

Disciplinary matters — Unacceptable behaviour on the part of employees which has to be handled according to the organisation's procedures in line with employment law.

Diversity — Difference or variety.

Duty of trust — The 'term of mutual trust and confidence' between employer and employee not to act in a way that could destroy, or damage, the relationship of trust and confidence.

Economic growth — An increase in the amount of goods manufactured and sold by a country.

Economy — The wealth and resources of a country.

Efficiency — A measure of how well a business uses its resources.

Electronic funds transfer — The transfer of money electronically from one bank account to another.

Employment contract — An agreement between an employer and employee setting out the terms of work, such as hours of work and wages.

Enterprise — A business venture.

Entrepreneur — Someone who looks for opportunities to set up a new business, and is prepared to take risks to make a profit.

Ethical consumerism — The process of buying goods or services that are made or provided with minimal negative impact on humans, animals or land.

Ethical consumers — A consumer who chooses to buy goods and services that will not harm the environment.

Ethics — Moral codes which guide an individual or organisation to act in the correct manner.

Expenditure — All money spent by an individual.

Expenses — Costs accumulated by a business.

Express terms — Terms in a contract that must be included by law.

External factor — A factor that affects the business but which is beyond its control.

Facilitator — A person who assists a group of people to plan to achieve their objectives, but without taking sides in the process.

Fairtrade — A world standard which ensures that producers are operating in acceptable working conditions and being paid a reasonable amount in return for their product and labour.

Features — Factual or technical pieces of information about the product, e.g. shape, size, colour, performance.

Financial transactions — Selling products and services for money.

Fixed assets — Things owned by the business that cannot be easily converted into cash such as property and equipment.

Float — The process whereby a company offers its shares to the public and lists itself on the stock exchange.

Formal authority — A concept whereby a hierarchy of power exists in a business and the power is used by managers to make directive change.

Formal channels — Based on the organisation's needs; the systems are normally planned by the organisation.

Functional area — A person, area or department, which carries out a specific business function, for example customer service, human resources, or production.

Generic name — Common or general name for a product, that has to be distinguished by the addition of a brand or company name, e.g. 'television' is generic and needs *Sony, Philips* or other name in front to make it distinctive.

Generic software	An off-the-shelf package designed to suit a range of companies.	**Jargon**	Technical words, often buzzwords, which relates to specific activities or groups and can be used to show you are a member of a group or an outsider. It is a barrier to effective communication.
Hierarchical structure	Where there are different levels in a treelike structure, with each level being accountable to another.	**Job description**	Document informing an employee what their job title is, their duties and responsibilities, who they will be working with, and the terms and conditions of the job (Unit 2).
Hierarchy	Employees ranked by order of level of responsibility.		
Implied terms	Terms that are customary to include in a contract.	**Job description**	Gives information about the job (Unit 9).
Income	All money received by an individual (Unit 3).	**Labour budget**	Forecast of monthly staff needs.
Income	Revenue generated by a business (Unit 1).	**Laissez-faire**	A concept whereby employees let the business operate without intervening.
Incremental change	Smaller scale change, e.g. looking at improving the way a task is completed.	**Legal tender**	Payment that, by law, cannot be refused in settlement of a debt.
Influence	Power to affect other people.	**Liabilities**	The debts of a business.
Informal channels	Based on the needs of individuals and groups; these can be designed to meet organisational objectives or satisfy social needs, and usually develop spontaneously such as the office grapevine (where staff discuss news, gossip and rumour).	**'Limited' status**	Privately and publicly owned companies which are registered at Companies House.
		Liquidity	A measure of how easily a business can pay its debts. The more liquid a business is, the more cash it has available to pay debts such as wages and bills.
Interest	A sum of money that the business pays to a lender in return for the use of their money as a loan. Interest is usually a percentage of the loan (Unit 4).	**Logo**	A distinctive graphic or piece of text (or combination of the two) that customers recognise immediately.
		Market	A specific group of customers that the business is aiming to attract.
Interest	The sum that you are charged for borrowing money from a bank or other lender (Unit 3).	**Market researcher**	The person who carries out the research on behalf of a business.
Interpersonal skills	Used when interacting with others in different situations; often referred to as communication skills or people skills.	**Medium**	The singular of media. In marketing, it is used to describe a type of communication that carries a message or information to consumers, e.g. print, audio, moving image.
Interviewee	The job applicant who is being asked the questions.		
Interviewer	The person who asks the questions.	**Minutes**	The written record of all the decisions made at a meeting.

Motivates — Encourages a person to do a task without pressure being applied from elsewhere.

Motivation — The reason why someone does something and what makes them want to do it.

Needs — Objective, functional requirements.

Non-governmental organisation (NGO) — An organisation set up to influence government and businesses. It has no connection to government.

Objections — Reasons that customers give for not buying something.

Opportunity cost — The value of the next best option that is given up when making an investment.

Organic change — Change that naturally occurs within a business through the efforts of an efficient workforce.

Pace — The speed at which you talk, e.g. fast or slow.

Participant — A person who is being surveyed as part of the research.

Patent — A business that is given the right to be the sole makers or sellers of a new product.

Person specification — Describes the type of person the business is looking for.

Policy — A formal, stated approach for dealing with particular situations that arise in a common way to meet the objectives of a business.

Population — The total number of people or organisations that can provide information relevant to a research problem.

Pressure group — A group of like-minded individuals who work together to campaign for a common cause.

Primary research — The process of gathering data first hand in a way that is specific to a business' needs.

Procedure — A step-by-step course of action that has been laid down to implement a policy.

Procedures — Either written or accepted methods of how to complete a job or task.

Product — What a business has to market and to sell. It may be bought or consumed in the form of physical goods or it may be a service.

Profile — A general description used to identify a group of people, such as a target market, based on a range of features that would be typical of that group, e.g. a simple profile of your class may be 'aged 14–19, 50:50 male and female, unmarried, live within 5 miles of centre, income spent mostly on entertainment'.

Profit — The amount of money left over in the business for its owners or shareholders after costs and expenses have been deducted from the income of a business.

Profitability — A measure of how profitable a business is.

Protocols — A set of rules or expectations setting out how you should behave in a given situation.

Redundancy — Where a company identifies that a person is no longer required for a particular job. The person is relieved of their duties and leaves the business. If the employee is eligible, they will receive a sum of money called a 'redundancy settlement'.

Rephrase — Reword a question in a different way to make it easier to understand.

Respondents — Individuals that you research, who provide you with results of your research.

Roles and responsibilities — The activities that are to be carried out to perform the job.

Sample	The number and profile of the people or organisations – the respondents – that you select to include in a survey.	**Team**	A group of individuals with a shared vision working together with specific roles and committed to achieving a common goal.
Segment	To divide up or split a market into smaller parts, then tailoring plans or products for each part of the market (each segment), so that each part is targeted in the most effective way.	**Team dynamics**	The strength of the team, how people get on together.
		Tone	The way you talk, e.g. a deep or high voice, do you sound serious or fun?
Self-regulating	The organisation or industry monitors and polices its own standards.	**Trade discount**	This is money off purchases given by one organisation to another. These discounts are usually given by businesses in the same trade, for example, within the building trade.
Self-reliance	Not relying on others to help.		
Shareholders	Individuals or corporate investors who buy shares in a business in the hope that these will increase in value.		
		Trade union	An organised group of workers set up to protect their interests in the workplace. Unions offer advice and support to their members, and may negotiate pay and working conditions with employers.
Span of control	The number of workers that a supervisor is responsible for.		
Step change	Large-scale change that has significant effect on the size and value of a business.		
		Transactions	The sale and purchase of goods or services for money.
Sterling	The currency of the UK – the pound.	**Unbounded problems**	Those that are new and for which information is incomplete.
Stockpile	Make more of a product than is needed at the time and store them for future sales.		
		Variance analysis	The analysis of differences between predicted costs and actual costs.
Surplus	The money made by voluntary organisations, as opposed to profit made by commercial organisations.	**Wants**	Subjective, qualitative desires.
		Will	A legal document declaring a person's wishes regarding the disposal of their money and possessions when they die.
Survey	The process of carrying out research which involves a large number of people.		
Sustainable resources	Materials that can be produced with little impact on the environment, e.g. fast growing wood – providing a tree can be planted straight after another has been felled, the impact on the environment should be minimised.	**Win-win solutions**	When both sides benefit from a compromise.
		Work shadowing	Learning how someone does their job by watching them.
Target population	The defined population from which research results are required.		

INDEX